MW00592452

Ferrari
CENTURY

The Story of The Prancing Horse
1898 to Today

MBI Publishing Company

"I am devoted to my land, dare I say it, fiercely.
Especially today, for reasons connected to my family's tragic history.
This devotion did not exist before, when I worked in Turin, Milan or Switzerland.
They were places which meant more to me than my flat, monotonous,
foggy land with its exaggerated summer heat, without a lake,
without a beach and with a few plain hills on the horizon.
However I don't know if I could have obtained the same results
if I had stayed there"

Enzo Ferrari
from his autobiography "Ferrari 80"

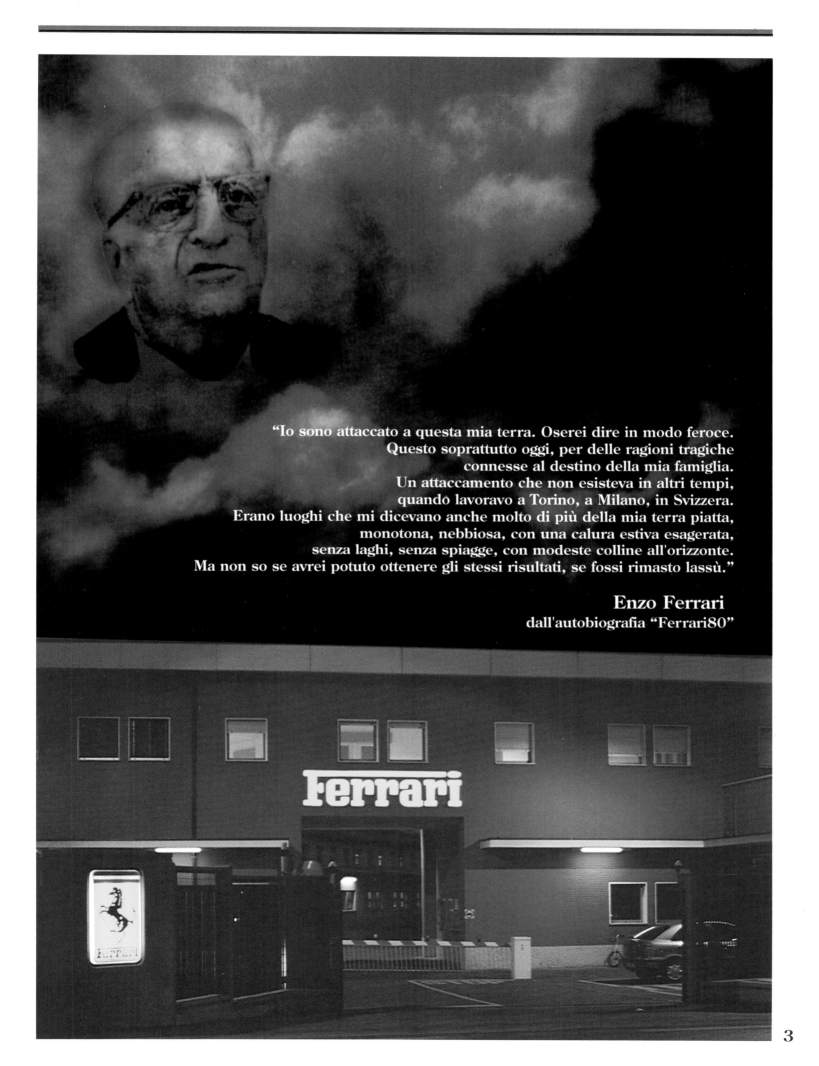

"Io sono attaccato a questa mia terra. Oserei dire in modo feroce.
Questo soprattutto oggi, per delle ragioni tragiche
connesse al destino della mia famiglia.
Un attaccamento che non esisteva in altri tempi,
quando lavoravo a Torino, a Milano, in Svizzera.
Erano luoghi che mi dicevano anche molto di più della mia terra piatta,
monotona, nebbiosa, con una calura estiva esagerata,
senza laghi, senza spiagge, con modeste colline all'orizzonte.
Ma non so se avrei potuto ottenere gli stessi risultati, se fossi rimasto lassù."

Enzo Ferrari
dall'autobiografia "Ferrari80"

CONTENTS

I would like to thank Roberto Boccafogli, the author of this book, for having understood the spirit of the project, which was not simply a "rewrite" of the history of Ferrari. It is instead an analysis of the legend through minor and major details, long-forgotten curiosities as well as a recollection of well-known and not so well-known fact ... always working closely with everyone who assisted us in the project. In producing the book, we met dozens of people and it was fantastic to appreciate the warmth with which they welcomed us, opened their homes to us and patiently put up with our interest and that of our photographers.

The Editor

Thanks to everyone and in particular to:

Renzo and Alvaro Cernesi, Gisberto Leopardi and Sergio Vezzali, Luigi Montanini "Pasticcino", all the men who have given their everything to Ferrari in the company and at the race-tracks, to Don Erio Belloi, parish priest of Maranello, to Riccardo Andreoni of Ferrari for checking the statistics and finally to Pietro De Franchi, Ferrari Club Italy secretary. Umberto Masetti, 1950 and 1952 World Motorcycle Racing Champion, Antonio Magro and Elvira Ruocco of Alfa Romeo, Paolo Montagna and Paolo Moroni of the Milan Automobile Club, Paolo D'Alessio, whose colour plates of Ferraris from 1948 to 1988 illustrate the book, Gabriella Coltrin, the wife of the late Peter Coltrin as well as our photographers, Serafino Celso and Giulio Guerrieri who often worked in technically harsh situations.

The stylized car designs in the headings were produced of Diego Galbiati.

Author: Roberto Boccafogli
English version: Julian Thomas
Photographic archives:
Gabriella Coltrin, C.O.N.I.Press Office, Expressen, Shell Italiana Press Office, Alfa Romeo archives, MilanAutomobile Club - archives, Bryn Williams - Colin McMaster, Ferrari Press Office- Maranello, Tazio Nuvolari Museum (Mantua), La Libertà di Piacenza, Mario Arquati, Auto Italiana, Sport Mecanique - France, Autosprint, Opel Italia Press Office, Williams Grand Prix (UK), Automobile Club de Monaco, UMI (USA), Corriere della Sera, Gazzetta dello Sport, Car Magazine (Japan), Autosport (Japan).
Photographs: Serafino Celso, Giulio Guerrieri, Carlo Rezzonico
Colour Plates and Technical Drawings: Paolo D'Alessio
Graphic Design: Diego Galbiati
Technical Coordination: Ermenegildo Chiozzotto
Editing and Information: Tina Caiazza, Chiara Mendella, Francesca Vallardi
Photolithograph: FCM - Marcallo C. (MI)   **Printing:** Alfa Print - Busto A. (VA)

© 1997 Worldwide - SEP Editrice - Milan (Italy)

•

This edition first published in 1998 by MBI Publishing Company, 729 Prospect Avenue, PO Box 1, Osceola, WI 54020-0001 USA.

Previously published by SEP Editrice - Milan (Italy)

Library of Congress Cataloging-in-Publication Data Available.

ISBN 0-7603-0550-1

Printed and bound in ITALY

CONTENTS

Ferrari Century:

The Story of the Prancing Horse
1898 to Today

BIBLIOGRAPHY
Many quotes in the text come from the following books:

- Ferrari l'unico
  Nada Editore 1988

- F1 33 anni di Gran Premi
  iridati - Conti Editore 1982

- Ferrari 80 - Edizione
  Fuori Commercio 1980

- Ferrari
  La Storia di un mito -
  RCS Supplemento della
  Gazzetta dello Sport 1996

- Marlboro Grand Prix Guide
  Edizione 1997

- Museo Alfa Romeo -
  Catalogo - Automobilia 1985

- Museo Storico Alfa Romeo -
  Alfa Romeo 1983

- Bandiera a Scacchi -
  Vallardi 1993

- The Legendary Italian
  Grand Prix - ACM 1989

INTRODUCTION

As you drive from Modena toward Maranello, near the Appenines and Mount Abetone, you can sense the soul of Ferrari here among the tidy fields, the quintessence of perfect productivity in every season. It is fitting that Enzo Ferrari and Ferrari were born in this area.

In the beginning, Ferrari was just a small idea, the result of a childhood dream. "When I grow up, I'm going to be a racing driver," said a young

Ferrari to his close friend Peppino one hot August evening. Together, the two boys were leafing through a newspaper that reported the exploits of Italian-born, Raffaele De Palma, a driver of the time and one of the stars of the Indianapolis race.

"A good idea," was the reply. "That must be a great job."

These were great expectations at a time when Italy almost had no experience with the motor car, let alone speed and racing. Those words, however, contained something special: a foreshadowing of a legend born not from chance but from real human ambition. It eventually turned into a reality that formed the story of a man, a marque and much of the sport of motor racing.

From the early years of the twentieth century until today, the wide-eyed dream of Enzo Ferrari has become a reality, which today guarantees worldwide fame and fortune for Maranello.

Every motor racing fan, especially the F1 enthusiast, knows about Ferrari, the flaming red Ferrari and the Ferrari legend with its drivers, its engineers, its victories, and defeats, which are all inextricably linked with a unique historical roll of honors.

Everyone who reads detailed newspaper accounts and follows the television commentary of the races can learn a lot about the technology, the aerodynamics, and the latest carbon-fiber applications. But they can never get the real feeling of Maranello that makes Ferrari something more than just a mere motor racing team.

All one has to do, however, is visit Maranello once. A short, unhurried visit is all that is required to understand the hidden but visible meaning of this small town in the Modena industrial hinterland. Some 1,800 of the slightly more than 15,000 inhabitants work for Ferrari, and for the legend and history of the Prancing Horse. A legend that will never die; a legend born in the nineteenth century and ready to race into the year 2000 in top gear; a legend rejuvenated by the alternating fortunes of Ferrari since the death of its founder almost 10 years ago.

At Maranello there is an overriding sensation: Ferrari is the phenomenon that helped to industrialize this predominantly agricultural before World War II, a pillar of industrial society on a world scale. At Maranello and throughout the surrounding areas, Ferrari means cars, races, and

Maranello, just a few minutes from Modena by car, at the foot of the Appenines. The legend of the Prancing Horse was born here and developed over the years. The Ferrari company was first a small-time firm, but then became a worldwide industrial and sporting phenomenon. Young Enzo Ferrari's dream ("I'm going to be a racing driver when I grow up") far exceeded his own expectations. . . .

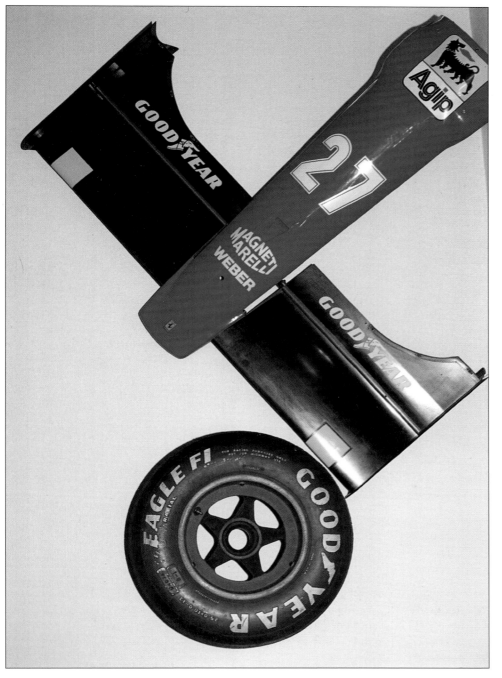

victories.

But it also means work: work and economic security, where until a half-century ago, only fields made the difference between making ends meet and widespread hunger.

Everything and everyone at Maranello "breathes" Ferrari: the factory; the racing headquarters; the Fiorano test track, just a few meters away from the monument dedicated to Gilles Villeneuve in the street named after him; the street dedicated to Ascari; the Ferrari Museum; the Ferrari shop, which is visited by customers from all over the world in search of Ferrari-related products; the Cavallino restaurant, in front of the

The "Cavallino" in front of the main Ferrari entrance is not just an excellent restaurant. Inside, life revolves around the scarlet red cars and their race wins. With trophies, helmets signed by drivers, and racing-car parts, the restaurant is a gallery of Ferrari.

7

The Ferrari Gallery appears on the road leading to Fiorano. It is the only official souvenir outlet for the Prancing Horse marque in the world. In Maranello, the shops sell motor sport articles, gadgets and items, but Ferrari-related products sell the most.

Other page: Enzo Ferrari has been depicted in stamps, bas-relief and statues, made from piston-heads. The bust which has special importance for the "tifosi" is the one dedicated to Gilles Villeneuve, put up in 1982 a few meters from the entrance to Fiorano.

INTRODUCTION

main company entrance, where even today it is not unusual to bump into Ferrari figures of the past and the present, such as the unforgettable Umberto Masetti, world motorcycling champion in 1950 and 1952.

Or you might meet Alvaro Cernesi, employee in the engine paint-shop department and son of a worker who accompanied Enzo Ferrari in the good old days. His father started work in the factory in the first half of the century with Registration Number 22. His son remembers this with pride and adds: "See these overalls? On the left there is the Prancing Horse, and I feel its heart beating next to mine." These overalls, which for an outsider are quite normal, for Cernesi are something quite unique and special and are never removed . . . except during working hours, so as not to get them dirty.
Similar sentiments are expressed by Gisberto Leopardi.
"Everything I have I owe to Ferrari,"

he says frankly, while showing us his pretty house on the outskirts of Maranello, immersed in the green countryside where the Abetone state road begins to climb. He continues, "I used to work in the rice-fields. The pay was meager, 20 kilos of rice to help the family get by."
Then suddenly, came Ferrari, in a way that could best be described as romantic. After successfully completing a mechanical engineering course, young Leopardi realized that his only hope lay in the newly created car industry. How could he get in? Simple: the most direct way possible. One day he waited for Enzo Ferrari on the steps of the town hall. He went up to him and said point-blank: "Ferrari, I've finished my course, but my stomach is empty. . . ." And that is how on April 10, 1947, 17-year-old Leopardi started work in the Cavallino factory. Almost 50 years of work and races, trips home and abroad full of adventure and hard work, and yet a marvelous experience. A story that only came to an end when he reached retirement age, but which has carried on today with a series of souvenirs, photographs, result-sheets, and circuit and pit passes. Items of memorabilia that in all parts of the world are exchanged at high prices by collectors and which for these men mean simply a succession of events in a life filled by a passiona-

Two "dynasties" of Ferrari mechanics. Left: Alvaro Cernesi with his father, who, in the 1940s, was registered worker Number 22 at Maranello. Bottom left: Gisberto Leopardi proudly stands before his personalized tools, and with his Ferrari employee's identity card.

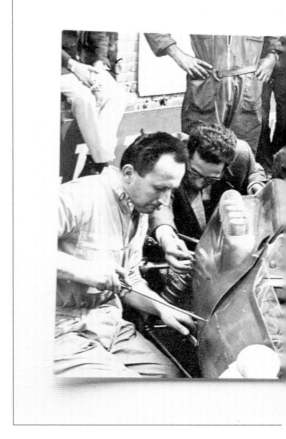

te love for their work. There are many others like Leopardi, men often linked by having their roots in Maranello and the surrounding area. But above all, they are linked by a history, the pace of which is dictated by the same metronome. Sergio Vezzali was Gilles Villeneuve's chief mechanic. Before he was with the Canadian, he worked with Niki Lauda, whom today he remembers as "the best, the most generous with us mechanics: after each win, he never fai-

*Sergio Vezzali,
Ferrari F1 mechanic
at the time of Niki Lauda
and Gilles Villeneuve.
The framed photographs portray
him in the pits in the 1960s,
in a briefing with Enzo Ferrari.
Alongside: Vezzali with the crown
and scepter of "King of the Box,"
as he was called affectionately
by his colleagues when he retired.*

*(8) and Villoresi (2) in the first two rows.
Below, Enzo Ferrari discusses 312 F1
with mechanic Sergio Vezzali in 1968.*

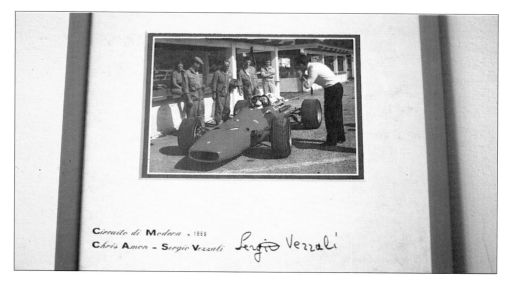

led to give us a present, sometimes a big one."

Vezzali's house, like Leopardi's and those of many other ex-colleagues, is packed with memories: souvenirs, photos and artifacts, trophies and copies of menus from the traditional and regular company meals offered by Ferrari to celebrate Christmas or other happy occasions, such as when they successfully completed a job within an impossible time-scale.

And what memories! Memories of days spent working on the racing cars, suddenly interrupted by a half-whispered word, or one that everyone could hear.

"Maraja, maraja!"

(Watch out! Watch out!)

"Daddy's coming."

That's what they called him: Daddy: a mixture of respect, fear and affection. Ferrari came into the factory and the chatter faded away, cigarettes smoked during work (absolutely forbidden!) were put out in a hurry.

He came every day at about 10:30 in the morning. And he always, at least once a day, visited every sector. A sudden and important presence, that brought everything to a standstill. On catching a worker hiding a cigarette in his pocket, he would say half-smilingly:

"You'd better put that out, otherwise you'll burn your overalls." Few words, often abrupt and without raising his voice. With a few exceptions. . . . "We all knew when there was a meeting going on," recalls Vezzali. I "If things were not going well, you could hear the shouting, sometimes even the cursing. There was no answering back. Shortly after, they all came out of his office, their eyes lowered. No one answered back to him: not even Forghieri or the young Montezemolo."

Ferrari instilled fear, but he also totally backed his workers.

"In all my years of working for Ferrari," recalled the ex-racing mechanic Leopardi, "I never received my wages late, not even in hard times for the company. For Ferrari, there was always money for those who worked. It was always the most important thing."

Thousands of different colors, shapes and logos. These are the circuit passes that represent years of activity for the Prancing Horse mechanics.

INTRODUCTION

These small memories also help to build the legend.

For Enzo Ferrari, an expert businessman, solidarity had absolute value. On his death, the parish priest of Maranello, don Erio Belloi, was approached by Ferrari's son, Piero: "Father has arranged for this check to be left to the parish."

Ferrari had shown this sort of generosity on many other occasions. The land where the parish sports fields are now situated was a gift from him.

A view from the bridge on the dividing line between Maranello and Fiorano. From this vantage point, one can see part of the circuit of Fiorano, where thousands of Ferrari fans gather when the scarlet cars are testing.

"Ferrari was very close to us," recalls the parish priest today. "On numerous occasions, he used to phone and say to me, "Father, things have gone well for me today. If you come and visit me, I've got something for you." This solidarity was not only addressed to the church.

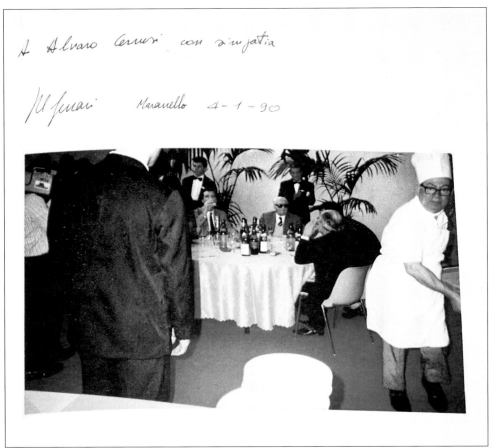

In Modena, you might meet up with one of the taxi drivers, Vincenzo Ferrari. No relation, just the same surname. Vincenzo tells his story:

"In 1982 Enzo Ferrari made a donation of 10 million lire to our new cooperative. He said he thought Modena should have a radio taxi cooperative, even though he would almost certainly never use it."

This relationship with Modena's public taxi system is one that has continued over the years. In front of the taxi rank can be found the barber's shop where Ferrari stopped every morning for a shave and a trim before going to work at Maranello.

Above: The barber's shop in Modena where Ferrari stopped every morning, and the adverts for the taxi company he financed.

The parish church of Maranello in a print from the first half of the century. The main entrance of Ferrari is on the avenue that can be seen on the left. On the death of Enzo in 1988, parish priest Don Erio Belloi had this beautiful stained-glass window fitted in the church in his memory.

MARANELLO - Chiesa Parrocchiale e Strada Abetone - Brennero

This is also Ferrari, and this is also his story. A story born in Modena, nourished by skill and inventiveness, and by the food and Lambrusco wine typical of the area, which Enzo Ferrari liked so much.

On his arrival at Ferrari in 1987, Technical Director John Barnard ordered a ban on the consumption of wine at the midday canteen. A small revolution ensued. The Maranello workers could not understand this restriction and maintained that it was an insult to their professionalism. Barnard had no way of knowing that the history that had beckoned him to that position had also been written at a table with a dream.

A DREAM BORN IN THE SNOW

Did Enzo Ferrari believe in destiny? A clear-cut answer on the subject has never been available, from him or his closest collaborators. Many clues however, first small and then increasingly larger, imply that destiny believed in Ferrari. This seemed to be the case in a freezing cold month of February 1898, the starting point for a journey toward a legend, toward an industrial, sporting and social phenomenon, an adventure that can only be called unique in the world.

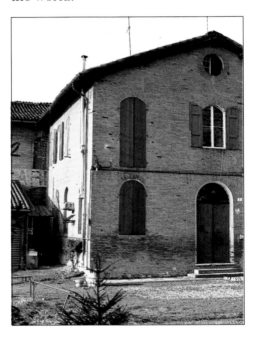

The snow was too high—recalled Ferrari himself, quoting his mother—and they had to wait a couple of days before heading for the registry office to report the happy event. It is strange then that the weather bulletins of the time, which can still be consulted in the town hall of the Emilian city, only speak of cold weather and rain, not snow. Was it the 18th or the 20th? The halo of mystery that surrounds this event is the best way to begin an exceptional story.

The news and the details of those days and those places are exact. They speak the language of Modena at the end of the nineteenth century: a city that was not particularly large, but already flourishing and open to the wonders of industrialization. Alfredo Ferrari would today be called a

Reginald Walker, born in Durban, South Africa, on March 16, 1889, won the 100-meter event at the London Olympics in 1908 with a time of 10.45 seconds, ahead of the American James Rector and Canada's Robert Kerr. Walker, 19 at the time, remains today the youngest-ever Olympic 100meters champion.

Half-hidden in the outskirts of Modena, Enzo Ferrari's birthplace is still perfectly preserved today. The only indication of its origins lies above the roof of the side of the building, where part of the writing "Officina meccanica Ferrari" is still visible.

Enzo Ferrari was born two years before the start of the twentieth century in a building on the outskirts of Modena, in via Paolo Ferrari 5. Here was the steel workshop founded by his father, Alfredo. The name of the street is purely a coincidence and does not justify any further research. The date of birth, however, is another matter.

According to his own personal version of the facts, and confirmed every year by the telegram of birthday wishes received from his mother, Adalgisa, Ferrari was born on Thursday, February 18. But files in the registry office record the date of 20th February 20. The reason for this discrepancy appears to be a purely technical hitch.

small businessman. His steel workshop occupied the ground floor of a building similar to many others in the outskirts of Modena. Above the road-level entrance, the sign read "Officina meccanica Alfredo Ferrari," still visible today, as the building has been saved from the industrialization of the area of the past few decades. Above are the windows of the first floor, where the Ferrari family lived a quiet middle-class life, thanks to the father's business: construction work for the state railways company. The early years of young Enzo had no connection with the motor car, which at the time was virtually unknown and would only become important to the family after the first decade of the twentieth century. The idea

of competition, however, came soon. Enzo and his brother Alfredo, two years his senior, had a very early passion, athletics. There was a canal behind the family house, and on its gravel bank, a row of poplar trees formed the backdrop to running races between the two brothers and their friends. Almost every evening, they would run the 100 meters, with the impossible aim of equaling or even beating the Olympic record of the day: 10.45 seconds, held by Reg Walker. Young Enzo was fast, but his brother was faster. In the long distance races, however, it was difficult to compete with their friend Carlo, the barber's son.

Life in those days was calm, well-to-do, and serene. One of father Alfre-

A young Enzo Ferrari with his elder brother Alfredo in the early years of the 20th century.

led Circuito di Bologna, deep in the countryside in the form of a triangle, two sides of which were the long straights of the via Emilia and the via Persicetana. Ferrari's official autobiography describes the emotion the youngster felt as having been "violent." Victory went to Felice Nazzaro after a perfect race, even though the fastest lap was set by Vincenzo Lancia. Ferrari watched, observed and made a note in his mind as if etching it in stone.

He was impressed by a measure stu-

died by the organizers to keep the massive numbers of spectators under control: a 15-meter strip of field running alongside the track had been flooded with water. A poor but genial idea. Spectators were always enthusiastic about being sprayed or soaked by water, but this solution made it safe for them, as the pool of water acted as a run-off area for the cars.

One year later, another race: the Record del Miglio. The setting for the race was a long straight of provincial

do's friends was Anselmo Chiarli, the owner of the wine-making firm of the same name and the godfather of Enzo, whose second name was in fact Anselmo. On top of his interest in athletics and a school performance which left a lot to be desired, Enzo spent long afternoons with his brother in the gym, roller-skating or fighting with sticks. He soon demonstrated ability with a pistol, which enabled the young Ferrari to be good at something and beat his brothers and friends. But his passion for cars and speed was just around the corner.

TENOR?
RACING DRIVER!

In 1908 Ferrari was 10 years old: everything was ripe for a revolution, which was destined to overturn the boundaries of the world he knew. The virtually unknown motor car started to take up young Enzo's thoughts.

One day his father took him and his brother to a motor race. The track wound its way around what was cal-

Journalism was one of Ferrari's earliest passions. This famous article was published in the Gazzetta dello Sport on Monday, November 16, 1914.

THE IDEA

road linking Modena with Ferrara. To get there, the Ferrari father and brothers had to walk across more than three kilometers of fields. Once they arrived at the scene of the action, the eyes of young Enzo began to record the details and etch them once again in his memory. There was no tarmac at the time, and neither was there the liquid called "Fix," a special mixture that would be spread on the surface to stop the dust from forming. The race was held on a gravel road, which dozens of voluntary workers from the Modena Automobile Association dampened with buckets of water and farm barrels to make it more compact and less dusty. Victory went to De Zara, whose average speed of more than 140 kilometers per hour, remarkable for the time, gave Enzo Ferrari a real thrill. A number of other steps had yet to be taken, however, before he entered the world of motor cars.

Basically there were two obstacles standing in his way. The first was the many temptations that every adolescent embraces, selects and discards.

April 14, 1923: Ugo Sivocci and Antonio Ascari finished first and second in the Targa Florio. Alfa Romeo celebrated with a team photograph: Enzo Ferrari is first left; alongside him is the engineer Rimini and the Baroness Avanzo.

One of Enzo's interests in the first decade of the century was music. At home, Saturday evenings were always dedicated to music, a family love that ended up involving the two sons. Many friends made a name for themselves in this field, such as the tenor Bussetti, a former farrier who performed at the New York Metropolitan. The other temptation was journalism. The years to come would demonstrate the connection between the future constructor and writing. In 1914, Enzo free-lanced with the daily newspaper La Provincia di Modena.

This was followed by service as football correspondent for La Gazzetta dello Sport: a memorable article, "Inter defeat Modena 7-1," published on Monday, November 16, 1914, is a historical testimony of this. But the second, more serious obstacle was represented by World War I. Ferrari went to war in a rather particular way: He was taken on as instructor in the turner's workshop of the Modena fire brigade, a position that at first enabled him to avoid military service. (Another sign of the destiny was that the turning workshop was to be converted into a factory, eventually to become the largest manufacturing plant for Fiat agricultural vehicles.)

The war tore through Ferrari's life like a tornado. The conflict left Italy far worse off, and 1917 brought a-

bout mass conscription for many young men who had managed to avoid being called to arms. Ferrari was forced to join the artillery on the Bergamo Alps.

He was only able to return home following a serious (and never exactly specified) illness, which led him to convalesce in Brescia Hospital and then, thanks to his mother's intervention, in nearby Bologna Hospital. In 1918, the final year of the war, Ferrari's life had totally changed. Two years previously, he had lost his father and his much-loved brother Alfredo almost at the same time.

Alone with his mother, young Ferrari had to start to get a grip on his life. He was not in any immediate difficulty, thanks to a small inheritance from his father's business, but he needed to find work quickly.

Twenty years old, without any real job experience but with a tireless resolve to do something important, Ferrari accepted with gratitude the help of his mother, who managed to obtain an interview for him at Fiat in Turin. It was the 1918-1919 winter, but not even his position as an ex-serviceman saved him from the courteous refusal of the Turin manufacturer, which was also in the reconstruction phase. In the biting cold, which swept throughout the main city of Piedmont, Ferrari felt disheartened, alone and without any hopes for the future.

Many years later, after a happier event that occurred in the same place, he told of how he had felt discouraged at Parco del Valentino, seated with his head in his hands on a snow-covered bench.

He didn't know at the time, but enthusiasm for the motor car and racing, long dormant, was about to break out. Enzo Ferrari remained in Turin and found work in the shop of an engine tuner from Bologna, na-

Enzo Ferrari's career as a driver began in 1919 with a C.M.N. car. Ferrari made his debut in the Parma-Poggio di Berceto mountain time-trial event, finishing fourth overall.

in the world

1898 - The Spanish-American War. Spain, under the rule of King Alfonso XIII, was defeated by the United States and lost control of Cuba, Puerto Rico and the Philippines.

1900 - OnJuly at 29 at Monza, the king of Italy, Umberto I, was assassinated by the anarchist Bresci. Victor Emanuel III was the new sovereign.

1900 - In China, the Boxer Rebellion led to the intervention of an international force, which occupied Peking and liberated the besieged western consulates in August.

in motor sport

1899 - On February 25, Marcel Fernand and Louis Renault founded the "Renault Frères" factory at Billancourt, near Paris.

1900 - National colors were for the first time associated with racing cars: blue for France, green for Great Britain, red for the United States and white for Germany.

med Giovannoni.

It wasn't much, just demolishing lorry chassis and turning them into motor cars. But Enzo soon began to make contacts in the world of racing by frequenting the Bar del Nord in Porta Nuova, where dozens of people from motor racing organized meetings. His acquaintances were mostly drivers, including the Nazzaro brothers, Bergese and Salamano; as well as Bonacini, who had been Bordino's mechanic before the war and was soon to become Ferrari's adviser.

Another bar, the Vittorio Emanuele in Milan, a city that attracted everyone looking for work, opened the door toward the Lombardy metropolis. Thanks to the insistence of former cyclist Ugo Sivocci, Enzo went to C.M.N. in Milan, where construction of tractors for wartime activity had given way to a factory which fitting engines on chassis derived from the Isotta Fraschini. Ferrari began work for C.M.N. as a test-driver, and then—despite his mother's objections—became a driver.

It was thanks to Sivocci, a driver who was destined to lose his life at Monza four years later, that Ferrari's passion became uncontrollable . . .

so much so that he invested his first earnings in the purchase of a racing C.M.N. and entered the first running of the Parma-Berceto mountain time-trial. It was 1919, and a fourth place overall convinced him to follow a path which he already felt was a vocation.

That same year, again on Sivocci's insistence, he took part in the Targa Florio. This is a magnificent story and deserves to be told. His participation in the classic Sicilian event began with him driving across almost all of Italy, then continuing from Naples to Palermo by ship. He finished the race, in which drove a C.M.N., over the time limit, when the grandstands had already been dismantled. The fault was partly mechanical, which lost him almost one hour, and partly due to a roadblock at Campofelice, where Carabinieri were monitoring a political rally. It was with this excuse that Ferrari, the day after the race, managed to obtain from Vincenzo Fiorio in person an overall ninth place, as well as reimbursement of his expenses and prize money.

While his career as a driver had begun with tireless resolve, it had now become a burning ambition.

A PASSION FOR ALFA ROMEO

Enzo Ferrari's career as a driver lasted from 1919 to 1931. Twelve years of passion, joys and even victories, some against drivers of the caliber of Tazio Nuvolari. Twelve years which also consolidated the relationship between Ferrari and Alfa Romeo, whose cars Ferrari raced throughout almost all of his career.

The first win with a car from the Alfa Romeo factory—the fifth race of his career—was the 1920 Targa Florio, after three races with an Isotta Franchini 4500 Grand Prix. Ferrari almost won the Sicilian race, but in the end was second with a twin-block four-cylinder Alfa 4500. The prize money was 12,000 lire ($750), a substantial sum for the time, the equivalent of 18,000,000 lire today ($11,250).

More importantly, this result opened

Sivocci's Alfa Romeo.
He persuaded Ferrari to become
a driver and shared the wheel
with him in several races.
Sivocci was killed in 1923
at Monza.

ALFA ROMEO

The Alfa Romeo logo

This is a stylized design of a snake, the symbol of the Visconti, the old noble family of Milan, together with a red cross against a white background, the ensign of the Municipality of Milan. The latter, created in 1045, in turn derives from the union of the ensign of the people (white) with that of the nobility (red).

1904 - The Russo-Japanese War for supremacy in the Far East ended (1905) with the defeat of Russia, which was forced to hand over to Japan the southern part of the island of Sakhalin and Port Arthur and surrender claims over the disputed territories of Korea and independent Manchuria.

1907 - Royal Dutch Petroleum Company and the Shell Transport and Trading Co. Ltd. (Britain) merged to form Shell, which today is the world's largest petroleum company for retail sales.

Kelly-Springfield transport truck, California USA, 1915

The evolution of the Alfa Romeo logo
1) *Alfa from 1910 to 1915.*

2) *Romeo was added from 1918 to 1925.*

3) *The World Championship laurels were added from 1925 to 1946.*

4) *From 1946 to 1971 the figure-of-eight knots of the ruling House of Savoy disappeared and were replaced by two insignia.*

5) *The current logo.*

in motor sport

1907 - On August 10, an Itala 7500 driven by Prince Scipione Borghese entered Paris in triumph after an adventurous 15,000-kilometer journey, which began in Peking two months earlier.

1907 - H.F. Locke King constructed Brooklands, the world's first permanent motor racing circuit, on his grounds in Surrey, England. The track was inaugurated on June 28, 1907.

1909 - The Indianapolis oval was founded in Indiana.
It was built in six months by four local firms. The track surface was brick.
On August 19, the first race was held over two laps of the track for a total of five miles. Lewis Strang won in a Fiat.

the doors to the official team of the Milan manufacturer, whose emblem at the time was the snake of the Viscount, an amaranth-colored cross and the name Alfa—which stood for Anonima Lombarda Fabrica Automobili. There was still no trace of the word which would complete the marque: Romeo, from the name of the Neapolitan industrialist and politician Nicola Romeo, who later was to enter the Alfa factory with full support for a sporting program that would become famous in the history of motor sport.

The glorious four-year period from 1921 to 1924 included most of Ferrari's career with Alfa. Wins at the Circuito del Savio (Ravenna), the Circuito del Polesine (Padua) and, above all, in the 1924 Coppa Acerbo (Pescara) make up a prestigious roll of honors. Ferrari could almost certainly have added another prestigious win, had he not suddenly withdrawn on the eve of the 1924 French Grand Prix in Lyon, where four P2 Grands Prix had been entered for the race. The drivers were Ascari, Campari, Wagner and Ferrari. For the world of motor sport, this decision was a bombshell. The withdrawal was announced with a simple telegram. Ferrari was by now a top-level international driver; exhaustion, the official reason for not racing at Lyon, did not fool anyone. It was rumored that the decision resulted from the insistence of Laura Garello, Ferrari's young and fascinating wife of the past three years, who had no love for the sport. The truth lies elsewhere. Even if one accepts exhaustion as the reason, at the time, Ferrari was not just content with being a driver and only a driver.

A MOTIVATOR OF MEN

The race in which he failed to take part in France in 1924 was, if not a pretext, at least a curious coincidence. For some time Ferrari had had a growing desire, which, given his character, was becoming an overwhelming ambition. He wanted to be more involved in Alfa Romeo's racing program—not only as a driver, not only as the final performer in a project that was born by chance. In 1923, he suggested to Alfa that they "poach" a young engineer, his great friend Luigi Bazzi, from Fiat. The move was a success, and Bazzi became the man behind the legendary 2,000-cc six-cylinder P1. It was also this engineer who suggested to Ferrari another young and brilliant engineer, who was also soon to defect from Fiat, Vittorio Jano.

Ferrari came to Turin in September

The Four-Leafed Clover

This symbol, a prominent feature on every Alfa Romeo sports car and racing car, appeared for the first time in 1923 on the front of the RL Targa Florio model, which dominated the race of the same name, finishing first, second and fourth. The same year, the Alfa RL won the Circuito del Savio race, driven by Enzo Ferrari. The 3,154-cc engine had six cylinders and 95 horsepower. Top speed was 157 kilometers per hour.

of the same year, as he had five years previously, although this time he came not to look for work but to offer it. With that typical look of his, despite being just 25, Ferrari knocked on the door of the Jano house on the third floor of a building in via San Massimo. To Jano's wife, who opened the door, he said candidly that he intended to convince her husband to leave Fiat for Alfa Romeo. Signora Jano began to laugh—the totally Piedmontese mind of her husband would never let itself be persuaded to upset the family in this way. Ferrari must have seemed like a madman. Then the engineer arrived and listened to Ferrari; they hit it off straight away and got on famously. The next day he signed a contract at Alfa headquarters.

This episode, a spontaneous one that had no profit-making or hierarchical aims, was just the first step toward making Ferrari totally independent in motor racing. Many years later, he rejected the label of "constructor" which many people called him. He always liked to call himself a "motivator of men," a continuous source of ideas, questions, ambitions and projects that sometimes were totally out of line. During the three years from 1924 to 1926, Ferrari kept far away from the steering wheel. Instead, he began to explore every detailed aspect of a racing program.

He also had to deal with the death of a number of close friends, events which were a severe test for his totally positive nature and his tireless energy.

In 1923, his close friend and great inspiration Sivocci lost his life in a crash at Monza, on what many years later would be called the Ascari Cur-

Lyons, 1924: Antonio Ascari's Alfa P2 in the French GP. Enzo Ferrari did not take part in the race, the first of two he decided to miss.

ve. This was followed by the deaths of Giuseppe Campari and Antonio Ascari; the former was a colleague at Alfa, the latter an acknowledged champion.

These events, however, only managed to slow down for a few days Ferrari's own professional drive toward his one ambition: to design and construct increasingly faster cars and assemble complete, perfect and winning teams around them. With this goal in mind, he even invented a number of totally new roles. He did not miss one important race.

He even started up the idea of sponsorship in motor racing, getting some of the leading technical suppliers to give financial backing in 1929 to his first great invention: Scuderia Ferrari.

1924 Parma-Poggio di Berceto mountain time-trial: Antonio Ascari and Ramponi immediately after the victory with the Alfa RLTF.

Vittorio Jano

The golden age of Alfa Romeo in racing started with Jano, who imme-

diately became the undisputed leader of the technical department in Milan. He would continue with Ferrari, where superb technical preparation would allow the thin and severe Turin manager—the method of work imposed by him at Alfa was defined by Ferrari as "military discipline"—to anticipate and perfect dozens of different theories and technical applications, including the 6, 8, and 12-cylinder World Championship-winning engines.

The Turin engineer was one of those many cases in which a man, an engineer, a driver, forged a bond with Ferrari that would go down in the history of motor racing.

More often than not, they were ties which went far beyond mere professional respect. Relations which were not always—in fact, almost never—serene, and were often prolonged to six or seven days of the week, from early in the morning to late in the evening; always discussing, planning, comparing projects during working hours, which were regularly extended to include lunch and often dinner.

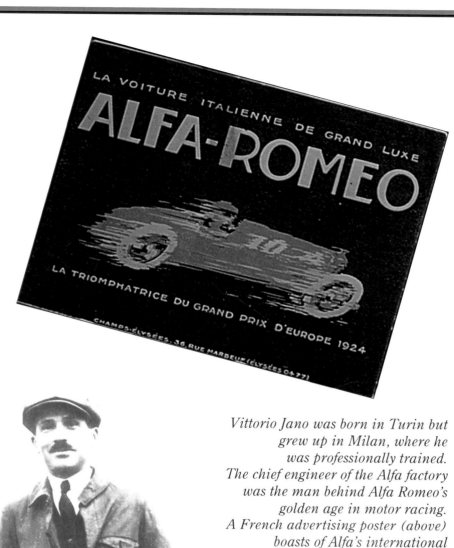

LA VOITURE ITALIENNE DE GRAND LUXE
ALFA-ROMEO
LA TRIOMPHATRICE DU GRAND PRIX D'EUROPE 1924
CHAMPS-ÉLYSÉES, 36, RUE MARBEUF (ÉLYSÉES 0477)

Vittorio Jano was born in Turin but grew up in Milan, where he was professionally trained. The chief engineer of the Alfa factory was the man behind Alfa Romeo's golden age in motor racing. A French advertising poster (above) boasts of Alfa's international successes in 1924.

25

Antonio Ascari

For Ferrari, and for every member of the Milan racing team in the 1920s, Antonio Ascari was known simply as "the master."

Born in Casteldario, province of Mantua, where Tazio Nuvolari also came from, Ascari began his career in his own workshop, where he prepared cars in the very early 1900s. He soon became part of the Alfa Romeo scene and was Alfa's representative for Lombardy. But he was also involved in other fields, as demonstrated by a spell in Brazil where, with his two brothers, he helped to build a narrow-gauge railway.

At the wheel of a racing car, Antonio Ascari showed all his talent: an exuberant, attacking driver, constantly going for top performance and maximum speed, rather than for tactics. One episode demonstrates this more than any other.

The 1924 Italian Grand Prix was held at Monza. Ascari was entered in an Alfa Romeo, and a message was received in his pits from Arturo Mer-

A child in the cockpit of the 1925 Alfa P2. From left to right, Antonio Ascari, Ferrari and Ramponi.

Spa-Francorchamps, 1925. Ascari's Alfa P2 refueling in the pits, and celebrations after winning the race.

canti, the race director as well as practically the founder of the Autodromo di Monza. "If Ascari continues to take the 'curvetta' in such a dangerous way," read the message, "I will be forced to disqualify him." The Mantua driver's control around the bend was slipping, as he tried to drive each lap faster than the last. Ascari was to lose his life on the circuit of Monthlery in France in 1925. He left a young son, Alberto, who would do more than just keep the family flag flying.

Monthlery, 1925:
The same bend and two dramatically different moments for Antonio Ascari, who was killed at the age of 37, when his car overturned.

in the world

1919 - In August, the Weimar Republic was founded in Germany.

1919 - Indian nationalists, dissatisfied with the Montague-Chelmsford reforms, sparked off bloody rioting; Gandhi took control of the situation and, adopting the principle of nonviolence, organized the first campaign of passive resistance and noncollaboration with the British.

1921 - In Persia, Reza Khan, after overthrowing the last Shah of the Qajar dynasty, became Reza Shah Pahlavi and set about modernizing the country.

in motor sport

1921 - The first motor racing circuit in Germany was constructed near Berlin. It was called the Avus and was inaugurated on September 24, 1921, with a German victory. Fritz von Opel, driving an Opel, set the fastest lap with an average speed of 131.9 kilometers per hour.

Giuseppe Campari

Giuseppe Campari became well k-nown in 1920. The Milan driver star-ted off his career in the automobile sector at Alfa Romeo, which he joined young as test driver. In his memoirs, Ferrari remembers him as an extraordinary driver, almost an acro-bat in a way. Tall, rather chubby, with black hair, very shy and incapable of speaking in public, he was always hot and sweating.

Campari however started off a friendship with Ferrari that went further than a mere commitment to the sport. Campari soon confessed to his young Alfa teammate from Modena his other two great passions: singing and cookery. His love for singing extended to his marriage, in the 1920s, to the famous opera singer Lina Cavalleri. His love for cookery would be remembered by Ferrari in a curious anecdote: One e-

*April 1931:
Giuseppe Campari
and Tazio Nuvolari during
a break in the Mille Miglia.*

vening, Ferrari was invited together with some friends to Campari's house in the San Siro area of Milan to try out his specialty: riccioline (a short, twisty pasta) in sauce.

A curious Enzo went into the kitchen, where the "cook" was bent over preparing the sauce, unaware that his sweat was dripping into the pan. Without saying a word, Ferrari was the only person present who managed to avoid eating the dish, claiming he was allergic to it. Campari lost his life at Monza in 1933, when he crashed on some oil, the same fate which befell Borzacchini and the Pole Czaykowski.

Campari just before the start of the 1933 Italian GP at Monza. He was destined not to reach the checkered flag. Campari lost his life in a tragic incident, when his car went off the road on oil and overturned.

1907 PEKING - PARIS RAID

The idea of this race had been suggested by the Paris daily newspaper Le Matin. It was an utterly crazy idea, because of its length (15,000 kilometers) and scarce knowledge of the route. The idea was taken up by only five teams (three French, one Dutch and one Italian, with the Itala). The route began in Peking (to be reached at the drivers' own expense) and then passed through the Gobi, crossing Asia, the Caucasus, and Siberia before arriving in Moscow, and then Warsaw, Berlin and Paris.

The Italian crew was made up of the 36-year-old Prince Scipione Borghese, a reporter from the Milan newspaper Corriere della Sera, 33-year-old Luigi Barzini and a mechanic, Ettore Guizzardi. The 7.5-liter, 100-horsepower Itala weighed 2,000 kilograms (4,400 pounds) fully loaded (with 400 liters of fuel and 100 liters of lubricating oil). After leaving Peking on June 10, 1907, the Italian crew was the first to arrive at the headquarters of Le Matin in Paris on August 10.

in the world

1927 - Charles Lindbergh completed the first nonstop solo flight from New York to Paris (May 20-21) in the single-engine mo-

noplane, Spirit of St. Louis.

1928 - Alexander Fleming discovered penicillin. He was awarded the Nobel Prize for medicine in 1945.

1929 - On October 24, the Wall Street Stock Market in New York crashed. It was the start of the Great Depression, which led to the collapse of thousands of firms and a

*Peking, 1907:
The start of modern-day
motor racing. The Itala,
driven by Prince Scipione Borghese,
accompanied by a mechanic
(Guizzardi) and a journalist
(Barzini), starts the
Peking-Paris Race from one
of the entrances to the Chinese
imperial city. They were the first to
reach Paris, after encountering
numerous difficulties along
the route, including
the crossing of this stone
bridge in Manchuria.*

massive increase in unemployment.

in motor sport

1927 - The International Association (AIACR) declared it was no longer obligatory to have two seats in motor sport competition. The figure of riding mechanic disappeared.

1929 - The circuit of Monaco-Monte Carlo was created. The street circuit would remain virtually unchanged until the present day.

31

THE INVENTOR

In 1929, Alfredo and Augusto Caniato would have found it difficult to believe that they were involved in something destined to become part of the history of motor sport. Hemp merchants from Ferrara, the two brothers were caught up in the wave of enthusiasm and ambitions which Enzo Ferrari managed to generate. It was the Caniato brothers who put in more than 60 percent (at the time 130,000 lire or $81.25, out of a total of 200,000 lire, or $125) of the share capital which set up the Scuderia Ferrari joint-stock company. Other shareholders, as well as Ferrari himself, were a driver, Mario Tadini and a photographer, Ferruccio Testi. Alfa Romeo and Pirelli were also minor, but important, shareholders.

Scuderia Ferrari was thus created on November 29, 1929, registered by the court of Modena. The initial idea dated back to a few months earlier, to a dinner in Bologna. The idea was to help the shareholders race by preparing and running the cars; to organize the necessary technical and sporting back-up, and race not only as an activity reserved for a rich élite, but as an outlet for anyone interested in racing, who from now onwards would only have to concentrate on just that.

Not even Enzo Ferrari could have imagined it, but his was a unique idea. Having taken Alfa Romeo to the top after removing it from the hands of Fiat, the 31-year-old from Modena became totally involved in motor sport throughout the second half of the 1920s by playing a variety of different roles. He took up racing once again and had a steady job in the Alfa factory working as commercial representative for Emilia-Romagna and the Marche. Above all however, he was thinking, elaborating and making plans. He was constantly inventing and instilling his enthusiasm in others to build up an organization that would top Alfa Romeo itself as far as both prestige and results were concerned. Moreover, his earlier passion for driving racing cars was becoming increasingly replaced by the desire to make his name in the sport with total authority and commitment.

The debate no longer revolved around whether Ferrari was a great driver or not: results show that although he might not have been an Ascari or a Nuvolari, he owed nothing to fortune on the track. By now the manager had replaced the driver, and the truth was emerging: Ability behind the wheel of a racing car was only the last—and decisive—phase of the road toward winning. The whole process began much earlier, with the choice of cars, their preparation and the knowledge of races, circuits and regulations; finally with the swift decision-making processes that understand and put into action everything required to arrive first at the checkered flag.

Ferrari at the end of the 1920s was basically an inventor. From his boundless imagination and his total ambition, a project was born out of nothing and grew to become a real company business. Just 10 years back, alone and lonely from the family misfortunes of the years of World War I, he could never have imagined this turn of events. Help obviously came from his new family. Married to the young Laura Garello from Turin, Ferrari was to become a father at the start of the 1930s. The birth of his son Alfredino would be the decisive factor in ending his driving career.

Right from the start, Scuderia Ferrari exclusively raced Alfa Romeo cars. After the pensioning off of the 6C with 1,500 and 1,750-cc engines, which Ferrari experimented with from

1927 when he resumed racing, the start of the 1930s saw the Scuderia involved with the Alfa Romeo P2 and P3. These cars were to become famous for the first epic battles between champions such as Tazio Nuvolari and Achille Varzi. "Nivola," in fact, won the Trieste-Opicina mountain time-trial on June 15, 1930, the first victory for the Scuderia, defeating an array of other Alfa Romeos and numerous Lancias and Bugattis. Two weeks later came the next win, with an Alfa P2, in the mountain race from Cuneo to Colle della Maddalena.

Ferrari was a young entrepreneur, 32 years old and full of hundreds of innovative ideas. The success of the Scuderia was quite exceptional, but one year's activity was sufficient to give cold feet to Ferrari's shareholders, who decided not to continue the business, due to the efforts required. Their pulling out, however, failed to discourage the Modena entrepreneur, who saw that it was necessary to capitalize on success.

In 1931, the Scuderia entered a total of 10 cars for the Mille Miglia. The following year, Ferrari managed to acquire all the P3s produced by the Milan constructor, becoming the te-

chnical-sporting arm of Alfa, which was more than happy to entrust its Modena partner with all of its sporting activity. The turning point came in 1932, on a company and organizational level, for Scuderia Ferrari. Ferrari began to employ professional drivers, in addition to his fellow shareholders. Antonio Varzi and Luigi Fagioli, Campari and Arcangeli, Borzacchini, and Chiron, as well as the brilliant Guy Moll, began to appear at the wheel of Scuderia Ferrari cars. But one name stood out amongst all the others: Tazio Nuvolari, who was always to remain "the alter ego" of Enzo Ferrari.

August 1930: Scuderia Ferrari has just been formed, and most road races were held on gravel surfaces, like these hairpin bends near St. Moritz.

NUVOLARI

Everything and more about Tazio Nuvolari has been handed down to the present day by historical news items. This means that the figure of "Nivola" has emerged from the legend itself. Six years older than Ferrari (he was born on November 16, 1892, at Castel d'Ario, a few kilometers from Mantua), Nuvolari was already a top driver when he joined the Scuderia. Small, with smiling eyes worn on a thin and nervous body, the champion from Mantua seemed to be born to be a part of motor racing history. He used to race and win on bikes. When he switched to cars, maybe because he was used to the superior balance required on two wheels, he did extraordinary things. He had no fear of speed; on the contrary, it spurred him on. But his class behind the wheel would be directly proportional to the number of curves waiting to be tackled. Curves. He called them resources of the track, and each one of them was for him a challenge, whatever the risk.

In October 1930, when he signed an exclusive contract for 1931, except for three motor bike races which he was particularly fond of, it was clear that Nuvolari was soon to become the flag-bearer of Scuderia Ferrari. This immediately led to the start of a string of events, sometimes sensational, which made Nivola's legend and motor racing history. At the 1930 Mille Miglia, he was driving an Alfa Romeo, identical to that of Varzi who started one minute before him. Nuvolari was to catch him by surprise at the end of the final night of the race, overtaking him with his headlights turned off so as not to be noticed. It was not important that the dark of the night had been replaced by the early light of dawn: The legend had been made.

Tazio Nuvolari won many races for Scuderia Ferrari. The historic victories were the 1932 Targa Florio, with a final time that was only to be bettered 20 years later. A sensational victory also came at the 1935 German GP, where Nuvolari's tiny Alfa managed to win on the impossible curves of the old Nürburgring circuit against the powerful and dominant Auto Union and Mercedes squads, the hosts, who were widely expected to walk away with an easy win.

At Brno in Czechoslovakia, again in 1935, Nuvolari finished second with his left rear tire down to the rim.

A special mention is reserved for his victory in the 1936 Vanderbilt Cup, organized in the United States, which aimed to start up motor racing competition between Europe and America.

The Italian driver was the driving force behind the growing technical

The Alfa Romeo P3 (1932).

side of the Scuderia, which was more and more involved in research and testing, even though always for Alfa Romeo. In 1935 Ferrari's organization constructed a "monster" of a car, fitted with two eight-cylinder Alfa engines (one at the front and one at the rear), capable of taking Nivola to a new maximum speed record of 364 kilometers per hour and an ave-

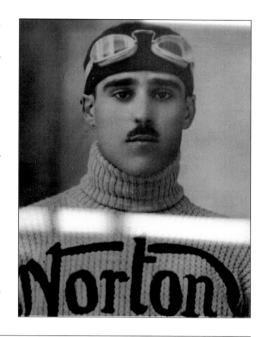

Tazio Nuvolari: The legend began on two wheels, but he soon switched to cars. This was the start of a unique relationship of friendship and rivalry, admiration and brotherly love between "Nivola" and Enzo Ferrari.

in the world

1936 - The Spanish Civil War broke out after the revolt of Generals Francisco Franco, Mola, Sanjurjo and Goded (backed by Germany, Italy and Portugal) against the Republican government of Manuel Azana.

1937 - The German Air Force devastated the Basque town of Guernica during the Spanish Civil War on April 26. The massacre provided the inspiration for a monumental oil painting by Pablo Picasso.

in motor sport

1936 - Tazio Nuvolari, driving an Alfa Romeo, won the Vanderbilt Cup in New York, 10 minutes ahead of Wimille (Bugatti 4900). Fiorello La Guardia, mayor of New York, thanked him publicly on behalf of millions of immigrants in the United States.

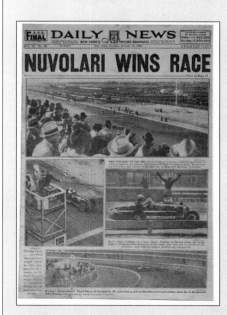

1937 - An Auto Union driven by Bernd Rosemeyer made history by breaking the 400 kilometers per hour limit for the first time on an autobahn near Frankfurt, Germany.

rage of more than 323 kilometers per hour over the mile, speeds which were reached on a stretch of the motorway from Florence to the coast.

The idyllic relations between Nuvolari and Ferrari were interrupted in 1936. The driver, aware that he was the reason for the fortunes of the Modena entrepreneur, wanted to become an equal partner in the company. But that wasn't all: He also wanted the new company to be called Scuderia Nuvolari Ferrari. This situation had its roots in a conflict of personalities, both strong and determined, between the driver and the businessman. A conflict only in part, full of mutual admiration and friendship, but one that had the capacity to surprise. Ferrari showed shrewdness and organizational and administrative ability; Nuvolari gave a constant display of extraordinary courage. On his departure for the 1932 Targa Florio from Modena, the driver discovered he had a return ticket, and he realized this was an opportunity to make a gibe at Ferrari: "They say you're a good administrator," said Nivola to an astonished Ferrari, "but I realize it's not true. You should have booked me a one-way ticket. When you leave for a race, there is always the possibility that you'll come back in a wooden coffin."

What an extraordinary personality! In any case, there are many such anecdotes aptly describing the relationship linking the driver and the constructor until 1953, the year of Nuvolari's death. A relationship between two giants of motor racing, who began to understand that they were just that, but managed all the same to respect each other.

After Nuvolari wanting to become partner of Ferrari, the relationship between the two was punctuated by divorces and reconciliation. At the 1936 Circuito di Modena, on the street circuit prepared on the narrow roads of the town in Emilia, the Monument Chicane was probably the most difficult curve, forcing the

1930: The Alfas of Scuderia Ferrari began to become more numerous. The 1750 SS of Lord Howe-Birkin (below) at the Le Mans 12 Hours, and the same car driven by Nuvolari at the Targa Florio (alongside), and the driver after victory in the Mille Miglia the same year.

12180

in the world

1939 - On September, Germany invaded Poland without declaring war. This was the beginning of World War II.

1940 - (August-October) In the Battle of Britain, Goering's Luftwaffe was unable to overcome the fighters of the Royal Air Force, who were helped by the discovery of radar.

1941 - OOn June 22, Hitler gave the go-ahead for Operation Barbarossa, attacking the USSR without declaring war.

1941 - OnDecember 7, the Japanese carried out a surprise attack on the U.S. naval base at Pearl Harbor, Hawaii. The United States entered the war the next day.

The New York Times.

JAPAN WARS ON U.S. AND BRITAIN; MAKES SUDDEN ATTACK ON HAWAII; HEAVY FIGHTING AT SEA REPORTED

1943 - On July 25, Mussolini was ousted after being outvoted by the Grand Council. Control of the Italian government was taken over by Marshal Badoglio, who with the consent of the king, opened peace negotiations with the Allies.

1943 - At the Tehran Conference on November 28, Roosevelt, Churchill and Stalin discussed the invasion of Europe, scheduled for May 1944, and postwar political issues regarding Germany and Poland.

THE TEAM

drivers to use their arms on the steering-wheel. The curve was also Ferrari's favorite observation point, but that year he was without Nuvolari, who had moved to Maserati. It was at the Variante del Monumento that the driver, oblivious to the difficult nature of the curve, on every lap passed his hand over his nose in a gesture mocking the astonished Ferrari. Memories of days gone by. . . . The two, in any case, took different paths. Nuvolari raced with other cars: Cisitalia and Auto Union, as a replacement driver after the tragic death of Bernd Rosemeyer. With the German car, Tazio amazingly won the race on October 22, 1938, at Donington Park in Britain, making up time on Lang's Mercedes after a pit-stop of almost a minute. He took the lead four laps from the end to the cheers of the spectators, thus earning the title of "master" from all the other drivers. Nuvolari and Ferrari found themselves back together again in 1947, the year of the birth of the first real Ferrari racing car. One year later Nuvolari dominated the Mille Miglia with a Ferrari 166 powered by a 2-liter 12-cylinder engine, but a few hours from the finish in Brescia, a broken leaf-spring pin interrupted the legendary cavalcade.

"Bad luck, you'll win next year," said Ferrari in an attempt to cheer up the 56-year-old driver.

"Ferrari," came the reply (he had always called him Ferrari). "At our age, there aren't many days left like this. Remember that, and try and enjoy them to the utmost, if you can." Nuvolari died five years later on August 11, 1953, in a way he would surely have preferred not to: in a bed. He had tried for many years to avoid the terrible destiny that had taken away both his sons at an early age, a destiny which made him lucidly but desperately in charge of his own fate.

With this letter, signed by Minister Falcone Lucifero, the Royal House expressed its condolences for the death of Tazio Nuvolari in 1953. Eighteen years before, in 1935, the contract between 'Nivola' and Scuderia Ferrari was three pages long.

AWAY FROM ALFA

Destiny often plays strange tricks, unpredictably yet inevitably taking its course. This was the case with Alfa Romeo from 1937 onward, a complex string of events with an initial serious consequence, that arrived at a turning point, deciding the fate of a man, a marque, and the future of motor racing.

Halfway through the 1930s, Alfa was in the middle of a serious crisis. The sporting regulations introduced in 1934 stipulated a maximum weight of 750 kilograms for cars. Everything else was free, including the type and power of the engine. The technical regulations by penalized the cars from the Milan manufacturer, especially against the German competitors—Mercedes and Auto Union—who made good use of

an avant-guard iron and steel industry and a budget far greater than anything the Italian manufacturer could pour into motor racing. The greater agility guaranteed by a smaller structure allowed Scuderia Ferrari to intervene more easily and, above all, more rapidly in this difficult technical scene. Already in 1935 the Scuderia had constructed the twin-engined "Bimotore," powered by two eight-cylinder units, whose main feature was its exceptional performance, although it also had major mechanical problems. In a lightened version weighing less than a ton, the "Bimotore" set the land speed record on the Florence-Livorno motorway. But in the heavier, more reliable version for racing, the car literally tore up its tires, thus requiring numerous pit stops, which wiped out the advantage from its greater

performance. One year later, Alfa Romeo commissioned Scuderia Ferrari to construct a new car, the 158, powered by a supercharged eight-cylinder engine. This was a car with a great potential, so much so that Alfa sent one of its top engineers, Gioachino Colombo, to Modena to design it, together with Ferrari's engineering staff.

The situation grew dramatic. The Milan manufacturer continued to support the Scuderia, but in a particular way and with particular agreements. It proposed the purchase of 80 percent of Ferrari's organization, leaving him with the task of representing Alfa in competition. Ferrari was waiting for this moment and replied with a counterproposal: close down the Scuderia and hand over to Alfa the technical material of the team, cars included. In exchange, he asked for a new structure in Milan, Alfa Corse, of which he would become sole director with full powers.

It was, in a certain sense, blackmail. "I will give you greater, more dedicated support," was Ferrari's reply, "on condition that from now, on the company guarantees its total commitment to competition, and I am the one who runs it."

The idea must have come as a shock to Alfa Romeo and its director-general, Ugo Gobbato, but in any case, it was swallowed and accepted. This transformed the moment of crisis of the Milan constructor into a clear take-over by Ferrari. In any case, Ferrari was the one who had the big ideas. The Scuderia itself, a splendid and revolutionary invention in the ever-changing world of motor sport, was limited by its size. Clearly, Alfa Romeo guaranteed a different future, other means and other possibilities. That was the start of Alfa Corse, but soon the expectations of the Modena constructor came face to face with cold reality. It was even colder in a way, because Ferrari soon discovered he was not the only real boss. Ferrari was put in charge of the sporting division, but as head of the special projects division, there was a certain Ricart, a man almost the same age as Ferrari, with whom he came into direct competition. Wilfredo Ricart, of Spanish origin, an extrovert, and an authoritarian engineer, had managed to obtain the total confidence of the Alfa Romeo director-general. Sparks immediately flew between him and Ferrari on a personal level. It was a clash that magnified the lack of synergy between the working methods of the man from Modena and those of Alfa. Ferrari maintained that the entire competitions program must be in the hands of a small and agile structure, capable of resolving problems in a short time. Gobbato thought differently, and in this he was backed by Ricart. The Alfa Romeo management maintained that races, although independent, must be run with cars that incorporated the technical capacities of the entire company.

Ferrari tried to prevail in every way possible. He attempted to convince the director general that Ricart was clearly a genius, and for this reason his efforts must be directed to higher activities than mere racing. He tried to make friends with the Spaniard, but to no avail. Ferrari was to remember this in one of his best books "Ferrari 80" with a few sharp words: "Ricart had smooth greasy hair. He dressed elegantly but looked rather oriental, with long-sleeved jackets which hid his hands. When he held out his hand, you could feel inert flesh, rather like that of a corpse."

He continued with a funny anecdote: "He used to wear shoes with enormous rubber soles. They were so big that one day I asked him why he wore them. He replied calmly that an engineer had to take certain precautions: A well-sprung step prevented disturbances and vibrations from going to the brain."

Ferrari was frustrated and felt he was reaching a boiling point. That was when the 158 began to cause problems. Ferrari wanted to exploit its potential, which he maintained was still vast; instead, Ricart thought it was outdated and pressed for the construction of a new car, with a 12-cylinder rear-located engine. This was never going to work. When En-

zo Ferrari pointed it out to the director general, the reply was what Ferrari expected.

Divorce came immediately: In September 1939, Alfa Romeo recognized the severance pay for almost 20 years of close collaboration, demanded a commitment from Ferrari not to become involved in motor racing for four years, and wound up the rapport with immediate effect.

Thus ended a chapter of motor sport history. Ferrari lost. The clash between his personal desire for innovation and inventive energy and the working methods of a large company placed him in a minority. The order to not become directly involved in motor sport for four years reveals just how much respect Alfa Romeo had for the 41-year-old "motivator of men" from Modena. On the other hand, Ferrari was a man of extraordinary sensibility and could see

that four years were soon to pass by in haste: World War II was just around the corner and all signs pointed to it being a long one. . . .

1935: A group photo for the first appearance of the Alfa Romeo Bimotore with Nuvolari at the wheel. A picture from Monza the same year (the other page, below) of the Trossi Monoposto, powered by a curious 16-cylinder engine with volumetric compressor that was capable of producing more than 250 horsepower. The following year, 1936, saw the first appearance at Monza of the Alfa Romeo driven by Dreyfuss, closely watched by Vittorio Jano. The Alfa 8C35, 12-cylinder of Nuvolari at Monza (the other page, above). Chicanes had already been invented.

Nivola's Secret

In 1931, Enzo Ferrari was still active as a driver as well as being the owner of Scuderia Ferrari. He was to hang up his gloves at the end of this season, helped a little in his decision by the birth of his son, Alfredino. One day, during practice for the Circuito delle Tre Province race, he asked Nuvolari if he could sit beside him in an Alfa 1750 leased to him by the Scuderia for that race. Nivola was suspicious. He had seen Ferrari at the wheel of a much more powerful eight-cylinder Alfa Romeo 2300. Nevertheless, he agreed to the request. From the tale of that experience as codriver, written by Ferrari in his book, Piloti, che gente . . . (Drivers, what people . . .), comes possibly the clearest and most colorful explanation of the mystery which made Nivola such a great and legendary driver. "At the first curve," wrote Ferrari, "I had the clear sensation that Tazio had made a mistake, and we were to end up in the ditch. I braced myself for the impact. Instead, we ended up at the start of the next straight with the car perfectly in line. I looked at him. His rugged face was calm and normal, not the face of one who has just luckily escaped from a spin. At the second and third curve, I had the same impression. At the fourth and fifth, it all became clear to me. Out of the corner of my eye, I noticed that throughout the Parabolica curve, Tazio never once took his foot off the accelerator; on the contrary, he pushed it flat to the floor. As the curves flashed by, I discovered his secret. Nuvolari went into the bend earlier than driver instinct would have told me. But he approached it in an unusual way, suddenly pointing the nose of the car at the inside edge, right at the point where the curve began. With his foot down—clearly in the right gear for the curve before pointing the car—he let the car go in a controlled skid on all four wheels, taking advantage of the centrifugal force and holding it with the traction force of the driving wheels. Throughout the entire radius of the curve, the nose of the car shaved the inside stone edge, and when the curve finished and the straight began, the car would be in the normal position to continue the race, without any corrective maneuvers." Just for the record, the Circuito delle Tre Province was won by Nuvolari. Ferrari was second.

Circuit of Biella, 1935.
The acrobatic driving style of Nuvolari was something that his rivals had no chance of emulating.

The Vanderbilt Cup

The Vanderbilt Cup, the first important motor race competition between Europe and America,. was well established on the U.S. side of the Atlantic, where it was more important than the Indianapolis 500. In 1936, it was even more prestigious than ever. The Roosevelt Field circuit on Long Island was set up for the event. A 34-strong American team lined up against the expedition from Europe, made up of Alfa Romeos, Bugattis and Maseratis. At the last moment, an entry was received from Scuderia Ferrari for three Alfa Romeo 12Cs for Nuvolari, Brivio and Farina. The result was sensational. Nivola totally annihilated the opposition: pole position, fastest lap, and victory in a race led from start to finish, almost half an hour ahead of the local favorite, Mauri Rose, the first of the Americans, but only sixth overall.

To drive home the sensational result, Nuvolari collected prize money of $85,000 (an exorbitant amount for the time), but broke into a cold sweat on the steamship on the trip home, when he thought he had left the winning check in his hotel. Luckily though, he found it.

When Nuvolari won the 1936 Vanderbilt Cup, the Italian press celebrated the victory. In the group photo on arriving in New York, the driver can be seen together with the captain of the transatlantic liner Rex, Brivio; on the right, Farina, Bazzi and the journalist Canestrini.

The Prancing Horse Emblem

A black horse on a yellow background, with its front legs in the air, viewed from the left. Today this is the universally recognized symbol of Ferrari and many other companies over the years have come to realize this—at their own expense—after having, maybe involuntarily, copied it to publicize their own products. The prancing horse appeared on Scuderia Ferrari cars in 1932 at the Spa 24 Hours race.

Ferrari remembered that the idea had been offered to him nine years before. On his first victory as a driver, at the 1923 Circuito del Savio, he was given the prize by Countess Paolina Baracca, the mother of the air force pilot and World War I ace, Francesco. The countess offered Ferrari the horse logo, which was on the fuselage of her son's fighter airplane, so that he could use it for his racing cars. Ferrari accepted with gratitude. Since 1932, the black horse on a yellow background—the historic color of Modena—has identified all the cars, competition and production, from Enzo Ferrari's activity.

"La storia del cavallino rampante è semplice e affascinante. Il cavallino era dipinto sulla carlinga del caccia di Francesco Baracca, l'eroico aviatore caduto sul Montello, l'asso degli assi della prima guerra mondiale.
Quando vinsi nel '23 il primo circuito del Savio, che si correva a Ravenna, conobbi il conte Enrico Baracca, padre dell'eroe; da quell'incontro nacque il successivo, con la madre, contessa Paolina.
Fu essa a dirmi, un giorno: «Ferrari, metta sulle sue macchine il cavallino rampante del mio figliolo. Le porterà fortuna». Conservo ancora la fotografia di Baracca, con la dedica dei genitori, in cui mi affidano l'emblema. Il cavallino era ed è rimasto nero; io aggiunsi il fondo giallo canarino che è il colore di Modena".

The Sponsors

History has already credited Enzo Ferrari's intuition in coming up with the idea of sponsorship. It was in 1929, the first year of the Scuderia; the involvement of Alfa Romeo and Pirelli in the initial share capital was aimed at ensuring maximum technical collaboration from the two companies. But as well as tires and cars, the two Milan companies also made a financial contribution: 5,000 lire ($312.50) from Pirelli and 10,000 ($ 625) from Alfa, paving the way for the numerous marques that were involved from then onward: Shell (fuels and lubricants), Bosch (electrical equipment), Rudge Whitworth (wheels), Champion (spark plugs), Siata (shock absorbers) and Memini (carburetors). In addition to supplying their material free of charge, these companies guaranteed financial support, in exchange for which Ferrari gave them advertising space in the end-of-season company magazine and their names on the lorries that transported the cars to the circuits. With this sensational new idea, Enzo Ferrari succeeded right from the start in financing his racing activity, improving the overall situation with the many "paying" drivers. The figures were quite substantial, with Shell in 1932 paying the Scuderia the tidy sum of 100,000 lire ($ 62.50). Today that would be around 150,000,000 lire ($ 93,750).

A Meteoric Guy Moll

It is no secret that out of all his drivers, Ferrari always loved the most instinctive and exciting ones, drivers who manage to put on a show thanks to their inborn sense of speed and their ability to overcome the risk threshold. Guy Moll, in this sense, would be paralleled by Ferrari to the recent phenomenon called Gilles Villeneuve. Born of an Algerian father and Spanish mother, Guy Moll began to make his name in motor racing and Ferrari immediately gave him an Alfa from the Scuderia. It was the 1934 Monaco Grand Prix: Moll won by overtaking Chiron on the final curve, repeating Nuvolari's victory of two years before. It was love at first sight between Ferrari and Moll. Unfortunately, however, it was not destined to last. Moll lost his life at the Coppa Acerbo that same year. The memory remains of Moll as a splendid, exciting meteor.

Victories of Ferrari at the wheel

Ferrari competed in 40 races from 1919 to 1931, with a break from 1925 to 1926. He won a total of 9 races:

1923   Circuito del Savio

1924   Circuito del Savio
           Circuito del Polesine
           Coppa Acerbo

1927   Circuito di Alessandria
           Circuito di Modena

1928   Circuito di Alessandria
           Circuito di Modena

1931   Bobbio-Passo del Penice
           mountain time-trial

Scuderia Ferrari raced from 1930 to 1937, competing—always with Alfa Romeos—in a total of 225 races, with 144 victories. The best year was 1935, with 30 victories out of 35 races.

Photo Album of Racing in the 1920s and 1930s

1)   *1936 Monaco GP: Brivio ahead of Farina and Nuvolari, all in eight-cylinder Alfa 3800s*
2)   *Enzo Ferrari and Nuvolari at the 1924 Circuit of Savio. The car is a Chiribiri, and Ferrari went on to win*
3)   *The prancing horse of Scuderia Ferrari can be seen on the Alfa Tipo B of Nuvolari, winner of the Circuit of Biella race*
4)   *1935: Enzo Ferrari behind Nuvolari, who is preparing for his first test with the Alfa Romeo Bimotore*
5)   *Monte Carlo 1935: the pile-up at the chicane in front of the port*
6)   *The triumph of 'Nivola' in an eight-cylinder Alfa 2300 at the 1931 Targa Florio*
7)   *1938 Le Mans 24 Hours: the eight-cylinder Alfa 2900 of Biondetti-Sommer*
8)   *1936 Hungarian GP: the Number 24 Alfa 8C of the winner Nuvolari, whose teammate Tadini finished fourth*
9)   *1933 Coppa Principessa di Piemonte: the Alfa 1500 SS of women drivers Peduzzi-Restelli*
10)   *The start of the 1932 Monaco GP: Nuvolari and Caracciola on the front row in eight–cylinder Alfa Romeo 2300Ms.*
11)   *Rome, 1931, the Autodromo del Littorio: Nuvolari drove the eight-cylinder Alfa 2300 Monza to victory in the duel with a Caproni 100 airplane*
12)   *1934 French GP: victory went to Luis Chiron, in the middle between Varzi and Trossi, all driving Tipo B Alfa Romeos*

THE NEW 12 CYLINDER ENGINE

Let us go back to the precise moment when Ferrari left Alfa Romeo. The amount of severance pay given to Enzo Ferrari by the Milan manufacturer was never officially made known, even though sources put the figure at about 1,000,000 lire ($ 625 at the time), a considerable sum that enabled Ferrari to purchase the beautiful Palazzo dei Cento Caproni, one of the finest buildings in Modena. It also allowed him to buy land at Maranello, and maybe just then the Modena constructor was unaware that he was laying the first stones of his legendary future.

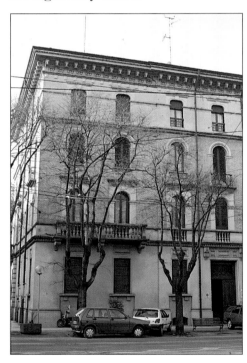

As mentioned, Ferrari left Alfa with one clear aim: to demonstrate to the management of the Milan manufacturer who Ferrari was and what he could achieve in motor racing. He was, of course, forced to abandon racing for four years, but this was easily got round by plans to build a car for private drivers: the 815. As he could not use the logo of the Scuderia, the Auto Avio Costruzioni Ferrari was born. With the first of the two 815s constructed, Alberto Ascari, the son of Antonio, who had flanked the Modena constructor in his first steps in the sport, made his racing

debut at the 1940 Mille Miglia. The race was much shorter, a triangle connecting the towns of Brescia, Cremona and Mantua. The 815 made a brilliant start before retiring with mechanical problems. The project was a good one, but the car was built too hastily. It was also spring 1940: Italy was about to become involved in World War II, and thoughts were lying elsewhere.

At the start of the conflict, the work of the small group of engineers in the headquarters at Viale Trento e Trieste in Modena became first difficult, and then impossible. The main cities of northern Italy were hit by bombs, and everything had to be moved to Maranello, especially after the new laws on industrial decentralization. Despite being caught up in a war, the workforce under Ferrari

grew from 40 to more than 150. Work was not hard to find. Ferrari was asked to construct mechanical parts for the National Aeronautics Company in Rome; later he also obtained the tender for the construction of industrial machinery for the production of ball bearings.

These weeks were packed with drama: bombing raids and war incidents quickly followed and not even the Maranello factory was spared, when it was hit in a couple of air raids at the end of 1944 and the start of 1945, the final year of the war.

The building in the center of Modena, purchased at the end of the 1930s, where Enzo Ferrari lived until the final days of his life.

When the engineer Colombo, the designer of the Alfa 158, came to Maranello in the summer, he found Ferrari impatient to get going again. By now he was thinking of racing cars day and night. He also had a new revolutionary aim in mind: a car constructed around a 12-cylinder engine. Raymond Sommer, a French driver who was very famous at the time, never failed to impress upon Ferrari his personal view of this particular engine configuration, which he considered to be the choice of the future. Convincing Ferrari was not difficult. In the 1920s he had already been impressed by an American car, purchased by Antonio Ascari, that had a V-12 engine. This was followed by the U.S. Army Packards, which arrived with the liberation of

Italy at the end of the war. Finally at Alfa Romeo, there was the idea of Ricart, who was convinced he could construct a rear-engined 12-cylinder 1,500-cc car. It was at this stage that Enzo Ferrari, not in the least perturbed by the events of the war, which had just ended after a period of terror in northern Italy, began to nurture splendid projects for the relaunch of motor sport.

The first real Ferrari made its debut at Piacenza on May 11, 1947: the local daily newspaper Libertà followed its early steps with great interest. Above, the Alfa 512 designed by the Spanish engineer Ricart after Ferrari's divorce from the Milan constructor.

THE FIRST REAL FERRARI

May 11, 1947, marked the debut of the first real Ferrari racing team at the Circuito di Piacenza. The race was a minor one and the spectators were unaware of the fact that the first chapter of a motor sport legend was being written. The Ferrari 125 at this debut had been designed two years beforehand. Since then, much importance had been given to the design, construction and testing of the 12-cylinder engine, which ran for the first time on the test bench in the autumn of 1946. At Piacenza there were two cars in the newly created colors of the Prancing Horse: they were driven by the future World Champion Nino Farina and Franco Cortese. The former decided to abandon the venture on the eve of the race, unhappy with the performance of the car in practice. Cortese, however, carried on and was leading the race until two laps from the end, when he retired with fuel pump problems. All things considered, it wasn't such a bad debut.

Two weeks later, on Sunday, 25th May 25, there was a race in Rome. At the Caracalla circuit, it was Cortese who again set the pace. This time there were no mechanical problems, and he won easily. The enthusiasm among the team members was evident, but nobody—not even Ferrari—could have guessed that this victory was the start of a legend. The run of victories continued. Cortese won again, as did Nuvolari soon afterward. After enthusiastically a-greeing to drive the new car, he triumphed in two races. In the autumn, at the end of the season, the Grand Prix version of the Ferrari 125 made its debut. It was driven by Sommer, who won the Turin GP. Success for the 125, a car that could be raced in different categories, thanks to simple modifications to the bodywork and the fairings, was complete and immediate.

This was in spite of the fact that the first real Ferrari had sprung from the Constructor's own technical conviction that the engine was always more important than the chassis.

He would only abandon this convic-

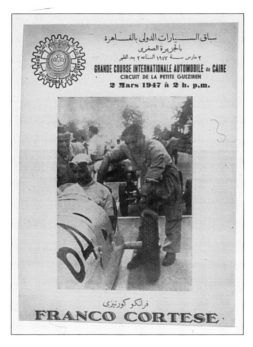

tion later, on the path toward technical perfection, paving the way to other wins and increasingly sophisticated cars, which would come to dominate in the technical sector.

For Enzo Ferrari, the Grand Prix won by Sommer stretched far beyond its technical importance. The finishing line for the 125 Grand Prix at the Circuito del Valentino was in fact just a few feet away from that famous bench where Ferrari had cried silent tears at the end of World War I. Then he was alone, af-

ter the death of his father and without his much-loved brother, Alfredo. He was unemployed without any immediate hope of finding work. That was 1919, now it was 1947. How life had changed over the years. .

That period of almost 30 years transformed the face of the world, society, the motor car, and motor racing; it was the 30 years in which Ferrari was "invented." Two years after the end of World War II, Ferrari was one of the new men on the Italian industrial scene. In racing, the stage for his real, indestructible ambition, the Modena constructor was the point of reference. He loved racing, but had abandoned the career due to a combination of professional and family reason.

A new profession, a motivator of men and ideas, had taken over. His driving ambition was to give life to a completely new role in racing: constructor, sporting director, technical adviser. The role of husband and father was not an easy one for a racing driver, who has to win, win, and win again. All of these conditioning factors undoubtedly influenced the decision to bring an end to his career as a racing driver. But all things considered, Ferrari himself felt he never had what it took to become a great champion.

"Even if I had worked hard at it," he admitted one day, "I wasn't sure I could have been a great racing-driver. I had my doubts at the time. . . . " The doubts, in a way, also involved a technical aspect. The racing driver in Ferrari respected the motor car and did everything he could to go easy

on it. A racing driver who wants only to win, who must win, thinks in a completely different way. The constructor in Ferrari could give his best to this role, dividing his massive desire to reach the top with this particular aspect. Furthermore, he was entirely at home in this role, and could totally respect the engineering techniques which were his guiding light. From this point onward, the scarlet red cars had become a cornerstone of road racing competition and were now ready to make a triumphant entry into the circuits.

FROM THE ROAD ... TO FORMULA 1

At the end of the 1940s Enzo Ferrari had reached a key point in his life. At 50 years of age, he was above all a lonely ma, but this time, not in the negative sense of the word. In the much more positive and reassuring sense of man and manager who did not have to ask for anyone's agreement before taking a decision. Ferrari was very much his own man. The racing team was based on various strong personalities, but only Ferrari was at the helm. The days at Alfa Romeo were long gone. And so were the days with the Spaniard, Ricart, with his crazy pretenses, with his absurd way of dressing, of speaking, of walking on rubber so as not to disturb his brain waves.

"I am in charge of Alfa Romeo," - said Gobbato at the moment of the

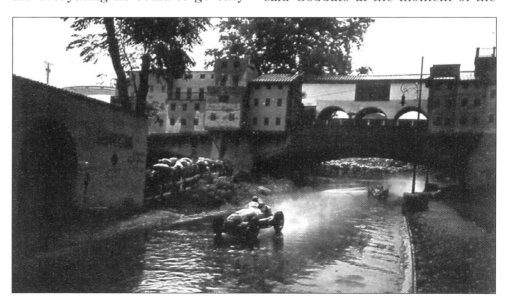

Racing at the Circuito del Valentino in Turin. On the other page, the 1948 Ferrari 125 Grand Prix.

disagreements leading to the divorce of 1939, "and I cannot accept your suggestions without reserve. Or in any case without discussion."

"I'm leaving Alfa," was Ferrari's reply, "and it's Alfa's decision. But for this reason I will not change my way of being and thinking."

History. Or maybe prehistory. The Milan manufacturer, which remained under Ricart's control, never again produced a winning racing car. The Spanish engineer, who stayed with Alfa until 1945 as director of special projects, was by then a man of the past. Ferrari, on the other hand, was looking with great interest toward everything that moved, changed, and promised innovation and developments in the competitions sector. On the horizon there was a new category of cars and races called Grands Prix, destined to become the first Formula 1 in 1950. The path toward Grands Prix on a continuous and worldwide basis was however still a long one. Ferrari approached it by dominating the road races of the day. In 1948 Clemente Biondetti and Giuseppe Navone won the Mille Miglia with a Ferrari 166S. For the Prancing Horse manufacturer, it was the first victory of international importance, but it was dulled by the disappointment which befell Nuvolari. Called upon to take part in the Mille Miglia just one day before the start, Nuvolari was given the Scuderia Inter 166S with Number 1049 on its bodywork. His codriver was the mechanic Sergio Scapinelli: together they took the lead on the stretch of road to Pescara. When they got to Rome, they had a 12-minute lead. At Livorno, the lead was 20 minutes. At Bologna, 35. Before Rome, the Number 1049 Ferrari had lost its bonnet, which they had never been able to close and which the drilowing the situation that was about to bring an end to Nuvolari. The racing driver from Mantua was 56 years old, Ferrari 6 years younger. They were linked by a special bond of affection. Eleven years before, in 1937, Tazio had been in the United States to defend the Vanderbilt Cup that he had won the year before. During those days, his oldest son Giorgio had died. Ferrari had had to inform Nuvolari in a touching telegram: "We have accompanied your Giorgio. Your mother and his mother have born the loss with great strength. Stay calm. Brotherly yours, Enzo Ferrari."

In 1948, after recovering from the disappointment of his retirement at Villa Ospizio near Reggio Emilia close to the finish of the Mille Miglia, Nuvolari asked the parish priest of the town if he could go and have a nap in the bed of his rectory. Nivola's season was over, but another reopened with renewed energy. The victory by Biondetti was the first of six succes-

sive Ferrari wins at the Mille Miglia. The red cars began to win regularly. In 1949, Biondetti repeated his victory in the Mille Miglia, this time co-piloted by Salami in a 166MM Barchetta Touring. Four more victories followed in the next four years. Meanwhile the Ferrari name was also beginning to be known at circuits on the other side of the Alps. Still in 1949, Luigi Chinetti and Lord Seldson alternated behind the wheel and triumphed at the Le Mans 24 Hours. A few weeks later Chinetti repeated the feat, this time with the Frenchman Jean Lucas, at the Spa-Francorchamps 24 Hours in Belgium. The Maranello cars were becoming enormously popular. Circuit races attracted massive numbers of spectators and received considerable coverage from newspapers and radio stations all over Europe. At the end of the 1940s and the start of the new decade, cars from Maranello also tackled the legendary Central American race: the Carrera, more than 3,000 kilometers from the United States to Mexico and then on to Guatemala, almost

ver pulled off while they were on the road at high speed. It is also possible that lack of a rear mudguard caused the breakage of the rear leaf spring pin, which was to prove fatal.
Ferrari, watching the race, was fol-

With the Ferrari 125,
Alberto Ascari obtained
a superb victory in
the European GP at Monza.

always in the middle of a festive and multi-colored tunnel of spectators. But Formula 1 was just around the corner and Enzo Ferrari could not—and did not want to—remain indifferent. Great Britain, Monte Carlo, Indianapolis, Switzerland and Belgium, France and finally Italy, with its Grand Prix at the Autodromo di Monza, which had seen Ferrari and Alberto Ascari take victory in 1949. The first season of the newly created Formula 1 in 1950 was a lengthy and complex one, imposing major production and technical efforts. The main competitors were Alfa Romeo and other important manufacturers such as Maserati, Talbot and Gordini. There was a real danger that the whole series would fizzle out. The Maranello manufacturer could only rely on the 125 Gran Premio, an updated but three-year-old car. The whole idea started off as a great adventure. If things went well, it would have been the right springboard for a young and ambitious factory such as Ferrari. If things went badly however, the whole project could have had dramatic repercussions.

One Soul, Three Faces

The Ferrari 125 was a twin-seater with the steering wheel on the right, long and bulky like all the competition cars of the early postwar period. A simple change of bodywork enabled the "Sport" to be turned into the "Competizione" version. The former was more massive and had covered wheels; the latter was thinner and with motorcycle-type mudguards. Under the bonnet of both versions could be found a 1,500-cc 12-cylinder 60-degree Vee engine. Power output was a respectable 90 horsepower for the Sport and around 120 horsepower for the Competizione version, with a top speed of close to 220 kilometers per hour. The Gran Premio version of the 125 had even greater performance.

in the world

1944 - On January 22, the Allies landed in Italy at Anzio, near Rome. On June 6, it was the turn of northern Europe. Under the command of General Eisenhower, the Allies landed in Normandy in Operation Overlord.

1945 - In Italy on April 27, Benito Mussolini was captured at Dongo, on Lake Como, while trying to flee to Switzerland. He was tried and shot by partisans. Three days later, Hitler and Goebbels committed suicide in a Berlin bunker, with the city surrounded by Soviet troops.

1945 - On May 7 and 8 in Reims, the Wehrmacht unconditionally surrendered to the Anglo-American forces and in Berlin to the Soviets; the new U.S. president, Harry S. Truman, with Churchill and Stalin, announced to the world the end of the war in Europe.

1945 - The U.S. Air Force dropped two atomic bombs on Hiroshima and Nagasaki on 6th and 9th August 6 and 9.

1945 - World War II ended on September 2 with the surrender of Japan.

1947 - In August, the independence of India and the secession of Muslim Pakistan was proclaimed.

1947 - BENELUX, a customs union between Belgium, the Netherlands and Luxembourg, was formed.

1948 - On January 30 in India, Gandhi was assassinated by a Hindu fanatic.

1948 - On May 14, the State of Israel was created, following the withdrawal of British forces from Palestine. David Ben Gurion was the new president.

1949 - On 1st October 1, the People's Republic of China was proclaimed, with Mao Tse-Tung as Chairman and Chou En-Lai as Prime Minister.

in motor sport

1946 - On June 9, the first postwar Grand Prix was held, at St. Cloud outside Paris. The race was won by Sommer in a Maserati.

1949 - Juan Manuel Fangio arrived in Europe from Argentina to race with "sponsorship" from the Automobile Club and the Argentine government. At 38, he immediately won the Pau GP in a Maserati.

1950 - The World F1 Drivers' Championship was created. The first winner was Italy's Giuseppe Farina in an Alfa Romeo. Farina won three races (Britain, Switzerland and Italy).

1951 - Disc brakes were fitted for the first time ever to a racing car at the Indianapolis 500.

75 Years of Monza

On February 26, 1922, Vincenzo Lancia and Felice Nazzaro laid the first stone of the Monza Racing Circuit, a dream come true for Senator Silvio Crespi, President of the Milan Automobile Club. Since that first stone, the circuit has always been under pressure from the supporters of the artistic heritage of the

Royal Park of Monza . . . as it still is today. In fact, just two days after construction started, the secretary of state for education asked for the work to be stopped. The real construction work began in May, and the track was completed in a record time of three months. Some 3,500 people were employed and a five-kilometer internal "railway" was used for the work.

On July 28, Nazzaro and Bordino tried out the track in a Fiat 350, and on August 20, the first race was held there. Since then, the F1 Italian Grand Prix has always been held at Monza, with only a few exceptions: the Livorno circuit for the 1937 race, Milan in 1947, Turin in 1948 and the Dino Ferrari circuit at Imola in 1980. In 1981, the Italian Grand Prix returned to Monza, while Imola has always hosted the San Marino Grand Prix.

6

7

THE ITALIAN GP FROM 1921 TO 1996

Date	Circuit	Distance	Winner	Car	Average
1921	Brescia (*)	km. 519	Goux	Ballo	144.737
1922	Monza	km. 800	Bordino	Fiat	139.853
1923	Monza	km. 800	Salamano	Fiat	146.502
1924	Monza	km. 800	Ascari Antonio	Alfa Romeo	158.896
1925	Monza	km. 800	Brilli Peri	Alfa Romeo	152.596
1926	Monza	km. 600	Charavel	Bugatti	138.204
1927	Monza	km. 500	Benoist	Delage	144.928
1928	Monza	km. 600	Chiron	Bugatti	159.898
1930	Monza (**)	km. 240	Varzi	Maserati	150.444
1931	Monza	10 ore	Campari-Nuvolari	Alfa Romeo	155.775
1932	Monza	5 ore	Nuvolari	Alfa Romeo	167.521
1933	Monza	km. 500	Fagioli	Alfa Romeo	174.740
1934	Monza	km. 500	Fagioli-Caracciola	Mercedes	105.175
1935	Monza	km. 503	Stuck	Auto Union	137.080
1936	Monza	km. 502	Rosemayer	Auto Union	135.352
1937	Livorno (*)	km. 350	Caracciola	Mercedes	131.310
1938	Monza	km. 419,5	Nuvolari	Auto Union	155.726
1947	Milano (*)	km. 345	Trossi	Alfa Romeo	113.194
1948	Torino (*)	km. 360	Wimille	Alfa Romeo	113.263
1949	Monza	km. 504	Ascari Alberto	Ferrari	169.039
1950	Monza	km. 504	Farina	Alfa Romeo	176.542
1951	Monza	km. 504	Ascari Alberto	Ferrari	185.910
1952	Monza	km. 504	Ascari Alberto	Ferrari	177.099
1953	Monza	km. 504	Fangio	Maserati	178.130
1954	Monza	km. 504	Fangio	Mercedes	180.210
1955	Monza	km. 500	Fangio	Mercedes	206.791
1956	Monza	km. 500	Moss	Maserati	208.787
1957	Monza	km. 500,250	Moss	Vanwall	193.563
1958	Monza	km. 402,500	Brooks	Vanwall	195.077
1959	Monza	km. 414	Moss	Cooper	200.177
1960	Monza	km. 500	P. Hill	Ferrari	212.534
1961	Monza	km. 430	P. Hill	Ferrari	209.387
1962	Monza	km. 494,500	Graham Hill	B.R.M.	198.940
1963	Monza	km. 494,500	Clark	Lotus Climax	205.575
1964	Monza	km. 448,500	Surtees	Ferrari	205.634
1965	Monza	km. 437	Stewart	B.R.M.	209.961
1966	Monza	km. 391	Scarfiotti	Ferrari	218.748
1967	Monza	km. 391	Surtees	Honda	226.119
1968	Monza	km. 391	Hulme	McLaren	234.022
1969	Monza	km. 391	Stewart	Matra Ford	236.523
1970	Monza	km. 391	Regazzoni	Ferrari	236.698
1971	Monza	km. 316	Gethin	B.R.M.	242.615
1972	Monza	km. 317	Fittipaldi	J. Player Sp.	211.812
1973	Monza	km. 317,625	Peterson	J. Player Sp.	213.449
1974	Monza	km. 300,560	Peterson	J. Player Sp.	217.420
1975	Monza	km. 300,560	Regazzoni	Ferrari	218.034
1976	Monza	km. 301,600	Peterson	March	199.749
1977	Monza	km. 301,600	Andretti	Lotus JPS	206.014
1978	Monza	km. 232	Lauda	Brabham	207.526
1979	Monza	km. 290	Scheckter	Ferrari	212.185
1980	Imola (*)	km. 300	Piquet	Brabham	183.440
1981	Monza	km. 301,600	Prost	Renault	209.045
1982	Monza	km. 301,600	Arnoux	Renault	219.500
1983	Monza	km. 301,600	Piquet	Brabham	217.548
1984	Monza	km. 295,800	Lauda	McLaren	220.514
1985	Monza	km. 295,800	Prost	McLaren	227.565
1986	Monza	km. 295,800	Piquet	Williams	228.373
1987	Monza	km. 290	Piquet	Williams	232.636
1988	Monza	km. 295,800	Berger	Ferrari	228.528
1989	Monza	km. 307,400	Prost	McLaren	232.119
1990	Monza	km. 307,400	Senna	McLaren	236.569
1991	Monza	km. 307,400	Mansell	Williams	236.749
1992	Monza	km. 307,400	Senna	McLaren	235.689
1993	Monza	km. 307,400	D. Hill	Williams	239.144
1994	Monza	km. 307,400	D. Hill	Williams	236.322
1995	Monza	km. 305,810	J. Herbert	Benetton	233.814
1996	Monza	km. 305,810	Schumacher	Ferrari	236.034

The first designs for the circuit of Monza were drawn up in 1921. It was a figureeight track made up of two perfect ovals, featuring long straights. These are some of the historic moments of the Autodromo and its races:

1) The internal railway used for construction work.

2) The underpass at the point where the two sections of the circuit crossed.

3) The construction of the banked curve.

4) 1923 Italian GP: The Mercedes Benz of Minoia follows the Miller of Murphy.

5) The first Italian GP dates back to 1921, but was held at Brescia, not Monza.

6) The Automobile Club of Milan was founded on June 3, 1903, and 19 years later, it gave the go-ahead for the construction of the Autodromo. In the photograph, the first president of the AC Milan, Augusto Massoni, behind the driver of a Serpollet with which in 1904 he made an adventure-filled journey from Paris to Milan

NOTES

(*) On five occasions, the Italian GP has not been held at Monza: the first edition in 1921 (circuit of Brescia), in 1937 on a decision by Benito Mussolini, "Il Duce" (Livorno), in 1947 on the streets around the trade fair in Milan, in 1948 in the Valentino Park in Turin, and finally in 1980 at Imola.

(**) In 1930 the Monza GP was held instead of the Italian GP.

ROAD-RACING DOMINATION

In 1950, Enzo Ferrari began to be just "Ferrari." In the sense that slowly, day after day, victory after victory, he began to unbridle his ambitions, his desire to tackle everything and everyone. To aim for victory without fear of showing what he was capable of doing. When Formula 1 started officially with the British GP on July 13, it was clear that Ferrari was aiming for a clear role: to be the thorn in the side of Alfa, the richer and more powerful Alfa. It was not going to be easy. The Milan manufacturer entered the famous 158 with Giuseppe Farina, Juan Manuel Fangio and Luigi Fagioli. The 158 was the car that had been constructed in the 1930s by Scuderia Ferrari for the Milan manufacturer, which then absorbed the entire sporting and technological side of the Modena group. Since then, 15 years had passed . . . and Alfa was still on the track with that single-seater. For Enzo Ferrari, that in itself was a major victory.

As far as performance was concerned, the Ferrari 125 could not seriously compete with the Alfa. Behind the wheel of the red Ferraris were drivers of the caliber of Alberto Ascari, Gigi Villoresi, Raymond Sommer and at Monza, Dorino Serafini. The English privateer Peter Whitehead also drove in two races. The 1950 Formula 1 World Championship was run over seven races. Six really: The Indianapolis 500 counted on an official level, although it was contested only by American drivers. Alfa domination was total: six victories out of six "real" races, three for Fangio and three for Farina, who became the first World Champion in the history of Formula 1. Farina, three years before, had refused to drive the Ferrari 125 on its debut at Piacenza, judging it to be poorly prepared and uncompetitive. Now, after having abandoned Ferrari for Alfa, where he was their favorite, he was World Champion.

There was not much news about Ferrari in that first World Championship year. It was, however, easy to imagine. With his inborn tendency to think ahead, almost always foreseeing events, the Modena constructor had perfectly understood that in Formula 1, the battle would be played out for the sporting power of tomorrow. For the moment, the field of play was almost exclusively Italian, with Alfa, Maserati and Ferrari. France made a contribution with Talbot and Gordini, but these manufacturers were echoes of the past. It was clear that the new category, born from the ashes of International Grands Prix, would attract new constructors. They would be British, above all, and not major manufacturers, but small factories that were already showing some interest in motor racing. Before the British, however, would come the Germans. For large manufacturers such as Mercedes, the wounds of World War II were still wide open, but they were seriously thinking about taking to the race tracks. Undoubtedly the memories of the prewar victories of Auto Union and the knife-edge battles with Italian industry around the 23 crazy kilometers of the Nurburgring had left their mark.

The expectation of this sensational rivalry enabled Ferrari to forget about 1950—no victories in the World F1 Championship, Alfa dominating with Farina, Fangio and Fagioli filling the top three places. Luckily, there were still road races, in which the red Sport Ferraris dominated. The Mille Miglia of that year saw a third successive victory: this time the 185S Touring driven by Giannino Marzotto crossed the finishing-line in Brescia first. A lawyer from the Veneto, a passionate racing driver and very fast in road races, Marzotto always took the wheel in an impeccable suit, jacket and tie. He won two Mille Miglias with Ferraris, and 1950 saw success in the Paris 12 Hours, thanks to Chinetti, who shared the wheel of a Barchetta 166 Touring with Lucas.

More glory and more victories, but Ferrari wasn't satisfied. The young man who had a dream without confessing it entirely, even to himself, had disappeared. In its place was a 52-year-old entrepreneur who had come from nothing and had chosen to remain true to his own ideas, realizing that he could count on a personal genius that in the racing world was second to none. As the second half of the century began, Enzo Ferrari was a man who had done a lot, but who still wanted to do a lot more. Even in his family, the situation was far from normal. Dino, the son born in 1931 from his marriage with Laura and the official reason for the end of Ferrari's career as a racing driver, was now a young man with a passion for engineering. He was soon to gain a degree in mechanical engineering, presenting a thesis on engines, much to the pride of his father. Ferrari also had a second son from Lina Lardi, Piero, who was born in May 1945. With his own personal life having stabilized, victories in Formula 1 now gradually became the Number One goal, to which every effort had to be directed and every hour of freedom sacrificed.

Mille Miglia: six out of six

From 1948 to 1953, Ferrari won six successive editions of the Mille Miglia. The series began with the unforgettable domination of Tazio Nuvolari, who retired not far from the finish at Brescia. A wide variety of Ferrari cars and drivers triumphed over those six years:

1948	Biondetti-Navone	166S
1949	Biondetti-Salami	166MM barchetta Touring
1950	Marzotto-Crosara	195S Le Mans-Touring
1951	Villoresi-Cassani	340 America
1952	Bracco-Rolfo	250S
1953	Marzotto-Crosara	340MM

OVERTAKING ALFA ROMEO

For Ferrari, the factory was everything, whether it was morning, midday, afternoon or evening, often after dinner. Work meant everything. It began with a detailed analysis of a technical design, continued with lengthy sessions at the engine test-bed or at one of the production or assembly divisions, and finished with testing on the track. Often, almost always, it was nonstop. Even lunch and dinner were the subject of endless meetings. In this way, the engineering staff worked as a team. Probably however, in this way they also wore themselves out.

In this atmosphere of full immersion, Ferrari began to change his technical staff and chief engineers over and over again, something which through the years became one of the hallmarks of the Ferrari factory in competition. Gioachino Colombo, responsible for the first 12-cylinder Ferrari engine, went back to Alfa. He was replaced by Giuseppe Busso, who was soon flanked by Aurelio Lampredi. The arrival of these two engineers marked the start of Ferrari's assault on the Formula 1 championship. Between one argument and another, Lampredi and Busso constructed the

375, which was entered for the 1951 Formula 1 World Championship. The single-seater was created in 1950. with a 3,300-cc 12-cylinder engine, and its capacity was increased to 4,500 cc for the 1951 championship.

The second season of Formula 1 began, as expected, with Alfa dominating. Fangio won on the circuit of Bremgarten in Switzerland, with Taruffi's Ferrari over one minute behind. The second race was at Indianapolis and was deserted by European teams and drivers. The third round was at Spa-Francorchamps: Alfa won again, this time with Farina; Ferrari finished second with Ascari and third with Villoresi, both on the same lap as the winner although some distance behind. Two Sundays later, it was the French GP: Fangio won again with Fagioli in an Alfa; Ferrari was second with the pairing of Ascari-Gonzalez, third with Villoresi and fourth with the British driver Reginald "Reg" Parnell. The positions at the flag were the same, but this time the gap was much smaller. The big event was on July 14 at Silverstone in England. The first surprise came from Gonzalez, who set the pole position for Ferrari,

Monte Carlo, 1950:
The second GP of the first-ever
World F1 Championship.

1954 - Stirling Moss won his first F1 race on May 29 at Aintree.

interrupting the domination of Fangio who had been fastest with the Alfa in the three previous races.

It was a tough race: 90 laps and more than 400 kilometers long. The fastest lap went to the Alfa of Farina, but at the checkered flag it was Gonzalez's Ferrari 375 which crossed the line first, 51 seconds ahead of Fangio.

It was a historic day for Enzo Ferrari and motor racing in general. The stocky Argentinian, nicknamed "Cabezon" because of his enormous head on top of a not particularly athletic body, took a victory that was to change the face of the sport. It was a victory that came about not through luck or the problems of the other drivers. The victories of Alberto Ascari in the next two Grands Prix, at Nurburgring and Monza (in Germany ahead of the ever-present Fangio; in Italy in front of the other 375 driven by Gonzalez), demonstrated without a shadow of doubt that the Ferrari phenomenon in Formula 1 was not destined to be a sporadic one. At the end of the championship, the title went to Juan Manuel Fangio, another victory for the Milan cars, but Ascari was second, and just six points behind. Ferrari had started to make everyone sit up and take notice.

FERRARI STARTS LIFE IN F1

At this point in time, another chapter has to be devoted to the famous, intense and difficult rapport between Enzo Ferrari and Alfa Romeo. It would not be out of place to say that after 1939, the year of his divorce from the Milan constructor, Enzo Ferrari had never for one minute ceased to think of Alfa Romeo cars. Especially how to beat them. It is easy to imagine Ferrari, on the evening of Gonzalez's great victory at Silverstone. In 1951, there was still no television in Formula 1 and the news would have come over the radio. Maranello would probably have been informed by phone. The first victory of a single-seater with Ferrari's name in a World Championship race, Alfa's domination finally interrupted. . . .

There was enough material here to touch a man who had devoted two-thirds of his life to the motor car in its various forms and to competition. A man who immediately grasped what Alfa Romeo had meant to him, the starting point for a career as a splendid soloist. He defined Alfa as his mother, a mother to whom he dealt a death blow at Silverstone. When Ferrari received a telegram of congratulations the next day from the President of Alfa Romeo, Quaroni, these sentiments uncontrollably burst to the fore. "My dear friends at Alfa," he began cautiously, "your telegram has prompted me to review the entire history of our memories. I lived 20 years with you, amongst events, facts and men . . . and I still remember everything clearly today. For our Alfa (yes, this is

what was actually written: "our" Alfa!) the adolescent tenderness of a first love, the pure affection for a mother." Years later, Ferrari mentioned that he thought the wheel had turned full circle. From Modena, where he was born, to Turin for his first job. Then to Milan, where he took some of the engineers who made Alfa great in the 1930s. Back to Modena, with only himself as the boss, without having to account to anyone. With him, the legacy of an engineering and sporting know-how picked up elsewhere and which he had brought to Maranello, to begin a new, exciting adventure. In a way, this adventure was only in its early stages, for 1952 was the year of the Prancing Horse's total commitment in competition, to Formula 1, as well as all the other most important international road and circuit racing events. Four Ferrari 4100s in the colors of Scuderia Guastella (a town in the province of Modena) went to Mexico for the Carrera Panamericana, to be driven by Ascari, Farina, Villoresi and Taruffi. At the Mille Miglia of that year, called "The Race of the Century" for the quality and quantity of cars and drivers entered, Ferrari notched up a fifth success with the pairing of Bracco and Rolfo. The team also went to the United States, where

Enzo Ferrari with the engineer Lampredi. Below, the front row of the grid in a heat of the third Autodromo di Monza GP. Note Bracco (8), Ascari (4), Fangio (16) and von Stuck (28). On the other page, the 1951 Alfa Romeo 159.

Ascari took part in an unlucky—and not particularly well-organized—expedition to the Indianapolis 500.

The most important result came from Formula 1. After the official retirement of Alfa Romeo, satisfied after the two successive titles won by Farina and Fangio, the Prancing Horse took on Nino Farina. With the Ferrari 500, a Formula 2 car as per the international regulations of that year, Ascari dominated the season, winning all the Grands Prix except two: the first on the Swiss circuit of Bremgarten, where Ferrari won, this time with Taruffi, and then the 500 Miles of Indianapolis which finished with the above-mentioned defeat. On September 8, the day after the Italian GP, the Italian press dedicated full-page headlines to the extraordinary victory of Ascari and the Ferrari 500 at the Autodromo di Monza. It was a triumph of the public to whom Enzo Ferrari was now a hero. The crown had, however, been mathematically clinched three weeks before with the Milan driver winning in Holland. Success in Formula 1 was accompanied by the title of World Champion in the Sport category (reported in the certificate from the International Federation, as the championship still did not have an official denomination).

At the end of 1952, Enzo Ferrari and Ferrari were one of the great names of motor racing, but they were not resting on their laurels. In 1953 Ascari won the World Championship in an even more impressive way. He won five Grands Prix in Argentina, Holland, Belgium, Switzerland and Britain, leaving one each to his teammates Farina (Germany) and Hawthorn (France). The final round was held at Monza and was won by Fangio in a Maserati. The second successive World Championship title for Ferrari was even more prestigious because it was accompanied by the title in the Sport category, which was finally made official and was conquered with wins in the Mille Miglia, the Spa 24 Hours and the Nurburgring 1000 Kms. This was definitive consecration for the Prancing Horse manufacturer. On the horizon for the 1954 season, however, the threat of Mercedes was looming....

The First Victorious Ferrari in F.1

The first Ferrari to win a Formula 1 Grand Prix was the 375, in the hands of José Froilan Gonzalez on July 14, 1951, at Silverstone.

The 375 was designed by Chief Engineer Lampredi to replace the 125, which campaigned the entire 1950 season. At first with a 3,300-cc engine, the 375 was powered by a 60-degree V-12 (obviously front-located at the time), which was then increased to 4,100 cc and then 4,500 cc, the version that notched up the first victory in F1.

The two valves per cylinder, carburetor-fed engine produced up to 350 horsepower at approximately 7,000 rpm. It also had a 4-speed gearbox. Suspension was transversal strut at the front and De Dion bridge at the rear. The Ferrari 375 only raced in the 1951 championship; beginning the following year, it was used for Indianapolis.

ASCARI

Alberto Ascari was unable to defend Ferrari honor against Mercedes. His story with the team, which made him great and which, thanks to his triumphs, reached the top of the World Championship, was a strange one. Like all strange stories, it was bound to end in an unusual, traumatic way. Alberto Ascari was the son of Antonio, who left him fatherless in 1925, when Alberto was just seven years old. Too old not to forget, too young to understand.

In any case, confirming the laws of genetic heredity, Alberto Ascari became a great racing driver. He was unable to demonstrate his talent immediately, because the Alfas were unbeatable and Ferrari was getting angrier race by race, month after month. When the technical picture changed halfway through the 1951 season and the red cars took over, Ascari sat on the throne and never gave it up even for one moment.

His tactics in the race were clear: If

A FERRARI IN EVERY CATEGORY

The 1950s: Ferrari racing production. Below, the Ferrari 500 F2 with which Alberto Ascari was crowned World F1 Champion in 1952 and 1953.

he took the lead at the start, no one could catch him. A total contrast to Varzi many years earlier, relentless in wheel-to-wheel battles and brilliant in catching up the leader. A total contrast to the Jim Clark of the 1960s, a racing driver who will never be forgotten for his incredible fighting back. Ascari did not exactly have the physique of a racing driver. Photographs from his two golden years in Ferrari, 1952 and 1953, show him as overweight, with a chubby face and body. Some people even called him "Ciccio Ascari" (Fatty Ascari). This nickname seemed more suitable for a shopkeeper than a racing driver who succeeded in winning two Formula 1 World Championships. Ascari himself didn't mind. He will be remembered as an almost comical figure under a blue helmet and with a woolen vest, also blue because he was superstitious. Another memory of Ascari, however, sticks in the mind: his impassiveness, his apparent indifference to tension, fear, and to what today is called stress. Monza, Silverstone, Nurburgring, sun, rain—nothing appeared to move him. As long as his Ferrari did not let him down, Ascari powered away and disappeared until the checkered flag. This happened repea-

tedly, with disarming ease. The red cars from Maranello won four World Championship titles (even though there was still no official title for the constructor) in the 1952-53 two-year period. In Italy, it was the era of Fausto Coppi, the champion cyclist. Apart from the two-wheeled sport of cycling, only football could command mass public attention. Motor racing, even Formula 1, came way down on the popularity scale. But the phenomenon of Ascari-Ferrari began to overturn this hierarchy of values. Television still did not exist, but the newspapers exalted the victories of "Ciccio" with the red Ferrari. Ascari became a personality; the connection with

his unforgotten father Antonio not forgotten, his popularity went beyond the Alps and spread like wildfire throughout Europe.

Maybe it was to this popularity that Enzo Ferrari referred to when in three words he defined the situation of Ferrari-firm and Ferrari-team at the end of 1953. Four years before, after Biondetti's great win at the Mille Miglia, a journalist wrote: "The Ferrari era has begun."

"No," was the immediate reply of the Constructor, "The Ferrari era begins now, and so do the problems of remaining at the top."

As 1953 came to a close, Ferrari again launched a message:

"It is easy to wake up in the morning as World Champion," he declared," but more difficult to demonstrate that you deserve it."

That wasn't enough. Evidently the person to whom that message was addressed did not hear, or pretended not to hear. The messages continued in an even more determined tone:

"One can die of hunger . . . or indigestion."

Historians tend not to agree on one point: Did Ferrari understand Ascari's intentions? If we consider the attention Ferrari devoted to the man instead of the racing driver, it is easier to answer yes. Ascari in fact was tempted by a stratospheric offer from Lancia, who wanted to build for 1954 a superteam capable of defeating Ferrari. In other situations, with other people involved, this problem could have been easily resolved. The Ferrari-Ascari pairing was unbeatable: why break it up? But certain arguments with the man from Maranello did not work.

On Christmas Eve, Ascari went to Morocco: together with Villoresi, he drove a Ferrari to victory at the 12 Hours of Casablanca. On returning to Italy, he did not go directly home to Milan: he stopped off at Modena for head-to-head talks. After the second, late in the evening, Ascari was seen coming out of Modena headquarters. He was alone and apparently confused: he said goodbye, wished everyone a Happy Christmas and burst into tears. This was, in the motor racing world, the divorce of the century.

This time there were no doubts: the real reason for the split was money. Only money. By joining Lancia, Ascari could earn a lot more than by staying with Ferrari.

"Talking about money," concluded the Constructor, "ruins friendships. I didn't want to lose Ascari's friendship."

Now it was 1954. The Lancia existed only on paper, not on the track. That meant that Ascari was a spectator. Fangio won the first two "real" Grands Prix for Maserati: Argentina (followed by the Indianapolis 500 for the Americans) and Belgium. On both occasions "El Chueco" (knock-kneed in Spanish) headed home a

Ferrari together with Gigi Villoresi. In 1952-53 however, the attention of the Italian and international press was focused on the Ferrari-Ascari pairing.

procession of Ferraris.

At Reims, the scene for the French GP on 4th July, the Mercedes made its appearance. Fangio, who had joined the German manufacturer, dominated qualifying and the race with the W196, winning ahead of his team-mate, the German Karl Kling, in a similar car. Ferrari was in difficulty, one lap behind with Frenchman Roberto Manzon. Two weeks later, Ferrari bounced back. At Silverstone, the aerodynamic Mercedes W196 for Gonzalez (him again, as at Silverstone 1951 against the Alfas) proved to be unsuitable for the circuit and the red cars were back on top. But it was only an illusion. At the German and Swiss Grands Prix, Fangio and Mercedes steam-rollered to victory . . . and Monza was just around the corner.

Something happened at the Italian race that was quite exceptional in the history of the Prancing Horse. Despite being contracted to Lancia, Ascari was given a Ferrari for his home race. It was a gesture of friendship by the Modena constructor, even though deep down, Ferrari knew that Ascari was just the right man to defeat Mercedes. Ascari knew what he had to do. Starting from the front row of the grid, alongside Fangio's Mercedes, he was right behind him for most of the Grand Prix. The Number 16 Mercedes led the race, but the constant counter-steer he had to use in the Parabolica was evidence that the Argentinian driver was having trouble holding off the Number 34 Ferrari's attacks. It didn't last long however: Ascari had to stop at the pits with a broken engine.

in the world

1955 - On May 14, the Eastern European countries signed the Warsaw Pact, a military alliance in clear opposition to NATO.

in motor sport

1955 - On May 26, Alberto Ascari was killed at Monza. The two-time World F1 Champion with the Ferrari 500-F2 in 1952 and 1953 was the son of Antonio Ascari.

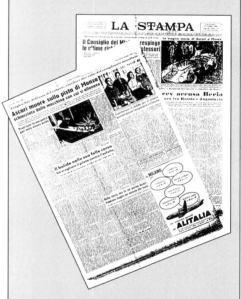

1955 - The most tragic motor sport incident ever occurred on June 12 at Le Mans. Two drivers, Levegh (Mercedes) and Macklin (Austin Healey) collided and flew off the track into the crowd. Levegh and 81 spectators were killed.

A FERRARI IN EVERY CATEGORY

His brief Ferrari interlude came to an end: seven weeks later, at the Spanish circuit of Pedralbes, he made his debut behind the wheel of the Lancia with pole position. For the record, Mike Hawthorn won for Ferrari. For Mercedes, it was a second defeat in a season dominated by Fangio, who won his second world title.

And Ascari? Although he remained great friends with Ferrari, the future was called Lancia. It was however to be a short future. On May 22, 1955, Ascari ended up in the sea at the GP of Monte Carlo in an accident that generated a lot of fear but few consequences, the worst of which was a fractured nose. On Thursday, May 26, he was at Monza, where Eugenio Castellotti was testing the Ferrari 750 Monza. The two drivers stopped for lunch together with Villoresi, who let

Ascari ahead of Marimon, Fangio and Farina at the 1953 Italian GP. Ascari was killed two years later. Alongside, his funeral in Milan. Below, Fangio with his road-going Mercedes at the time of his wins with the Stuttgart manufacturer in F1.

them go back to the pits without following them.
"After an accident," said Ascari, "it's better to get back behind the wheel as soon as possible. Let me have a few laps in your Ferrari."
Was this the reason that led Ascari to try out the Ferrari Sport? Was it that Castellotti had asked Ascari to try out the car? Or was it that Castellotti and Ascari, both official Lancia drivers, had obtained permission from their team to race with that very Ferrari at the Supercortemaggiore GP at Monza the following Sunday?
The mystery will never be solved.
Ascari decided to drive during the midday break. He was not wearing overalls but he did have a helmet and a pair of gloves, lent to him by Castellotti, in total contempt of his superstition that required wearing the same colors and items of clothing. He got in the cockpit of the still unpainted Ferrari.

Three laps later, the Sport went off the road at the braking-point for the Parabolica, a few hundred meters after the long curve, which would be later called "Ascari." The only things that remained of that fatal moment for the two-times World Champion were a mangled Ferrari and two long rubber tire-marks on the tarmac.
For the rest, there were only doubts. Some people maintain that his fractured nose could have caused a blood clot. Another possibility is that a circuit-worker did not expect any cars on the track during the lunch-break and walked over, causing Ascari to brake suddenly to avoid him. A third version, denied by Ferrari himself at the end of the year, maintained that the 750 Monza was a nervous, difficult and unpredictable car, even capable of betraying a two-time World Champion. It is of no importance: Alberto Ascari was killed at Monza on May 26,1955.

The Only Indy 500

Apart from the purely political operation in 1986, when Enzo Ferrari announced to the whole world that he had constructed a Formula Indy single-seater for the U.S. race, in response to the hotly contested regulations in force in Formula 1 at the time, Ferrari has only raced once in the legendary Indianapolis 500. It was in 1952, with a 375 for Alberto Ascari, and run at the Brickyard with almost pioneering methods.

Only one positive memory remains of that Indy expedition, the classic image of Ascari at the wheel of the single-seater before the race, because the result itself was certainly best forgotten.

In fact, Ferrari was not really interested in racing at Indianapolis, but Ascari and Luigi Chinetti, Ferrari's man in America, insisted and persuaded the constructor to give the green light to the expedition. Only one car was sent to Indianapolis, with virtually no spare parts and with a technical preparation not up to the specific demands of the ultra-fast 500 Mile oval race.

It was necessary to organize a sort of on-the-spot back-up, and it was clear that any attempt to find potential sponsors who were interested in putting their logos on the red car was not going to be successful.

The race was a disaster for Ferrari. Ascari barely managed to qualify and started way down on the grid. A broken joint soon put paid to the expedition. For the record, the race, which also counted for the F1 World Championship, was won in an Agajanian by local ace Troy Ruttman, who with this victory was classified seventh in the World Championship at the end of the season.

Indianapolis, 1952: Alberto Ascari drove the Ferrari 375 at the 500 Miles, but the improvised nature of the Prancing Horse manufacturer's expedition to America prevented good results from being achieved.

Sporting Director in a Double-Breasted Suit

It is impossible not to remember the sporting director of Ferrari in the years of the first world titles, Nello Ugolini, as a trim figure, always dressed in a jacket and tie, an exception to the rule even at that time. He had already been sporting director with Scuderia Ferrari from 1934 to 1937, then became involved in football with the Modena and Fiorentina teams until 1952. He returned to Ferrari and stayed there until 1956, when he moved to Maserati. He always wore "civvies" and was never seen without a jacket and tie, even when he had a stopwatch around his neck. Ugolini was the symbol of sportsmanship in races of the time.

LANCIA THEN DRAMA

The 1955 World Championship season was shaken by the death of Ascari. But things remained the same on the track: the Mercedes were too powerful to fear any other cars.

Apart from a victory for Ferrari, with Trintingnant at Monte Carlo, and the Indy 500, the Silver Arrows scored a string of victories in the other Grands Prix: in Britain at Aintree with Stirling Moss; in the others with Fangio, who took his third world title. The Ferrari of that year was David against Goliath. In the previous year, it had managed to contain the German "general offensive," rather like in total warfare, better than had been expected. In Ferrari headquarters at Modena, the Constructor, however, began to think that the Silver Arrows could be beaten . . . were it not for Fangio.

The Argentinian driver had by now become a legendary figure and this had led a generation of drivers to emerge from the South American country. It produced champions such as José Froilan Gonzalez, the man behind Ferrari's two "historic" victories: Great Britain 1951 against the dominant Alfas; the same race in 1954 against the Mercedes powerhouse. But Fangio had something extra, especially in his character. When another Argentinian driver Marimon, was killed during qualifying for the 1954 German GP, Gonzalez broke down in uncontrollable tears; Fangio also suffered, but barricaded himself behind a mask of stone.

Ferrari understood that Fangio was the key to the situation: if he had him in his team, his cars could beat the Mercedes. But the Argentine champion was, for many reasons, not available. The first reason was cost: "In 1955 Ferrari will be present in races where its means allow it to be present," he announced at the end of 1954, "means which are very modest."

This was true, but not entirely. In that period, Ferrari was an industrial phenomenon that employed around 250 people. Racing was possible thanks to a long list of technical suppliers—today they would be called sponsors—which he thanked punctually and publicly after each victory, receiving in return generous financing. Another form of help came from private drivers: those who bought a Ferrari to race, especially on the road but also in circuits. Giovanni Bracco, the famous winner of the 1952 Mille Miglia, one day declared that he had spent—from the 1940s to the 1950s—around 600 million lire ($ 375,000) to race. A considerable amount, close to 1 billion lire in today's money ($ 625,000).

But from a technical point of view, the Mercedes of 1955 were on another planet. They dominated the Formula 1 World Championship, and as if that was not enough, won the World Constructors Championship, thanks also to victory in the Mille Miglia by Stirling Moss and Denis Jenkinson in an SLR300. This situation underwent a sensational revolution in July when Lancia retired from motor racing. The Turin company was beginning to have financial problems and the death of Alberto Ascari was the "coup de grace." On June 5, there was the Belgian GP, where Castellotti set the fastest time in qualifying with the Lancia D50. But the decision was in the air. The team run by Gianni Lancia, son of Vincenzo, who was one of the first idols of Enzo Ferrari, found itself without any points of reference. No one was capable of guaranteeing the right technical development. Lancia therefore decided to retire, immediately. The outcome of this decision, which many people said was an unjustifiable surrender, was that Lancia handed over all its cars and material totally free of charge . . . to Ferrari, who accepted. In the last few days of July, six of the eight existing Lancia D50s were transported to Maranello. One month later, the Turin cars were tested at the Modena circuit, in preparation for the Italian GP, scheduled for September 11 at Monza.

The Ferrari F1 of 1954-55: The 625 (other page); the 553 Shark (above) and the 555 Supershark (below), in detailed pictures from the weekly magazine Auto Italiana in 1955.

FANGIO: A LOVE-HATE RELATIONSHIP

As 1955 drew to a close, fortune brought Ferrari a second unexpected gift. As well as inheriting all of Lancia's technical material, the Maranello team found itself virtually alone in battling for the 1956 World Championship. Its rivals for the new season were called Maserati and Vanwall, the first of the small but innovative British teams (the famous "tuners") who were soon to rewrite the book on motor racing.

THE DRIVER DRAMA

The sudden absence of Mercedes in 1956 helped Ferrari to win the World Championship. Officially the reason was " . . . the lack of valid competition," according to a meager and pompous farewell statement from the German manufacturer and its Sporting Director, Alfred Neubauer. The superiority of the Stuttgart cars was unquestionable, but other events had a destructive role. Amongst these was the tragedy at Le Mans. That race will be remembered as the 24 Hours of the "Apocalypse," the most tragic in the history of motor sport. A Mercedes was involved in an incident and crashed into the stands. The death toll was appalling:

July 1955: Six of the eight Lancia D50s produced were presented free of charge to Ferrari. They were transported to Maranello, where they underwent various modifications and became known as Ferraris, one of which (alongside) Fangio took to the world title in 1956.

ver, led to Mercedes formally withdrawing at the end of the season. After inheriting cars and equipment from Lancia, Ferrari also inherited from the German team the three-time World Champion Juan Manuel Fangio. At the traditional end-of-year gathering with the presentation of the program for

81 people lost their lives, wiped out when the Mercedes turned into a fireball. Public opinion turned against the sport . . . and began to make itself heard. From all sides, criticism was leveled at the races, the risks, the speed and the audacity. Races were canceled all over Europe after feelings ran wild. Enzo Ferrari chose to speak, and publicly defended the Stuttgart manufacturer. Figures at hand, which no one chose to consult after the wave of accusations, demonstrated that Mercedes was not to blame. It was not a gesture of courtesy; Ferrari knew more than ever that at that moment motor racing risked extinction. And without races, his work over the years would have been in vain, and he too would have died. This series of events, howe-

D50: From Turin to the Prancing Horse

The Lancia D50 was born on paper in August 1953. The car began to interest Alberto Ascari and Gigi Villoresi almost immediately, and the Ferrari drivers were soon contacted by Gianni Lancia to form part of his future motor sport plans. When it took to the track for first shakedown tests at Turin's Caselle Airport in February 1954, it was characterized by having large side fuel tanks, enveloped by the bodywork but clearly visible. It was also powered by a load-bearing 2,488-cc V-8 engine.

It was these two features, lateral fuel tanks and load-bearing engine, which were changed by Ferrari as soon as he took them over. The

front-located engine was balanced by a single fuel tank of almost 200 liters in the rear and was uprated to 280 horsepower at slightly more than 8,100 rpm.

With this reborn Ferrari car, Juan Manuel Fangio won three Grands Prix (Argentina, Great Britain and Germany) and was crowned 1956 World Champion.

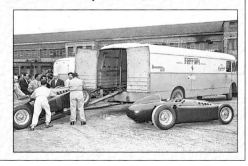

mechanical engineering and collaborated with the production of a Formula 1 engine: the 2,500-cc six-cylinder unit powering the 246, which won the championship in 1958 with Mike Hawthorn. Later, a Prancing Horse car was named after him. After the death of his son, Ferrari was on his knees. His countless victories could not lessen the feeling of emptiness caused by the death of Dino, a death which was expected due to the advanced state of the illness. His anguish can be recalled in several of the letters written with difficulty by the Constructor at the time: always worthy of attention, but particularly moving given the circumstances. Ferrari on his knees however was not the real Ferrari . . . and a reaction was forthcoming; sudden, violent and not devoid of controversy. It was not surprising, therefore, that the divorce came as it did, falling at the end of the year like a mature fruit. "We will no longer have Fangio," confirmed Ferrari in the traditional end-of-year meeting. "We will no longer have him because we are not rich enough."

We will never know if the motives were financial or not. It was certain, however, that Maserati, where Fangio opted to move for 1957 to guarantee him a fifth world title, would pay him generously as well as give him total control over prize money and retainers. This was a treatment no Ferrari driver had ever had, and no one ever would.
The split was clouded in controversy. In the publication with which Ferrari celebrated its seasonal results, Fangio was only granted a few lines of subtle insinuations: "With the help of the other drivers of Scuderia Ferrari and all of Ferrari Automobili," he wrote, or someone wrote for him, "he won the 1956 World F1 Drivers Championship." Just that and no more. References to the other drivers came in abundance: Von Trips received a lot of space, Castellotti was described as "generous and daring," Gendebien, "exceptional," followed by kind words for Phil "Filippo" Hill and De

Portago, for whom he predicted "a great future." And finally Musso, the most celebrated, whom Ferrari described as having "special driving skills." In any case, the news of the time reported that the Constructor and Fangio harmoniously went their separate ways. A book published several years later in France by the driver, My Life at 300 kilometers per hour, was therefore an underhand trick to play. The book's pages were littered with direct accusations and insinuations against Ferrari. The driver maintained that the Maranello manufacturer wanted to prove that even without Fangio his cars would have won. He also wrote that an eventual victory in the World Championship by Peter Collins would have given more satisfaction to Ferrari because of the beneficial effects it would have had on the British car market, which was, unlike in Argentina, not closed off to imports. To confirm these ideas, he even accused the team of attempted sabotage, leading to Ferrari, who wanted to sue him, harboring a grudge. But things eventually turned out differently. In 1962 a book was published entitled My Terrible Joys, a tale of drivers, emotions, races, cars and hopes . . . with a special section dedicated to the Argentinian driver.

FROM CASTELLOTTI TO DE PORTAGO

Four dates written in blood: March 14 and May 12, 1957, and July 6 and August 3, 1958. In that order, in the terrible space of 1 year, 4 months and 20 days, Ferrari and motor sport lost Castellotti, De Portago, Musso and Collins. The causes, where they could be found, were different. The places and the details of the tragedies were all different. The consequences, however, were identical: terrible mounting charges leveled against Enzo Ferrari, his racing cars and his criminal logic of striving to win at any price, while sacrificing his drivers' lives.

Eugenio Castellotti lost his on the second lap of a test session organized at the Autodromo di Modena. His Ferrari went off the road at the chicane, flew into the air and landed on a grandstand, luckily empty. The Constructor learnt of the accident by phone from Technical Director Amorotti. The incident was so incredible that hundreds of suppositions have been put forward. Ferrari denied mechanical failure; even a sudden illness could have been the reason. Castellotti, whose fiancée was the show-business star Delia Scala, seemed to be going through a difficult patch: continous, almost daily, journeys between Modena and Florence, where his girlfriend was on tour. Hours without sleep (the north-south Autostrada del Sole motorway had not yet been built), stress and tension.

Fifty-nine days later, Alfonso Cabeza de Vaca, the Marquis De Portago, was killed in the final stages of the Mille Miglia. This was another mystery, which aroused the interest of the judicial authorities. They dragged Ferrari through a trial from which he only emerged when he was acquitted four years later on July 27, 1961. The events preceding the incident are well known. Five top Ferraris were entered for the race, dominated by Peter Collins, who however retired after more than 1,000 kilometers. The Ferraris of Taruffi, Von Trips, De Portago and Gendebien were still left, in

69

THE DRIVER DRAMA

that order. Ferrari, present as always at the Bologna halt, the last one before the finish in Brescia, imposed team orders: victory was to go to Taruffi, who had made a specific request and who with this victory wanted to wind up a long career. Von Trips argued against the team orders but was then persuaded. Nothing was heard from De Portago, but he was still out there racing. At Marmirolo, shortly after Mantua, his Ferrari 315S almost spun off the road in a fast curve. His tires left a rubber mark on the cat's eyes in the middle of the road. Ten kilometers later, at Guidizzolo, a tire exploded, and the car went off the road toward a row of trees and curbstones, where De Portago and his codriver, Nelson, were killed outright. Incited by the press, public opinion suddenly realized that motor racing was dangerous and this even gave rise to parliamentary lobbying and a series of accusations. The first result was that the Mille Miglia would no longer be held as a race. It would be held in 1958, 1959 and 1961 as a time trial, and then in its "historic" version many years later. The second outcome was that Enzo Ferrari was dragged up to the defendant's bench. His cars were seized: the accusation regarded the tires, produced by the Belgian company Englebert, which were considered to be suitable for normal use but not for the demands of racing cars. The trial finished as expected, with the acquittal of Ferrari. But it was to be four years of accusations and insults to which the Modena

constructor reacted with energy and firmness, not without many moments of grief, regrets and sense of guilt. As 1957 drew to a close, Enzo Ferrari licked his wounds. The two racing drivers who had been killed at the wheel of his cars filled his heart with anguish, and there were a number of other matters to be dealt with. To the attacks from those who called him the murderer of his "children" (i.e. his racing drivers), he reacted without his usual verve. He was particularly moved by an article called "That's enough blood!," published in the Turin daily newspaper La Stampa; in the piece, he came under attack from a journalist who had always been a fan of motor sport as well as a personal friend of Ferrari. These were difficult days for the Constructor. Not only were there the attacks from the outside, but his conscience was weakening him from the inside. On top of this, results on the track were not particularly good either. The World Constructors title was won, thanks to victory by Taruffi in the Mille Miglia and two races in South America by Collins-Phil Hill and Musso-Castellotti. But in Formula 1, nothing could be done against the Maserati of Fangio, who became World Champion for the fifth time: a result which no one will be able to repeat, at least in this century. But above all, the long list of disasters was yet to end. At Reims on July 6, the French Grand Prix saw the death of Luigi Musso. The Italian driver had a chance of winning the World Cham-

pionship, together with Mike Hawthorn, who had arrived at Ferrari largely due to the support of the Prancing Horse distributor in Britain. Unlike Hawthorn, Musso had a warm and affectionate rapport with Enzo Ferrari. The blow for the Modena constructor was tremendous. Its impact deepened the grief from the tragedies of 1957: As well as Castellotti and De Portago, a young engineer, Fraschetti, who loved to try out his own cars, lost his life in a crash at the Autodromo di Modena in a Formula 2 single-seater. The list continued. On August 3 at the Nurburgring, Peter Collins was killed while making up ground in second place on the Vanwall of his fellow-Englishman Brooks. For Enzo Ferrari this was another mortal blow. He was in no way consoled by the world title, which was won by Hawthorn by one point from the competitive Vanwall of Stirling Moss. The string of losses was for Ferrari a sort of mortal embrace. Even Hawthorn, who retired from motor racing at the end of 1958, affected by the long series of deaths as well, lost his life on January 22, 1959 in a road accident in his Jaguar. This happened following a duel organized between Hawthorn and Rob Walker, the owner of the team of the same name, on a bend in the English countryside near Guildford. Twenty-eight years later, near to that town and not far from London, Ferrari's first "technical center," built for John Barnard, was to have its headquarters....

The 1957 Ferrari 801

The Tragedy of Le Mans

Tragedy struck Le Mans at 6:28 pm. A few weeks after the death of Alberto Ascari, terror hit motor racing along the pits straight of the French circuit, where the 1955 24 Hour race, one of the most exciting ever in its history, was taking place. Ferrari took part in grand style, with five cars, driven by its top drivers, Phil Hill, Trintignant, Castellotti, Marzotto and Maglioli. On the eve of the race, no one could have imagined that it would have been overshadowed by drama. It all happened by chance, the result of one of those banal incidents that happen at every race, on every circuit, in any conditions. The Jaguar driven by Hawthorn was about to enter the pits. Before reaching the pit entry lane, he found Macklin's Austin Healey in his way, but overtook him anyway. Macklin was boxed in and made a sudden move into the path of the two Mercedes of Fangio and Levegh, who were arriving at speed. Fangio managed to avoid the obstacle, but Levegh plowed into the Austin. The impact was tremendous. The Mercedes hurled into the air, burst into flames and crashed into the crowd. The death toll was the worst ever in the history of the sport: 81 victims, including Levegh, with more than 300 spectators injured. The catastrophe clearly had worldwide repercussions. The fact that Mercedes was involved was a contributing factor to the German manufacturer's decision to abandon motor racing at the end of the season.

The 246 of the Fourth Title

In 1958, Mike Hawthorn won Ferrari's fourth World Championship title with the Ferrari 246. It derived from the F2 car of the previous year and was powered by a 2,41-cc V-6 engine, designed and constructed using suggestions mode by the constructor's son, Dino, who died in 1956. The 246 had a 4-speed gearbox and its engine produced more than 280 horsepower of power at approximately 8,300 rpm.

THE REAR REVOLUTION

PULL OR PUSH?

At the end of the 1950s, Enzo Ferrari was rich and famous. But he was alone in his affections, battered by the loss of his much-loved son, Dino. He was also alone in motor racing circles, which did not forgive him his fame, his authority, his power and the fact that he was an "awkward" personality. When Mike Hawthorn won the 1958 world title, Ferrari was more than 60 years old.

The memories of drivers who had lost their lives with his cars in rapid succession made him think seriously about retiring. Maybe not a total retirement; the passion for racing, the will to win, never ceased to fill his dreams. But a measured and gradual absence from the spotlights was certainly a tempting idea. These were months of personal, unconfessable suffering for Ferrari. An internal grief that ended up by bringing him closer to religion: Ferrari had always been a believer, but also a bad example.

In brief, the challenge proposed by engineering technology and racing held the upper hand and Ferrari once again became "Ferrari." At the end of 1958, the Maranello constructor was the undisputed "King" of Formula 1: of the nine World Championships held so far, the red cars had won four: Alfa Romeo and Mercedes two each and Maserati one. During 1958, Fangio said goodbye to motor racing. He would reappear occasionally for competitions here and there, but his age, his financial position, the fame and glory he had achieved with five titles, as well as the satisfaction of being still alive and well, convinced "El Chueco" to hang up his gloves and helmet. Even looking toward the future, Ferrari was still the "King" of motor racing, but technical and sporting changes on the horizon were destined to revolutionize the history of Formula 1. One step backward. On May 13,1957, 24 hours after the death of De Portago at the Mille Miglia, a Climax-engined Cooper made its debut at the Grand Prix of Monte Carlo. It was driven by an unknown Australian, Jack Brabham. But the real sensation was that the single-seater, going against current technical trends, had its engine mounted at the rear. Small and nimble, Brabham's Cooper was based on a slender tubular chassis frame. The driver sat on this frame and was enveloped by the bodywork. The Cooper seemed like a metallic spider, with its uncovered suspensions and wheels which held it anchored to the ground. For Formula 1 and motor racing, it was a revolution. With less weight and smaller dimensions, the rear-engined "spiders" swept away the engineering techniques of a half-century.

Enzo Ferrari is reputed to have said something which went down in history: "The horse is in front of the cart, it doesn't push it."

He is alleged to have said something like that, because there are thousands of different versions, as well as of the time and place he said it. Ferrari himself (in his splendid autobiography, Ferrari 80,) however, denies ever having said these words.

"I have been accused of having stubbornly underestimated the true worth of a rear-engined car," he wrote in his book. "In fact, some time earlier, I had prepared designs for a rear-engined car, but I feared commercial repercussions on my Granturismo production, which was at its initial stages and which was based on a rear engine."

True? It is undeniable, however, that in 1958 the rear-engined Coopers began to seriously trouble Ferrari, who lost out to Vanwall in the Constructors' Championship, but won the Drivers' with Hawthorn. The situation deteriorated the following year. The line-up for the start of the Monte Carlo GP, the opening round of the championship, saw eight rear-engined cars. One of these, the Cooper-Climax of Jack Brabham, won the race 20 seconds ahead of Brooks' Ferrari, and began its march towards the world title. The red cars won two Grands Prix that year, France and Germany, both with Brooks, the "Flying Dentist." The British "spider" cars won five races: two for Brabham, who won the world title; two for the eternal runner-up Stirling Moss and one for Bruce McLaren. The latter victory was in the final round of the championship: on the Sebring circuit in Florida, Brabham finished fourth after pushing his Cooper over the line because it had run out of petrol.

In 1960, the situation began to get really difficult, even embarrassing. The Coopers won 6 of the 10 World Championship rounds: five with Brabham, who won his second successive title, and one with Bruce McLaren. Ferrari had to settle for a single victory: at the Italian GP with Phil Hill, a race which was deserted by the British constructors because they refused to race on the banked high-speed curves of the Autodromo di Monza. Two victories went to Stirling Moss' Lotus, which was also

The Ferrari Dino 412Mi "posing" for photographers at Monza and (other page) in the pits at the 1958 Italian GP with Hawthorn, who was to become World Champion. The rear-engined Cooper of Moss (alongside) sets the pace in the 1959 Italian GP.

powered by the Coventry Climax engine. The remaining race on the calendar, the third chronologically, was the Indianapolis 500 for American cars and drivers, which was won by Jim Rathmann.

A REAR REVOLUTION: THE 156

At this point, faced with the spectacle of his 246 losing from the start against the Coopers, Enzo Ferrari decided to make a move. His policy of having the most powerful engines, something of which he had always been proud, no longer guaranteed success. The greater equilibrium from this new weight division, thanks to the engine located at the rear, made the British cars unbeatable, not only on medium-fast twisty circuits, but also on fast ones. According to Ferrari, in 1957 the newly appointed engineer Chiti had already been given a brief to design a future rear-engined car. The project slowed down in 1958, but was then resurrected in 1959, despite not being satisfactory at a technical level, thus

causing further delays.

In the late spring of 1960, the first rear-engined Ferrari Formula 1 carried out lengthy testing at the Autodromo di Modena. On May 29, it made its debut at the Monaco GP: Richie Ginther, a 30-year-old American, finished sixth. But he was also fourth last in an elimination race and the 30-lap gap between him and the Lotus of winner Moss made it clear that the Ferrari needed a long period of preparation.

For the next Grands Prix the old front-engined 246 was dusted off.

For 1961, the Ferrari 156 was ready and immediately competitive. At the opening GP in Monte Carlo, Moss won again with the Lotus-Climax, but Ginther's Ferrari was second, just 3.6 inches behind, and third was another Ferrari, driven by Germany's Wolfgang von Trips. At the next GP, in Holland, von Trips won in a dash to the line ahead of his teammate Phil Hill, who took his Ferrari to victory in the next race on the Belgian circuit of Spa-Francorchamps. It was clear to everyone that the music had changed: Ferrari was back.

France and Great Britain brought another two victories for Ferrari: the first with the young Baghetti, who a-

mazed everyone by winning on his GP debut in France, the second with von Trips. Moss won at the Nurburgring but at Monza, the seventh and penultimate round of the championship, Phil Hill won the race and the championship. Celebrations were dampened, however, by the tragedy which befell Wolfgang von Trips, who died after a terrible crash in which he was hit by a Lotus on the second lap. These were again hours of high feelings. The German driver, who started from pole position and who had a good chance of winning the title (in the end he was second, one point behind Hill), was thrown out of the cockpit of his 156, which went up the bank and crashed into the crowd. Once again, the death toll was appalling: 13 spectators and von Trips lost their lives. The Prancing Horse was back at the top of Formula 1, but mourning inside the team left no room for celebrations.

The Ferrari 256P F1 from 1960.
On the other page (below),
last-minute modifications to the 156
under the watchful eyes
of Enzo Ferrari, on the wall,
and engineer Chiti.

MAKE WAY FOR THE YOUNG

The end of 1961 marked a new phase in the legend of Ferrari. Almost 64 years of age, the bastion of the old guard in a sport whose lead was being challenged by younger, more dynamic and revolutionary men, the Engineer took home a number of triumphs in one fell swoop. He wiped out three years of late Ferrari development by convincingly winning the 1961 World Championship with his first real rear-engined single-seater racing car. He took Phil Hill to the title, the first American to succeed at this level. He won a fifth world title (in 12 championship seasons), leveling the score, in a certain sense, with Juan Manuel Fangio. Above all, he realized that Ferrari had to undergo a renovation, in order to continue to win in this world, which was increasingly characterized by the innovations from the British constructors.

Alongside, from top to bottom: 1961 Dutch GP, von Trips took the Ferrari 156 to its first victory in F1; testing at the Modena circuit; the car in the version that would take Phil Hill to victory in the 1961 World Championship.

There was just enough time to recover from Monza. The tragedy of von Trips could not fail to dampen the day of joy for Phil Hill's title. From Germany, Countess von Trips, the mother of Wolfgang, asked for her son to be brought back the day of the race. She wanted to receive him in a coffin ".. with a glass window, to see him." The request was granted by the team, which in the agitated post-race atmosphere managed to organize this unusual and sad funeral journey.

Once the team had returned to Maranello (Ferrari had already been there since Saturday evening, as per tradition), the Constructor began to tackle the problem. His ideas were

THE REAR REVOLUTION

Monza 1961: Triumph and tragedy. Two Ferrari 156s, driven by Ricardo Rodriguez (8) and Wolfgang von Trips (4), started from the front row of the grid. Von Trips' Ferrari (below), hit by Clark's Lotus, goes off the road and into the crowd. Thirteen spectators, in addition to von Trips, were killed, and the tragedy left a mark on Phil Hill, the new World Champion. Enzo Ferrari at the wheel of a 250 SWB (other page) at the Modena circuit.

clear. He realized that the world of motor racing, especially Formula 1, had changed more rapidly than Ferrari. Formula 1 was moving into its second decade. The heroic years, with drivers already themselves in part legend and races organized on a wave of enthusiasm, had all given way to new teams, new men and new technology. The switch to rear-mounted engines was only the first step toward a new type of car. The search for smaller cars and engines

and more refined aerodynamics had begun. As well as the Cooper phenomenon, the Grand Prix world was already familiar with future legends, such as the designer and ex-driver Colin Chapman with his Lotus; Graham Hill, the BRM driver and future constructor; Jim Clark, who became a track hero with his Lotus; Jack Brabham and Bruce McLaren, successful drivers who would also become successful constructors. These were the men of the future.

The generation had changed. Ferrari, at an age that made him resemble a pensioner rather than a dynamic engineer, could not change his birth certificate . . . but he could change the men around him. At the end of the day, the skills he needed to "motivate" men and ideas—a definition that was dear to him—were still intact.

As for the drivers, the operation had already begun. On July 2 of the year that had just concluded, Giancarlo Baghetti made his debut in the French Grand Prix at Reims. A young man of 27, Baghetti will forever go down in history as the first and only driver to win his debut race. The previous March, a test had been organized at Monza to evaluate the most interesting new Italian drivers. Amongst these was Eugenio Monti, a bobsled champion who set some interesting times. But there was also Lorenzo Bandini, who was destined for a great career. With Richie Ginther moving to BRM, it was Bandini and Baghetti, as well as the reconfirmed Phil Hill, the Mexican Ricardo Rodriguez and Willy Mairesse, who made up Ferrari's 1962 F1 driving squad.

Before concentrating on the new championship however, the team had to be revamped. At the end of the year, Enzo Ferrari simultaneously said goodbye to eight of the top men in the team and the company. Some of them came from the commercial and administrative areas, but others were closely linked to activities on the track. Carlo Chiti left the company, for which he had designed the 156 and its V6 1,500-cc engine, which won the World Championship with Hill; the 246, which won the 1958 title with Mike Hawthorn; as well as the cars which won five titles for the Prancing Horse in the World Manufacturers' Championship for Sports Cars. Others to go were the engineer Giotto Bizzarrini, who was responsible for prototypes, Sporting Director Romolo Tavoni and Director of Production Federico Giberti.

Such a "purge" (even though Ferrari commented on it by saying "I've lost my generals . . . ") could not have taken place without the men to step into the various roles. Halfway between courage and irresponsibility, and maybe to satisfy that need for youth that he, as a 64-year-old man could have no longer, Ferrari promoted a number of young men to the most sensitive positions. One of them was the engineer, Mauro Forghieri, who joined Maranello in 1959 immediately after graduating and who was appointed Technical Director of the team at the age of 26. He would perform brilliantly and would become one of the most important figures in the history of motor racing right up to 1987.

FORD WANTS THE PRANCING HORSE

At this point, it is impossible to continue the story without touching on the subject of Ford and Ferrari. The 1962 and 1963 Formula 1 seasons were unsuccessful for the Italian manufacturers. As predicted by Ferrari, the new generation of British constructors had revolutionary ideas. The 1962 championship ended with just one second place for Phil Hill and Ferrari, at Monte Carlo. The Ferrari 156, which had dominated 1961, suddenly looked old. The more agile and modern BRMs and Lotuses had things easy, and divided the spoils of the Grand Prix victories between them. In the end, it was Graham Hill with the BRM who won, but the Lotus and its genial owner-designer Colin Chapman took revenge in 1963, which was dominated by Jim Clark and the revolutionary "25," the first single-seater in history to be constructed on a monocoque chassis, designed around the driver. This was the new frontier in motor racing. With the Lotus 25, Jim Clark was forced to drive on the straight with his head leaning to the left, to improve the aerodynamics. Ferrari considered these cars dangerous, as they were too narrow a-

THE REAR REVOLUTION

round the body of the driver. But he was soon to adapt to the new situation. Meanwhile, Ferrari continued to win in the Sport category, picking up world titles in 1962 and 1963. On the horizon, however, there was a gigantic deal looming. On April 10, 1963, the Director of Ford Italia telephoned Maranello. His name was Filmer M. Paradise . . . and he wanted a meeting with the Engineer. The meeting happened two days later in the Prancing Horse offices in Modena. The proposal was simple: an industrial agreement, extended to racing activity. Ferrari was immediately interested.

"I replied that I was interested," he wrote in his autobiography, Ferrari 80 - "I had never thought of myself as an industrialist, just a constructor. The production of my company interested me only as long as it was run by others. I was interested in only one thing: being able to devote myself entirely to prototypes and racing cars, but only by being totally independent and with an abundance of technical and financial means, which were not at my disposal. I remember that in 1962 I spent 450 million lire, ($281,250—about 7.5 billion lire or $4,687,000 of today's money—Ed.) total madness for such a small company. A visit to Maranello followed. We parted by agreeing that he and his colleagues would return to have a look at each sector."

Business was brief and frenetic. For a month, a task force from the U.S. manufacturer had free access to every

division of the Prancing Horse. It carried out checks, estimates, controls, counts and made lists. Ford was serious about the deal. Ferrari was calm about it; if the deal went through, the future of the company would be in good hands, and he could continue to enjoy himself in racing as his structure would have been strengthened. The Modena constructor would later say that he had also, out of scruple, spoken to all the leading Italian car companies to see if they were interested in competing with Ford in the deal. But to no avail.

They arrived at the meeting on May 15. Three top management representatives of Ford and Enzo Ferrari signed an agreement at Maranello to set up two new companies: Ford-Fer-

rari, which would manufacture Granturismo cars for the Italian and European market; Ferrari-Ford for the construction and running of racing cars. For Ferrari, the position of Vice President in the former company and that of plenipotentiary President (and 90 percent of the shares) in the latter. The Italian and international press had managed to "sniff" out what was brewing and had written about it without prompting any denial or approval from Ferrari. The deal was nearly completed, but the meeting for the signature spoiled everything.

On the evening of May 20, a swarm of translators were hard at work to make every comma for the two different sides comprehensible . . . and then it was time for the signature.

1962: A difficult year for Ferrari. Phil Hill drove the 156 to second place at Monte Carlo. At the Targa Florio, Vaccarella left his car in this state. Celebrations for Colin Chapman (above) at Monza in 1963 for the victory of Jim Clark, who became World Champion.

The Americans telephoned Detroit before every signature, for authorization from Henry Ford II, the grandson of the founder and boss of the American manufacturer. Everything was going smoothly, until they arrived at the file marked "GS" (Gestione Sportiva), which stood for Sporting Administration.

"It had strangely been kept for last," remembered Ferrari.

There was something wrong. At the crucial moment, the Modena constructor read the passage regarding his independence of action as plenipotentiary president. He discovered that he would not have full powers at all, and that the programs would have to be submitted for the consensus of the partner. Ferrari didn't understand. He tried and tried again: The formula of "consensus of the partner" irritated him, but he just could not believe that the Americans were "taking him for a ride." Racing and associated decisions had to be his responsibility, and his alone. It was all too clear. . . .

To cut things short, amidst the growing irritation of Ferrari and his entourage, it was clear that neither side was going to back down. The agreement stalled. The first to realize

this were the Ford representatives, who left the room with a few abrupt words for the Modena constructor: "Mr. Ferrari, you are selling your company and you expect to continue to do what you want with it?"

One of the representatives of the American manufacturer appeared to be the most interested in finding a way out of the impossible situation. Ferrari turned to him, for one last attempt. He explained that the demands of racing required immediate action, agility and the specific knowledge of certain problems: They were not compatible with the organization of a large company. The American hesitated. Finally Ferrari asked him: "What is the limit you can commit yourself to without prior authorization from Detroit?." The reply filled him with disappointment: "Up to $10,000." Ten thousand dollars: less than 7 million lire at the time, about 100 million in today's money ($ 62,500) . . .

It was all over. In five minutes, the agreement between Ford and Ferrari, the detailed preparation of which had required 40 days of exploratory talks, projects, alternatives and variants, was in tatters. It was all over. But Ferrari, in a certain sense, was saved.

1963 Italian GP: Hill (BRM) ahead of Surtees (Ferrari). Surtees with Mike Parkes (above).
The eight-cylinder Ferrari (top).

The Comfort of Religion

"I believe in God, not the beyond," were the words of Enzo Ferrari, replying to the numerous questions asked over the years about his relationship with religion. They provide only a small clue about the Constructor and his faith.

On one occasion, Ferrari admitted he had not been a good Catholic. On another occasion, he said he had prayed with these words: "God, help me to be a better man." At a certain moment, he would admit his lack of belief in the existence of "something" up there after death. Reports from the last few years depict Ferrari not only as a believer, but also an observer of the sacraments. This was maintained by Don Erio Belloi, the parish priest of Maranello, with whom the Constructor had a deep and warm relationship in last few years of his life, and from whom

in 1988, with death just around the corner, Ferrari expressly chose to receive the Last Rites.

In any case, Enzo Ferrari asked for and got help from religion. In the dock after the death of his drivers in 1957 and 1958, religion came to the rescue of the besieged man. In particular, in the Catholic publication Horizons, Father Giacomo Perico, a Jesuit, wrote an article which was a sort of panacea for all of Ferrari's troubles.

"In the chance cases which characterize motor racing," it could be read, "the integrity of man can not be attributed to anyone in particular, if everyone involved has done his utmost to guarantee safety and protection. The unexpected is the inevitable result of progress." He continued by praising the quest for progress, which is inherent in every intelligent human being, concluding, "In the face of these deaths, (Catholic) morals do not condemn."

Don Erio Belloi,
parish priest of Maranello

All-Rear One-and-a-Half Litres

The first rear-engined Ferrari, which enabled Phil Hill to win the 1961 World Championship, was the 156. The first two numbers stood for

1,500 cc, the cubic capacity of the engines imposed by the new regulations, which fixed maximum cylinder size at that limit.

The final "6" indicated the number of cylinders. The design of the car dated back to early 1960 and was the work of the engineer Carlo Chiti, who had arrived at Maranello three years before and who penned the first designs of the rear-mounted 6-cylinder engine.

The single-seater, a total innovation for the Maranello constructor, was designed after lengthy studies in a small wind-tunnel for models, and its development required the angle between the two banks of 3 cylinders to be changed from 65 degrees to 120 degrees to lower the center of gravity.

The maximum power output of the engine was slightly less than 200 horsepower at approximately 9,500 rpm. The car had a 5-speed gearbox.

Honorary Engineer

It was in the middle of a disappointing patch, resulting from failure to match the technical evolution of the British rear-engined competition, that Enzo Ferrari was awarded an honorary degree in engineering at the University of Bologna. The ceremony, on July 7, 1960, came just after the victory at the Le Mans 24 Hours and was emotional for the "new" engineering graduate, who could not hold back a few tears. His father Alfredo had insisted, unsuccessfully, that Enzo finish his studies. In the years to come, Ferrari regretted over and over again that he had not had a real education and a diploma.

A report by Enzo Ferrari, How To Construct a Racing Car is the memory that lingers of that emotional day in 1960. Twenty-eight years later, on February 11, 1988, he received a second degree, this time in physics, awarded by the University of Modena. But on that occasion, Ferrari was a sick old man (he died just over six months later), and it did not give him the same amount of pleasure.

THE 8-CYLINDER EPISODE

At the end of 1963, Enzo Ferrari was the undisputed "star" of international motor sport. His presence went far beyond the results achieved by his scarlet red cars. As well as Ferrari the constructor, there was also Ferrari the writer. His book, My Terrible Joys, a clear-headed response to the "j'accuse" of Fangio a few years before, was extremely successful, and led to a series of other books. At the traditional end-of-year press conference, the Engineer came out with all guns blazing. He didn't have much to say about Formula 1, which was monopolized by

Jim Clark and Lotus, but he did have a few words about the new Grand Prix car, to be presented on April 7 the following year. The 158 had the ambitious task of bringing back the world title to Ferrari. In the Sports Car category, they were celebrating yet another victory in the Le Mans 24 Hours. This time however, it was for the all-Italian triumph of Lorenzo Bandini and Ludovico Scarfiotti with a Ferrari 250P, the first prototype of a long series characterized by the letter "P" and which in the years to come would have great success.

But that wasn't all. The end-of-year "meeting," held in the presence of Italian and international journalists, whose numbers multiplied year after year, also saw the presentation of the

Dino Ferrari Journalism Award. Officially, the aim was to honor the best press article of the season. As the years went by, the award would be given for personal relations, because of the enormous quantity and quality of positive articles about the Prancing Horse, and would end up by ignoring anything other than just that.

Back on the motor sport scene, 1963, which was drawing to a close, was a special year for Ferrari. Apart from the victories (and defeats) in races, the road cars the Maranello factory was producing began to really come into their own. The numbers were plain for all to see. Road-going Ferraris were being sold in Italy, in almost all other European countries, in North America (thanks to the sales network of Luigi Chinetti) and also in South America, the Far East (especially Japan, which was starting to become a major market) and in Australia and New Zealand. At the start of 1964, there were more than 400 Ferrari employees. Enzo Ferrari used to maintain that the ideal number of manufactured road cars was the same as the number of employees in the company.

*Graham Hill in a BRM.
A group of drivers
(alongside) before the start
of the 1963 Italian GP.
From left to right,
Hailwood and Brabham
(from behind), Clark, Surtees,
Hill and Ginther.*

Over the year, the company increased that number of cars to more than 650, and every single one of them was sold. With the growing success and prestige of the road division, racing remained the Engineer's Number One passion. In Formula 1, the "offensive" by British constructors (the famous "garage-owners"), who with Graham Hill (BRM) in 1962 and Jim Clark (Lotus) in 1963 had kicked GP racing (and Ferrari) in the face had to be wiped out. The reaction of the Modena constructor was immediate.

Initially viewed with skepticism, the first Ferrari monocoque single-seater was created at the end of 1963. It was called 158: design work was by Angelo Bellei with the elderly Vittorio Jano as consultant. Jano was also behind the choice of the eight-cylinder engine, inherited from the Jano-designed V-8 used almost 10 years beforehand for the Lancia D50, which was then entered by Maranello and which had taken Fangio to the 1956 title.

Despite his 66 years of age, Ferrari continued to be the incarnation of the role he liked the most: "motivator" of men and ideas. On a technical level, the Prancing Horse was a reality acknowledged the world over. Its innovative capacity was renowned and feared by its rivals. Going back to the 158, winter tests between the end of 1963 and the start of 1964 showed that the ex-Lancia engine needed "freshening up" a little.

Carburetor feed was abandoned and replaced with direct fuel injection. The results were immediate and plain for all to see: around 210 horsepower at more than 11,000 rpm, not bad for a 1,500-cc engine.

With the Ferrari 158, John Surtees and local hero Lorenzo Bandini competed in the 1964 World Championship. The Constructor had a lot of

Ferrari 1964: Make way for the youngsters! Drivers Bandini and Scarfiotti together with engineer Forghieri. (Above) Hill (BRM), Gurney (Brabham) and Surtees (Ferrari) on the front row of the grid for the 1964 Italian GP.

faith in the ability, both on the track and as a tester, of the seven-times British ex-World Motorbike Champion, Surtees. His origins on two wheels evoked memories of a past era for Ferrari: Nuvolari and Varzi, but also Ascari and Serafini. . . .

The ability to race and win on two wheels proved the existence of two overriding qualities: boldness and aggression—two natural gifts which the Engineer, despite having total respect for the mechanical side, admired and would always admire in some of his drivers. Alongside Surtees, Bandini underlined the importance

for Ferrari of having an Italian driver in the team. The grief of a half-decade ago, with the tragic deaths of Castellotti and Musso, as well as De Portago and Collins, had by now almost disappeared. The Surtees-Bandini pairing worked well. The World Championship got under way with the British teams in evidence: Graham Hill won in Monte Carlo for BRM and Jim Clark took Lotus to victory in Holland and Belgium. At the Rouen circuit in France, Dan Gurney won with a Coventry-Climax engined Brabham. In Great Britain, Clark returned to the top of the podium. For the Scottish ace, the championship was downhill all the way. At Maranello, Enzo Ferrari was nervous: constant hard work and testing, yet the British continued to win. Surtees only managed a second place in Holland and third in Britain, where Bandini was fifth, picking up his first championship points. But the recovery was just around the corner.

In Germany, on the thousand curves of the legendary Nurburgring circuit, where he had won the previous year, Surtees triumphed ahead of Graham Hill and Bandini. In Austria, Bandini won his first GP. It would be his only victory. At Monza, Surtees was back at the top, with his young Italian teammate again on the podium in third place, behind Bruce McLaren in a Cooper. The World Championship would be decided in a sprint finish. The next round was the U.S. GP at Watkins Glen. Clark set pole position and fastest lap in the race, but victory went to Graham Hill, who took the lead in the championship in front of Surtees, who finished second. On to the final round, the Mexican GP. Here, Clark was a steamroller. He dominated qualifying, set fastest lap and led for 64 laps. The Grand Prix, however, was made up of 65 laps, and the last lap saw Dan Gurney's Brabham take the flag ahead of the Ferrari of Surtees. The British driver became World Champion after Hill retired from the race after a clash with Bandini, who then let his teammate through. Surtees finished just two points ahead of Clark, who pulled out one lap from the end with a broken engine and who was classified fifth.

For Ferrari, this was total glorification. Three years after the first title won by his rear-engined car, the Constructor had left his mark with a victory worth its weight in gold. The British "garage-owners" had been defeated, Ferrari technique and technological superiority had been confirmed, and his first monocoque single-seater was immediately victorious against the very people (Chapman and Clark) who had been responsible for bringing it into the Grand Prix world. It was also a triumph for the eight-cylinder engine against the identical technology of the British constructors.

As if that wasn't enough, Ferrari also had the pleasure of taking a former motorcycle champion to the F1 title. The year concluded with victory in the World Championship for Makes, dominated by the Prancing Horse cars against the massive Ford works team, which was also defeated by the Ferrari 330P of Vaccarella-Guichet in the Le Mans 24 Hours.

Monza 1964: The Honda F1 of Bucknum. (Above) Fooling around at the Modena circuit. From left to right, Scarfiotti, Surtees, Parkes, Vaccarella and Ferrari.

THE ONLY NON-RED FERRARIS

It happened about halfway through 1964, the year of triumph in Formula 1 with Surtees. Ferrari was involved in a number of different categories: the World Championship for Makes and the Granturismo Championship, as well as Formula 1. It was in the GT series that the problems arrived. In this category, the red cars were racing (and winning) against the Porsches with the Ferrari 250 LM, but they ran up against a bureaucratic hitch. The regulations, in fact, stipulated that to obtain homologation for a car in this category, 100 models had to be produced. The Maranello factory failed to do this and the International Federation immediately decided to disqualify Ferrari, handing the GT title to Porsche.

Enzo Ferrari exploded in rage. Not so much against the federation and the regulations, but against their total lack of flexibility: All that was needed was to consider Ferrari different to a large constructor, because it did not have the material capacity to construct 100 cars in a year. According to Ferrari, therefore, the regulations were intolerable and his anger was directed above all against the Italian Motor Sport Federation,

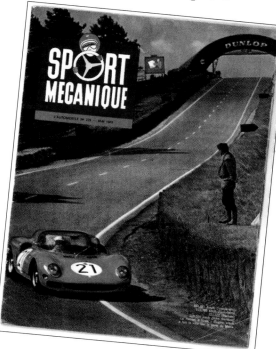

The Ferrari in the white and blue colors of NART at the final two Grands Prix of the 1964 season. Below, the four-liter Ferrari at Le Mans on the cover of a French newspaper. Center page, a technical meeting between the drivers and Forghieri.

which failed to come to the defense of Ferrari in the international body. He protested . . . and in a sensational way. With a clamorous gesture, Ferrari resigned from his position as member of the national federation and renounced his Italian competition license in international races. This was, to all appearances, suicide Without a license, Ferrari couldn't race, especially in Formula 1, where Surtees had a chance for the title with the 158. But the Constructor clearly had an ace up his sleeve. He contacted his friend Luigi Chinetti, the American Ferrari distributor, and asked if he could "borrow" his competition license. He removed the national red color from the cars (something which has never been missing from the company's origins to the present day), painted them the blue and white of the American national colors and sent them across the Atlantic for the final rounds of the championship.

So at the Mexican and U.S. Grands Prix, decisive for the outcome of the championship, the F1 Ferraris raced in the colors of the North American Racing Team of Chinetti, who couldn't believe his eyes at the publicity he was getting for his commercial and sporting activities. This publicity continued in 1965, with a blue and white Ferrari 250LM at the Le Mans 24 Hours. This was the last-ever victory of the Prancing Horse at Le Mans, with future World Champion Jochen Rindt and Masten Gregory.

THE ENTRY OF FIAT

The failure to obtain homologation for the Gran Turismo 250LM would not be the last obstacle for Ferrari. It was followed by the problem of the 275GTB, a car that won on the track but was thrown out for irregularities by the international federation, which didn't really care much about Ferrari's protest and decision to abandon his competition license. When it was time to construct a Prancing Horse single-seater for Formula 2, Ferrari had to find another idea, possibly less controversial and blatant but just as strong. The regulations for the F2 category stipulated that the engines of the cars taking part had to come from a production model, produced in at least 500 examples. Once again, this was an impossible figure for Ferrari and his limited production means.

At this point, Fiat entered the stage. March saw the signing of an innovative agreement between the Turin manufacturer and the Prancing Hor-

se for the production of road cars which would take the very name which was so dear to the Modena Constructor—Dino. It was a two-way agreement. Ferrari gave to Fiat the six-cylinder engine, which would equip the spyder and coupé Dinos, with bodywork designed respectively by the constructor's old friend, Pininfarina, and by Bertone. With more than the required 500 examples produced, this engine ended up by powering the Ferrari Formula 2 cars, to be piloted by numerous drivers: Bandini, Andrea de Adamich, Brian Redman, Clay Regazzoni, Jackie Ickx and Chris Amon. To all appearances, this deal was a great success: an innovative and important partnership. But it was only the prelude to a future, much more important agreement between Ferrari and Fiat. This would be finalized four years later after the elimination of the famous Ferrari Sefac company (Società Esercizio Fabbriche Automobili e Corse) and the creation of Ferrari SpA (Società per Azioni/Joint-stock company).

Fifty percent of the shares belonged to Ferrari, 40 percent to Fiat and the **85**

NO TO FORD, YES TO FIAT

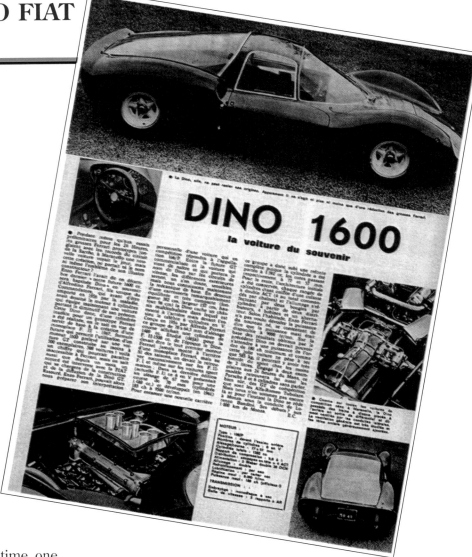

remaining 10 percent controlled—according to the official communication—by "a person very close." At least this was the official version. To a well-known Italian journalist and very close friend, Ferrari confided that he himself had 49 percent and the rest was split between Fiat (40 percent), his son Piero (10 percent) and Pininfarina (1 percent). The other part of the agreement was that on the Constructor's death, his 49 percent would go to the Turin manufacturer.

True? False? Utter fantasy? One thing is, however, certain: Pininfarina has never possessed shares in Ferrari SpA. The answer to the mystery, as this book goes to print, remains a secret.

Whatever the share division, the Ferrari company for the end of the century was created: A company ready to take on the sporting and market challenges of the early 1970s right up to the present day. For Enzo Ferrari, the agreement meant everything . . . but it was also without limitations.

"On June 18, 1969, I went up to the eighth floor of Corso Marconi in Turin, and I was shown into the office of Gianni Agnelli," —recalled Ferrari in one of his books. "It was the concluding act of a story that had come about through a number of different situations." He continued: "I left Turin late in the evening to go back to Modena. I felt happy after finally having found the right future for my company, and calm because I had ensured continuity and development at work for my collaborators."

This is most probably one of the thousand different truths mixed with "convenient" versions that are in the tradition of the history of the man and the Constructor himself. But there is certainly one element of truth: In 1969, Ferrari was more than 71 years of age. On the international markets, as well as in motor racing circles, almost all the competition rested on the shoulders of men who were a lot younger than him. Most of them had worked, constructed and developed on an already-existing industrial and entrepreneurial basis.

Enzo Ferrari was different. In 71 years, he had built from nothing a splendid, sensational and sound reality. He had built it up one brick at a time, one drop of sweat after another, tackling one problem after another. He had given life to it by sacrificing an entire life for the aim, to reach his dream, to satisfy an ambition. He had not even taken one day's holiday, because living in that way, in total control of himself and his creature, was probably already a holiday for him.

The end of the 1960s was approaching and Ferrari was virtually alone. He was without Dino, his much-loved son who had been taken away from him 13 years before by a terrible destiny. That was June 30, 1956: the next day at Reims, a Ferrari driven by Collins won the French GP, a major step toward the world title, which in the end went to Fangio. Life went on.

He was without his much-loved drivers: Nuvolari, Moll, Ascari, Castellotti, Musso. And with them many others. Life went on.

He was without Vittorio Jano, his technical alter ego of the early days, from the heroic days of the Ferrari adventure, when the cars were also scarlet red but were called Alfa Romeos.

Jano departed from this world in 1965, together with his friend Giovan Battista Pininfarina.

Life went on.

He was without his mother, Signora Adalgisa, who died in October of the same year at 93 years of age.

Even after this, life went on.

A constant point of reference for her son, a "spiritual guide" as he himself called her, Adalgisa left in her will the desire to have her much-loved grandson Piero at her funeral. Piero was the son of Enzo Ferrari and Lina Lardi and had for a long time had been kept away from the eyes of those who were not close family. This was the moment when Piero Ferrari "entered the company."

He was young and had always been attracted by cars, drivers and racing, and was to earn his place in the shadows of the Prancing Horse before taking up important roles after a lengthy and not entirely tranquil apprenticeship.

Cautious and modest, bashful even, at first the heir to the "motivator of men" was present only for a close circle of people.

But he was there.

Life went on.

The First Monocoque

Enzo Ferrari had looked upon the Lotus 25 with which Jim Clark dominated the 1963 F1 championship with dread. The first single-seater constructed on a monocoque frame, which virtually enveloped the driver, the "25" evoked danger. In fact, the biggest threat was for its opponents, who were totally outclassed by Clark, thanks to this idea from Colin Chapman, a man who was to come up with many others over the years.

In any case, the Ferrari 158 was created—at least on paper—in the autumn of 1963, when Lotus domination was total and had pushed aside any thought of danger.

With Mauro Forghieri concentrating on sports cars, Ferrari entrusted the design of his new F1 car to Angelo Bellei. He was flanked by engineer Vittorio Jano, who had remained at Ferrari's side. Jano was also the designer of the eight-cylinder engine, first mounted on the Lancia D50 (called a Ferrari in the year of Fangio's title in 1956), which was then remodernized to power the F1 car for the 1964 championship. Powered by a 1500-cc V-8 engine with a 90-degree head angle, the Ferrari 158 developed more than 210 horsepower.

In addition, it was successful from a weight balance and aerodynamics point of view, as the results in the races demonstrated. For 1965, a new 12-cylinder engine was constructed.

The Ferrari 158:
The first F1 car from
the Prancing Horse manufacturer
with a monocoque chassis won
the 1964 title with John Surtees.

THE MOTORCYCLISTS

John Surtees used to say over and over again that had it not been for his friends in British motor racing circles, he would have abandoned competition for good. Seven times World Champion on two wheels (three in the 350-cc and four in the 500-cc class, always on MV Agustas), Big John had no intention of making the move to four wheels, but he was persuaded by Mike Hawthorn and Tony Vandervell.

From that moment on, it was all too easy: tests with Vanwall, as well as Aston Martin; a debut in the 1961 World Championship with Lotus, and an offer from Ferrari. The offer was first refused, then accepted in 1963, the year of his first GP victory in Germany with the Prancing Horse.

Surtees was the first driver to win world titles on both two wheels and four. Others had tried before him. Nuvolari himself, before the World War II, began to win in cars only after triumphing on bikes.

Varzi was the same. Even Ascari managed to win in both disciplines. In the second half of the century, several other riders tried to be successful with racing cars: pluri-titled Giacomo Agostini was never entirely convincing behind the wheel; his eternal rival Johnny Cecotto reached F1 (the first and probably only competitive teammate of Ayrton Senna) but had to lower his aims after a terrible accident in a race.

For all these drivers, Enzo Ferrari had always had special admiration, probably similar to that reserved for forms of extraterrestrial life landing on our planet. Boldness and aggression: These were the main characteristics of riders who switched disciplines in the eyes of the Modena constructor.

They were not totally essential in a driver because one can even win by calculating better, by adopting a better strategy or just by being in perfect tune with the car. But they had always been admired in a special way by Ferrari, as in acrobats or jugglers.

He would one day have the same feeling for another driver, not from the world of motorbikes, but from motorsleds. His name was Gilles Villeneuve . . . .

Images of Umberto Masetti: Below, with the MV Agusta in 1955; on the other page, the celebratory postcard of his two motorcycle racing world titles. Above, the trophy won at Monza by the motorcycle racer before he switched to four wheels.

Masetti:
From World Championship to Ferrari

It was no secret that Enzo Ferrari had always held special admiration for motorcycle racers, and more than one ended up driving the scarlet red cars. Tazio Nuvolari was the best example in the early years. Ferrari adored the superior balance, the capacity to drive like an acrobat and the confidence when going to the limit which "il Mantovano Volante" and two-wheeled riders in particular possessed.

Ferrari had a similar infatuation in 1953 for Umberto Masetti. Twenty-seven years old, born in Parma and World Champion (with Gilera) in 1950 and 1952, Masetti caught the attention of the Modena constructor at the new Imola circuit, where he was testing bikes. Alberto Ascari and Gigi Villoresi were trying out the 250.

The request came out of the blue: "Would you like to test the 250?," Enzo Ferrari asked the rider.

The answer was clearly yes. Masetti, after a few laps of the circuit alongside Ascari and then Villoresi, took the wheel of the Ferrari and soon managed to set some interesting times. The logical consequence was that he was invited to Maranello.

In 1953, Umberto Masetti signed a contract to drive sports cars. He was the first two-wheeled champion to drive a Ferrari racing car. His first race was the Tour of Sicily, better known as the Targa Florio.

"They put a boy alongside me." remembered Masetti. - "and as soon as he arrived in Sicily, he was overwhelmed by the natural beauty of the place. In the race we had a few problems. We stopped after brushing against a bridge parapet. There was no real damage, but the radiator tap was broken and we had to stop."

That was the start of the four-wheeled career of Umberto Masetti, who went on to drive with Osca and Alfa Romeo.

It was also the start of Ferrari's fascination with motorcycle racers, which continued with John Surtees, who became Formula 1 World Champion in 1964 . . .

UMBERTO MASETTI
Campione del mondo assoluto
1950 - 52

SURTEES, THEN THE FLOOD

It has been said that in 1965 Enzo Ferrari was no longer the man he used to be. Certain rough edges of the past had disappeared; certain essential traits had changed, leaving room for him to enjoy life, friends, success and solid economic security. Maybe they were all just stories, because it was the world that had changed. The poverty of postwar Italy had given way to the economic "boom." Financial security had never left Ferrari since the end of the World War I. People "who know him well" say that Ferrari halfway through the 1960s no longer put on a black tie, which he had worn as a continuous sign of mourning after the death of his son Dino. Maybe the new ties and suits in lighter colors were a sign of a renewed spirit. Or maybe not. What had not changed, however, was the will to win . . . in races, in competitions and in confrontations. Victory was the pretext for this will.

"The best victory," he used to say, "is the one that is still to come."

Having turned 70 some time before, Enzo Ferrari now only had eyes for success. As his personal life had stabilized some time ago, his life in racing now became a unique and total mission. Most men in their 70s begin to enjoy old age. Not necessarily slumped in an armchair, but certainly without worries, no timetable to respect, no fixed obligations.

This was not the case with Ferrari. Every morning, on Saturday and often Sunday as well, he repeated the same habits over and over again: a quick visit to the barber's shop in the center of Modena, then off to Maranello in the car of his loyal driver, Peppino.. He wore the same dark sunglasses, even in the midst of winter, on the top of a nose that appea-

red to separate "him" from "everybody else." So he could see, observe, scrutinize and take mental notes without being seen, observed or scrutinized. He had the typical expression of a person who is absorbed in things: his chin resting on an upturned hand, thumb under his throat and little finger between his lips. A key expression both in the 1930s and

Ferrari at the table, wearing one of his typical expressions. Below, Mike Parkes in the 1966 Italian GP won by Scarfiotti. Alongside, Jackie Stewart.

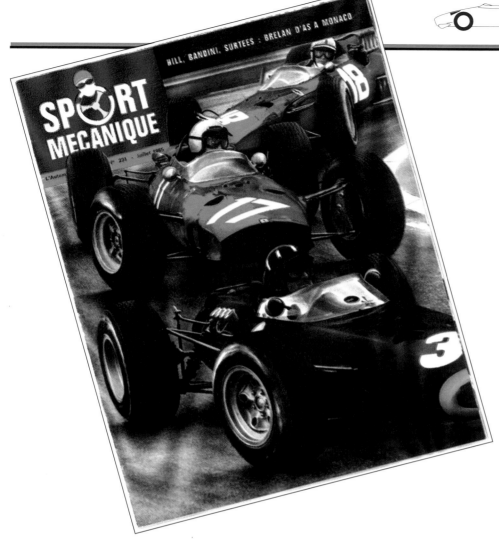

*Graham Hill ahead
of a Ferrari at Monte Carlo,
from the cover of a 1965 French
magazine. Below, a close-up
of the twelve-cylinder Ferrari
engine at Monza, 1966.*

at the start of the 1970s. It meant concentration, meditation, and balance in weighing up the elements.
The man, even though he was old, had not changed.
John Surtees realized this in 1966. The year before, Big John had been unable to, or did not know how to, repeat the triumphs of 1964. The season was marked by Clark and his Lotus dominating again, followed in vain by the BRM of Graham Hill. For the record, third was a certain Jackie Stewart, who won at Monza with a BRM. Luckily, a title came in the World Championship for Makes. The curtain was drawn on the 1965 season, and 1966 got under way with strained relations within the team. Especially between Surtees and the Sporting Director, Dragoni, who lost no opportunity to show up the driver in a bad way. Moreover, the idyllic rapport between Big John and the team appeared to be over. The driver stood his ground: He wanted to race with the six-cylinder engine instead of the V-12 unit, which the team entered and which enabled Bandini to finish second at Monte Carlo.

Things reached boiling point with Sports Cars. Under pressure from Ford, which was launching a massive technical and economic offensive in the category, Ferrari looked toward the World Championship for Makes with particular interest. From 1953 to the start of 1966, the red cars had won the title every year, apart from two: 1955, when Mercedes won, and 1959, with the turn of Aston Martin. Now there was Ford. . . .
Surtees, however, started off well. He competed in a Grand Prix not valid for the World Championship at Siracusa, taking the 312 to victory. Then he won at the 1,000 Kilometers of Monza, driving a P3 together with Mike Parkes. The situation deteriorated after a stormy Monte Carlo GP, the scene of numerous arguments between the British driver and Dragoni, who returned to Maranello and said that he had seen "a Lola sports car (in England), which was virtually identical to our Ferraris."
For the Engineer, this accusation—if proved—would be sufficient to get rid of Surtees, a partner in Lola with its owner Eric Broadley. At the end of 1965, Surtees even managed to escape unhurt from a massive accident in Canada, testing the famous Lola Sport. It was decided to announce the separation between Surtees and Ferrari at the end of the next GP in Belgium. But at Spa,

THE LEAN YEARS

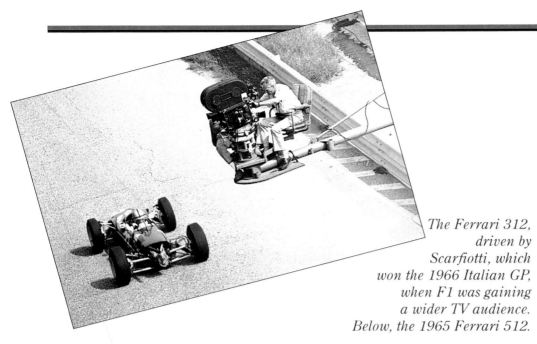

Brabham and his Repco-powered car of the same name. There was another win for Surtees in 1967: at Monza, giving Honda their second (the first was Richie Ginther in Mexico 1965) and final victory in Formula 1. Afterward, there was nothing, or almost.

The same could also be said of the scarlet red cars, which would not see another world title until 1975 with Niki Lauda.

The Ferrari 312, driven by Scarfiotti, which won the 1966 Italian GP, when F1 was gaining a wider TV audience. Below, the 1965 Ferrari 512.

to everyone's surprise, Surtees won, and the order from Maranello was "Let's wait."

A few days later, qualifying got under way for the Le Mans 24 Hours. Here, Dragoni used the first excuse he could think of to get rid of the driver, whom he prevented from taking part in the race. This was just the first step. On June 22, Surtees came out of Ferrari headquarters at Maranello for the final time. The real reasons for the divorce remain a secret, both for the team and the driver. What is certain is that an unresolvable personal split had emerged between Big John and Dragoni. Fer-

rari's decision to get rid of Surtees was amazing: In these cases, it is usually the Sporting Director who packs his bags. In any case, Dragoni didn't have long to go either. The following year, he was replaced by Franco Lini.

A photo remains of John Surtees on that day, the driver with an unfathomable look, impeccable in jacket and tie, his left arm holding what appears to be a heavy leather briefcase. Surtees returned to the victory rostrum that very same year, in Mexico, with a Maserati-engined Cooper, and he finished second in the World Championship, behind

FROM DEFEAT TO TRAGEDY

Ferrari in the post-Surtees period was a team searching for its own identity. From a number of quarters, even within, accusations were leveled at the 312; if Surtees had not left and his rapport with the team had continued to be positive, maybe the car could have challenged for the 1966 title, which instead easily went to Jack Brabham. As an immediate consequence of the split with the British driver, Ferrari had to pin most of his hopes on the fast, yet fragile, Lorenzo Bandini. The Italian driver was under a great deal of stress, as he was Number One Ferrari driver. In addition, he had a dual commitment: Formula 1 and World Championship for Makes, the latter in the midst of a tremendous battle with the American giant, Ford.

The U.S. manufacturer had geared up its industry, to what seemed like a wartime level, to win the World Championship for Makes. The small but agile and powerful MkIIs were rapidly improving and causing problems for the scarlet cars, which in the meantime were also facing a challenge from the powerful American Chaparrals: a car powered by a 5,700-cc engine with an automatic gearbox, which won the Nurburgring 1,000 Kilometers after a long duel with the Ferrari P3 of Bandini and Scarfiotti. The title, however, would be fought out between Ford and Ferrari and the last round—the Le Mans 24 Hours—would be decisive.

The 1966 edition of the Sarthe marathon was a classic. Three Ferrari 330 P3s were entered to be driven by Bandini-Guichet, Scarfiotti-Parkes and Rodriguez-Ginther. Ford had a massive entry of 13 cars, split between the MkII prototype and the GT40 Sport. Above all in the pits, it had put together a task force that was destined to revolutionize the spirit of competition. Where Ferrari counted on a staff of a few selected engineers and mechanics, who had to stay awake for two days on the run, the American manufacturer turned up with

Chris Amon at the 1967 Italian GP. Below, the fast Chaparral ZF of Hill-Spence at the 1000 Kilometers of Monza sportscar race the same year.

in the world

1968 - Student unrest broke out in Europe with street fighting in France.

1968 - Republican Richard Nixon became President of the United States.

1969 - On July 21, Neil Armstrong became the first man to set foot on the moon.

in motor sport

1968 - On April 7, during a Formula 2 race at Hockenheim, Jim Clark's Lotus skidded on the wet tarmac and crashed into the trees bordering the track. He died before reaching the hospital.

1968 - The great Ferrari driver Ludovico Scarfiotti was killed while testing a Porsche.

1969 - The Italo-American Mario Andretti won the Indianapolis 500.

1971 - The prize money for the Indianapolis 500 amounted to $1 million.

field kitchens and a quantity of men and means to enable six-hour shifts per person to be organized. During the night, it was strange to see fresh and well-rested Ford mechanics in the pits, which were usually populated by tired, sleepy personnel, ready to wake with a surge of energy when their car arrived for refueling or a tire change. In brief, all the Ferraris had mechanical problems and all except the two 275 GTB Granturismos retired. The Fords ran like clockwork.

The French press churned out comparisons of biblical proportions. In the annual publication, Année Automobile, a cartoon portrayed the titanic battle between David and Goliath. The logical conclusion was that the Fords took the flag in parade formation, even though not in the agreed order. The top podium slot went to the New Zealanders Chris Amon and Bruce McLaren, who crossed the line with the sister car of Denis Hulme and John Miles alongside. The Kiwi pairing only won because they had started 12 meters behind Hulme-Miles on the grid and had therefore covered a greater distance over the 24 hours. The immortal photographs of those days show Henry Ford II on the podium together with McLaren and Amon. Three years after the failure to buy Ferrari, revenge was total. Thirteen years later however, a letter full of respect was sent by the American tycoon to Ferrari for his 80th birthday. The year concluded for Ferrari without even the traditional victory in the World Championship for Makes. Although things looked promising in the Sport category for the following year thanks to the almost-ready 330 P4 (the legendary P4), in Formula 1 the situation was bleak. As mentioned before, Bandini was nervous about being the team's leading driver. As a replacement for Surtees, Ferrari had called upon Mike Parkes, who was not a great individual driver, but a good finisher to obtain points for the red cars and above all, a good teammate, who helped Ludovico Scarfiotti to win the Italian GP at Monza on September 4. Still today, this remains the last victory of an Italian driver (Switzerland's Regazzoni scored two in

1970 and 1975 and Italo-American Mario Andretti one in 1978) at the Autodromo. The red cars' season more or less ended here. Ferrari finished second in the World Manufacturers' Championship, one point ahead of Cooper, but 11 behind Brabham.

The Australian driver-constructor won the Drivers' title; Surtees, the ex-Ferrari driver was second, with Bandini and Parkes tied for eighth, ahead of Scarfiotti.

At this point, Maranello decided to sign Chris Amon. The New Zealander had been victorious with sports cars, but remained an unknown factor in Formula 1. In the 17 Grands Prix he contested between his debut in 1963 up until the end of 1966, he had raced for three teams (Lola, Lotus and Cooper, all with different engines) and scored two points with a Lotus-BRM at the Dutch GP in 1964. The story of Amon and Ferrari was a strange one. Three years together, but no victories. Undisputed class behind the wheel, maybe lacking in aggression, Amon had a few problems when the track was wet. The partnership between the two was destined to end amidst mutual reproaches:

"I lost three years with Ferrari," he declared at the end of 1969, as soon as he signed for March.

"Amon?" thundered Enzo Ferrari. "We supported him and tolerated him, because we were convinced we were on to something good. If he

thinks he made a mistake, then we all made a mistake . . . . "

Let's go back in time to 1967. The year began with two important and, in a certain sense, historical victories. Bandini and Amon won both the Daytona 24 Hours and the Monza 1,000 Kilometers. They were a strong and well-sorted pairing, but Bandini had other aims in sight: He wanted to prove he could be Number One in Grands Prix as well. With these premises, they arrived at the GP of Monte Carlo, the first European round of a championship that

Monza 1967: The Ferrari 330 P4 of Bandini-Amon at the 1000 Kilometers sportscar race. For the Prancing Horse, it was a difficult moment and the Italian weekly magazine Autosprint summed up the situation in this way.

began in far off South Africa. Ferrari did not take part in the South African race, but on the curves of the street circuit, Bandini started from the front row, seven-tenths of a second off the pole position of three-time World Champion Jack Brabham. "What's the difference between Bandini and Baghetti?," it was asked at Ferrari in 1962, when both were at the wheel of Ferraris. "Bandini, unlike Baghetti, would agree to die for Ferrari," was the blunt answer. These words were prophetic on the eve of the 1967 Monte Carlo GP. The Italian driver wanted to win at all costs. After an accident in Friday qualifying, when the car was almost totally destroyed, Lorenzo beat everyone off the line at the start. Behind, Brabham had a broken engine and dumped oil all over the track. The group had difficulty in passing after the marshals had waved the oil flags. Bandini came round, unaware of what had happened behind him. He arrived on the scene flat-out, slid on Brabham's oil, spun and was overtaken by Denny Hulme's Brabham and Jackie Stewart's BRM. The Scot retired, leaving second to the Ferrari driver, who began a furious fightback. He got close to Hulme, but then the gap widened again. On lap 82, there was drama. The race was an exhausting one: the following year, it would be reduced from 100 to 80 laps. Bandini was probably tired and made a mistake entering the chicane after the tunnel on the waterfront. The Ferrari crashed in fifth gear (it was a third-gear curve) into one of the bollards used for mooring the boats in the port. The car overturned and caught fire. Bandini was stuck inside; several minutes passed before the fire was under control. Ferrari was watching the race from home on television. When the cameras picked up the column of smoke down in the port from a distance, he exclaimed:

"Oh God, it's Bandini!."

The Grand Prix finished with victory for Hulme, who took the championship lead and stayed there right until the end. Second was the Lotus of Graham Hill, third Amon in the Ferra-

ri. When the checkered flag fell, Bandini was in an ambulance, heading at full speed toward the hospital, where three days later he was to die of incurable burns. No one knew at the time, but the death of Bandini took Ferrari back to the time when he was on trial, not only in court, but following the death in rapid succession of some of his drivers in the 1950s. The fear of having to account for the injury or the death of one of his drivers began to spread again at Maranello. In the following years, apart from the brief appearances of de Adamich and Giunti, the Prancing Horse manufacturer would only have one other Italian driver in F1—in 1972, when Arturo Mer-

zario joined the team. Then nothing for 11 seasons, until the arrival of Alboreto in 1984, and he was the last Italian to drive the scarlet cars full-time until the present day.

A disastrous 1967 Italian GP: Surtees (14) won in a Honda, Amon (2) was only seventh for Ferrari.

The legendary P4

The Ferrari 330 P4 only campaigned one season in the Sports Car category. The car will simply be remembered as the P4, with admiration for the fantastic results obtained in 1967. Born as a development of the P3, the first sports car built on a semimonocoque chassis, the P4 repeated this technical solution but it was more powerful. The power output of the 12-cylinder 60-degree engine (at 3,989.5 cc, not quite 4 liters) was almost 450 horsepower and it was positioned at the center of the car, immediately behind the driver's back. The charac-

teristics of the chassis and the suspension, as well as its refined aerodynamics, virtually made the P4 a covered-wheel Formula 1 car: nimble and easy-to-drive on every type of circuit and in every condition. It also had a massive amount of power and an efficient Ferrari-made 5-speed gearbox. The brief life of the legendary P4 can be explained by the change in the Sports Car regulations, which from 1968 onwards limited engines to a maximum 3 000-cc cylinder-size. The P4s, which had already been constructed, were then transformed for use in the North American Can-Am sports car championship.

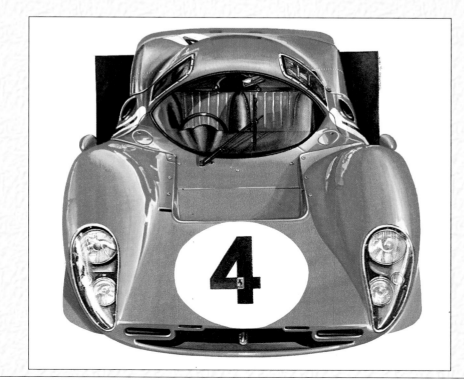

Revenge at Daytona

The finish of the 1967 Daytona 24 Hours will have a permanent place in history, with three 330 P4 Ferraris in perfect side-by-side formation at the checkered flag. Bandini and Amon won with the number 23 car, ahead of Scarfiotti-Parkes (24) and the 412P in the white and blue colors of the North American Racing Team, driven by Rodriguez-Guichet. For the Prancing Horse, badly beaten the year before at Le Mans and in the World Championship for Makes by Ford, the triumph at Daytona assumed a particular significance because it was achieved on the home turf of the A-merican giant. It was also the first step along the road toward recaptu-ring the Makes title at the end of the season. During the race, the signifi-cance of the event was growing hour by hour. The newly appointed team manager, Franco Lini, organized the parade finish. He then repeated it with a static photo after the flag, and this image was also sent around the world. The local press celebrated the event: the Daytona Beach Morning Journal dedicated a full-page headline to the victory—in Italian: "Ferrari: Primo, Secondo, Terzo."

A 1-2-3 that would go down in history: Three Ferrari (P4 and P3) win the Daytona 24 Hours in a parade finish. Below, the 312 F1 of the 1967 World Championship.

A 312 for Four Years

Three victories in four seasons: Sur-tees in Belgium 1966, Scarfiotti at Monza in the same year and Ickx in France 1968. This was the roll of ho-nor in Formula 1 by the Ferrari 312, the precursor of the series which, with a transversal gearbox, would become successful in the 1970s but which was disappointing in the se-cond half of the 1960s.

The 312 was put together in the win-ter of 1965-1966. The choice of the 3,000-cc 12-cylinder engine (not yet flat but with a 60-degree cylinder head angle) was the cornerstone of Maranello's technical thinking. It would generate more than 410 hor-sepower at around 11,000 rpm: a lot more than the eight-cylinder Ford Cosworth engine, which scored its first victory at the 1967 Dutch GP (Clark with a Lotus) and which im-mediately became the technical leit-motif of almost all the British teams until the arrival of the turbo engines at the end of the 1970s.

But even without the hoped-for re-sults, the Ferrari 312 will remain in the annals of F1 thanks to the conti-nuous flow of technical innovations.

The first version of the engine was in fact two valves per cylinder (Surtees' victory in Belgium 1966), but the 36-valve version, capable of more than 370 horsepower, made its debut at Monza (Scarfiotti's win). The engine was further developed at Monza 1967, with the four-valve per cylinder version capable of producing more than 410 horsepower . In 1968, starting from the Belgian GP, the fourth round of the championship, the 312 was the first single-seater to adopt wings, and this was the main innovation four weeks later in Ickx's victory in the French GP at Rouen.

End of the 1960s:
Mauro Forghieri was by
now the main engineering brains
of the F1 Ferraris.
From top to bottom,
the F1 312 respectively in its 1966,
1968 and 1969 versions.

AMON AND ICKX

Chris Amon and Jacky Ickx were two faces of the same Ferrari, a Ferrari in the midst of a driver crisis. The New Zealander, Amon, has already been mentioned. Signed at the end of 1966 on the strength of his performances in Sports Cars, he ended up a disappointment. Not a single victory, a record in the history of Formula 1, given the often technically outstanding material he had available and given the number of races he dominated during his three years with Ferrari, from 1967 to 1969. The words "bad luck" have often been used to describe the phenomenon of Chris Amon, but the driver himself was not convinced: "Bad luck does not exist," - he tried to persuade his colleagues. "It's our conviction, an excuse. In reality, we call bad luck that negative run of events we are not prepared for, and which we are unable to predict."

Nice words, but the suspicion remains. Amon's class, his brilliant and elegant driving style, came as a shock. To someone who appeared an artist on the track, his chronic inability to win can even be pardoned.

A few drops of rain were all that was needed for Amon the Stylist to turn into Amon the Beginner. At this point, even Enzo Ferrari's sturdy patience began to run out. His trust in the driver wavered, and a great relationship gave way to the traumatic divorce at the end of 1969, as mentioned before. Amon was, above all, a human being, and was therefore prone to mistakes, professional mistakes, as well as personal, business and family ones. Ferrari was not going to go back on his decision.

Jacky Ickx's period in Ferrari was different. He came to Maranello at the end of 1967, when the marriage between the Prancing Horse and Amon appeared still to have a few more surprises up its sleeve. A young man at 22 years of age, Belgian, from a wealthy family, good-looking and brilliant, Ickx had a difficult character, soon to come to the fore: he entered the Engineer's office and immediately caught Ferrari's eye with his impudence. His career was, until then, almost embarrassing: four F1 races, just one point in 1967 with a not particularly competitive Cooper-Maserati. Despite this, Ferrari judged him to be the right man for the job of taking the team back to the top . . . immediately. For his part, Ickx was certainly a man who feared no one. His strong self-confidence was a weapon that would turn out to be double-edged, but it was too early to realize that. He stayed with Ferrari five seasons, from 1968 to 1973, with one at Brabham in between (1969) and won a total of six races in Formula 1, numerous rounds of the Sports Car championship, and hundreds of arguments, small and large. The period was full of obstinacies, whims, about-turns, vitriolic declarations and rapid denials, and small and big lies. Not for nothing were his six years with Ferrari to be remembered as "terrible" years.

At the moment when Amon was picked, as well as when Ickx arrived, Formula 1 was a totally different world from what Ferrari had been used to in the past. Until the end of the 1950s, Ferrari could do and undo things as he pleased, pick and choose the best drivers, force them to adopt his strategies and his policies. From the 1960s the increase in the number of British teams (the famous assemblers or, even worse, "garage owners" who were not "creators" like Ferrari, but who in any case raced and won with single-seaters) revolutionized Grands Prix and motor racing in general. Ten years before, leaving aside the Fangio phenomenon, drivers would have paid out of their own pockets to race for Ferrari. At the end of the 1960s, they knew they could race and win with other cars, irrespective of the fact that the engines were all the same or that their allure was not as fascinating as Ferrari's.

Above all, they knew that racing without earning money in this new market was unthinkable . . .

Ferrari found himself unprepared for this new reality.

"Drivers have never had to pay to race for us," the Modena constructor used to say. "On the contrary, they have always been paid. Maybe not very much, but certainly regularly. We are a small company. We don't have money to burn."

This was the truth. Ferrari did not have money to burn by following the market trends. Or in any case it did not want to. The situation changed much later, when Jody Scheckter

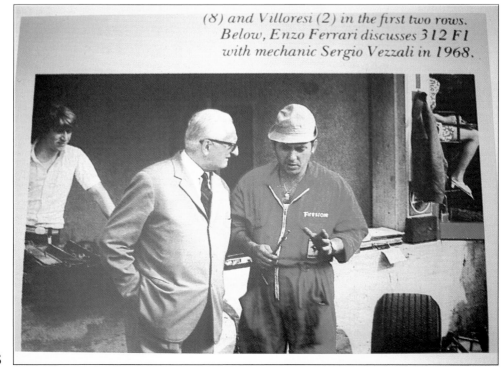

(8) and Villoresi (2) in the first two rows. Below, Enzo Ferrari discusses 312 F1 with mechanic Sergio Vezzali in 1968.

Monza 1968:
Enzo Ferrari together with
the mechanic Sergio Vezzali.

came to Maranello in 1979 with a contract that was in tune with the market. Before him, a long list of drivers either said no or left, even (for some it would be better to say only) for financial reasons. One name stands out above everyone: Jackie Stewart. He was signed to race for Ferrari in the World Championship for Makes in the final round of the 1967 championship, but the future three-time World Formula 1 Champion never drove a Grand Prix Ferrari.

Finance played a major part in this. Another factor was Emerson Fittipaldi. The Brazilian driver, World Champion in 1972 with Lotus and in 1974 with McLaren, was often to be seen at Maranello, but nothing ever came of it. Niki Lauda left at the end of 1977, officially because he no longer had any motivation, but the massive sum of money offered to him by Brabham at the time was certainly one of the reasons.

The barrier between Ferrari and the British teams in 1968 was not only financial. The 1967 Dutch GP saw the debut of the Ford Cosworth engine (from a combination of the names of

Monza 1968:
Wing fever hits
Formula 1.
From top to bottom,
Derek Bell's Ferrari,
Jack Brabham's
"Biplane" Brabham,
and Jackie
Oliver's Lotus.

its two designers: Mike Costin and Keith Duckworth). The debut was a positive one—Jim Clark took pole position, victory and fastest race lap with a Cosworth-engined Lotus 49. The title went to the Brabham-Repco of Denis "Denny" Hulme, a New Zealander like Amon and McLaren. The Cosworth era had begun and was to last all through the 1970s and even longer, before the invasion of the turbo engine. In 1968 Graham Hill, who had already been World Champion in 1962, returned to the top driving a Lotus-Cosworth. The first of three world titles for Jackie Stewart came in 1969 at the wheel of a Matra-Cosworth MS80. Then, 1970 saw the return of Lotus with the 72, with Jochen Rindt and with the Cosworth engine once again. This was exactly the same engine as the Tyrrell 003 of Jackie Stewart, the 1971 champion; the Lotus 72D of the 1972 champion, Emerson Fittipaldi; and the Tyrrell 006 of Stewart, who was champion for the third time in 1973.

What had happened to the famed engine superiority of Ferrari? Where was the general technical superiority of scarlet red cars? The number of British cars increased. During this astounding string of defeats, the cars from won only one victory in 1968 (with Ickx in France on the wing-car debut) and were none the following year—not a single victory, pole position or even one fastest lap. They returned to the forefront in 1970, when the brand new 312B showed to the world the competitiveness of the 12-cylinder Boxer engine, with its opposing cylinder heads and a flat 180-degree angle. Four victories were notched up that year: Austria, Italy, Canada and Mexico, all thanks to Ickx, except for the race at Monza, which saw

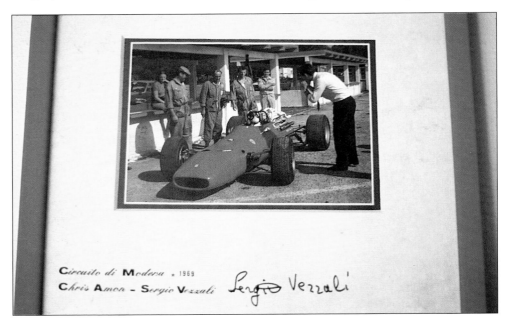

Circuito di Modena · 1969
Chris Amon - Sergio Vezzali Sergio Vezzali

Testing at Monza
for Amon's Ferrari 312.
Below, the 312
in "Biplane" version.

*The 1970 Ferrari 312B:
Below, the car driven
to victory by Clay Regazzoni
in the Italian GP at Monza
that year. Saturday's qualifying
session saw the tragic death
of Jochen Rindt, killed in
a terrible crash (below)
in his Lotus.*

a win for the young and brilliant Italo-Swiss driver, Clay Regazzoni. Ickx and Ferrari finished second respectively in both the Drivers' and Manufacturers' championships, beaten only by Lotus and the Austrian, Jochen Rindt, who lost his life at Monza and won the title posthumously.

The illusion didn't last long. The Prancing Horse entered the fray in 1971 with the 312B2 and then again with the 312B, which was more competitive. The number of races won was rather meager: only two in 1971, in South Africa with the newcomer, Mario Andretti, and in Holland with Ickx. Things were worse in 1972, when Ickx the Terrible triumphed at the Nurburgring, where he had already won in 1969 with a Brabham. On to 1973, another "annus horribilis." Ickx and his new teammate, Merzario, could only score a fourth place in Germany and two thirds in Brazil and South Africa. On the horizon, 1974 would be the year when Ferrari bounced back, but no-one at Maranello could have imagined it at the time. In the six years between 1968 and 1973, Formula 1 had completely changed, and Ferrari had passed through an extraordinarily lackluster period. In 1968 Jim Clark lost his life in a Formula 2 race, after winning the opening round of the season in South Africa. Clark had set a record for GP victories: 25, one more than Fangio, who with 24, had held the record since 1957. That same race in South Africa saw the debut of Andrea de Adamich: he stopped after just 20 minutes of the race and would never drive a Ferrari again in the World Championship. A Ferrari was involved in Regazzoni's splendid victory at Monza in 1970, and in the tragic death of Ignazio Giunti, who was killed in the 1971 Buenos Aires Sports Car race. It was Jean-Pierre Beltoise's fault, after the Frenchman pushed his Matra along the curve leading to the pits and was hit head-on by the 312PB of the Italian driver. In the same year, Pedro

Clay Regazzoni in the Ferrari pits at Monza in 1971. Below, Enzo Ferrari at the tests of the 312 B2 at the Modena circuit. At the foot of the page, the revolutionary refueling system for the Alfa Romeo Sport at the 1971 Monza 1000 Kilometers.

Rodriguez also lost his life at the wheel of a Ferrari 512 Sport in the 200 Miles of Nuremberg.

At Maranello, Enzo Ferrari was licking his wounds. His absence from the race tracks was now a matter of course: his future appearances at a circuit would only be on special occasions. But his attention and will to win were just the same as 10, 20, 40 years ago. The passage from the 1960s to the 1970s had brought him further success in the World Championship for Makes, victories that further strengthened a company that had become one of the most prestigious in the world, even though its production numbers were limited. But in Formula 1, things were not so rosy. At the end of 1973, the Constructor was 75 years of age. The desire to get back on top was more important than his age. And he was ready for a new, even more splendid challenge.

THE LAST WORLD CHAMPIONSHIP FOR MAKES

We have to go back to 1972, the year of the last victory of the scarlet cars in the World Championship for Makes. Although Ferrari was in the midst of its blackest crisis in Formula 1, in endurance racing it entered the field with the 312PB. The sports car was the work of Mauro Forghieri, whose technical importance within the company had grown year by year and was now at its peak, to the point where the Modena engineer would soon be moved onto the Formula 1 cars.

The 312PB steamrollered the opposition. The Prancing Horse entered at least three cars in almost all of the 10 rounds of the Sports Car championship: one singleton entry, driven by Arturo Merzario and rally driver Sandro Munari at the Targa Florio, which they won; four cars at the Zeltweg 1,000 kilometers, which finished in the first four places: the red cars won all the races on the calendar and brought back the World Championship for Makes to Maranello for the first time since 1967. The 1972 World Championship for Makes was also important for the quality of the drivers who alternated behind the wheel of the 312PB in that particular series. In four races (Daytona 6 Hours, Sebring 12 Hours, Brands Hatch 1,000 Kilome-

ters and the Watkins Glen 6 Hours), success went to the pairing of Mario Andretti and Jacky Ickx; the Buenos Aires 1,000 Kilometers, the opening round of the season, to Sweden's Ronnie Peterson (another driver who came very close to driving a F1 Ferrari) together with Tim Schenken, and they repeated the feat at the Nurburgring 1,000 Kilometers. Ickx and Regazzoni won the 1,000 Kilometers of Monza, Merzario triumphed in the 1,000 Kilometers of Spa and at the Kyalami 9 Hours, together respectively with Brian Redman and Regazzoni, as well as in the Targa Florio with Munari. The Zeltweg 1,000 Kilometers in Austria saw victory go to Ickx and Redman. The 1972 triumph was followed by confirmation of the Prancing Horse's involvement in the World Sports Car Championship the following year. The 312PB won at Monza and the Nurburgring, with Ickx and Redman, but overall victory went to Matra and the reduced prestige of endurance racing convinced Ferrari to pull out of the category. For 1974, a new and more competitive version of the 312PB had already been designed by the incredibly creative Mauro Forghieri, but the new year would mark Ferrari's exclusive commitment in Formula 1, where there had been no victories for a very long time.

1971 Italian GP: Pratt & Witney turbine-engined Lotus T56B driven by Emerson Fittipaldi.

THE END OF THE SPORTSCARS

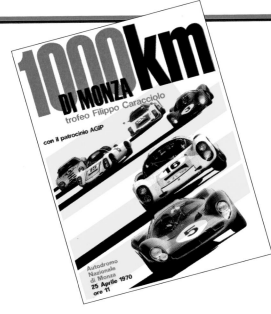

The 312 B2: With Ickx at the wheel and with Peter Schetty during tests with a curious "snow-plow" nose. Ferraris in endurance racing. Arturo Merzario reading Autosprint together with Ickx and Redman. Fiorano, April 1972: The presentation of the 312P with the sportscar drivers. From left to right, Regazzoni, Ickx, Munari, Peterson and Schenken. 1970 Monza 1000 Kilometers: a pitstop for the 512S of Giunti-Vaccarella. Below, during the 1968 Monza 1000 Kilometers race.

FIORANO AND THE MEMORY OF DINO

It was 1972. Amongst the many signs of Enzo Ferrari's total commitment to return to the top, was one which had a particular significance: the inauguration of the Fiorano test track. It was a figure-eight circuit, with a bridge passing over the main straight, alongside which was a small pit garage for the cars. There was also a data-processing room, with monitors covering every part of the track and a sophisticated time-keeping system. But the most important feature of Fiorano was that it had curves extremely similar to some of those on Europe's Formula 1 circuits. There was a hairpin bend similar to the "Rascasse" at Monte Carlo, a jump that resembled the "Brunnchen" at the Nurburgring, a wide corner like the "Tarzan" at Zandvoort. On the side of the track there was a modern steering-pad for the study of lateral acceleration and centrifugal force. The circuit was located in front of Ferrari headquarters. To reach it, the car transporters only had to cross the Abetone state road. An agricultural area in the Municipality of Fiorano, bordering on

104

Maranello and obviously Ferrari property, was used for its construction. For Formula 1 and motor racing in general, Fiorano was of outstanding value. Never before had any manufacturer had its own circuit to test racing cars and the Autodromo di Modena, built years before thanks also to funding from Ferrari, was not as convenient and useful. The true worth of Fiorano was immediately evident, with long, detailed test sessions taking place in its first year. It also had an advantage in that the cars and the squad could be back in the factory in just a few minutes, the technical changes suggested by the test program could be carried out quickly, and the cars could be back out on the track again without wasting time with flights, cargo travel and the availability and cost of other circuits. Among the drivers to benefit the most from Fiorano was Niki Lauda, who between the winter of 1973 and the end of 1977, carried out endless test sessions to make the scarlet cars unbeatable. Gilles Villeneuve, between 1977 and 1982, also

used Fiorano on an almost daily basis, putting in tens of thousands of kilometers of tests.

In 1972, Fiorano completed the series of buildings near Ferrari headquarters, which also included the 1972 extension to the main building used for the production line.

There was also the Dino Ferrari Te-

chnical Institute, with sports equipment for students. Furthermore, the Old Man promoted a campaign informing the public about muscular dystrophy, the genetic disease that killed Dino and which for Ferrari himself became the subject of study and philanthropic initiatives, such as the donation of a high-tech machine

THE END OF THE SPORTSCARS

for preventative diagnosis to Modena Hospital. All these activities would be continued by Piero Ferrari, the son who was destined to become the Constructor's sole heir.

Monza 1972: The Ferraris of Ickx-Regazzoni (1) and Peterson-Schenken (2) in a downpour at the 1000 Kilometers race. Alongside, Peterson together with Fittipaldi, his 1973 Lotus F1 teammate.

Above, testing at Modena: From left to right, Enzo Ferrari, the engineer Caliri and the reporter of the Italian magazine Autosprint,

Giancarlo Cevenini. On the other page: the 312P of Reutemann-Schenken at the 1973 Monza 1000 Kilometers.

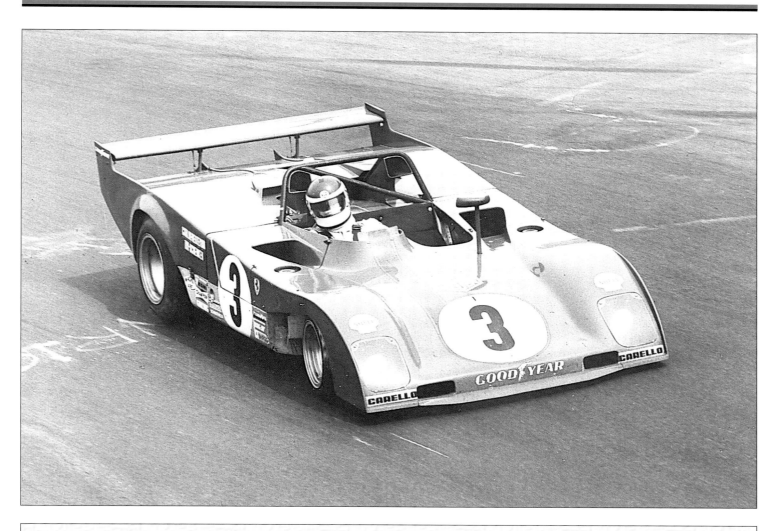

The Arrival of the Boxer !

The first F1 Ferrari powered by a 12-cylinder boxer engine, with a flat 180-degree angle between the two banks of cylinders, was called 312B. The car was designed in 1969 to race in the 1970 World Championship. The idea to use this type of engine came from the Ferrari 212E "barchetta," which won the European Championship of the Mountains in 1969 with Peter Schetty and which had a 2,000-cc 12-cylinder boxer engine. Its transformation into a circuit-racing engine was immediately successful: 1970 will be remembered for Ferrari's second place in the Constructors' championship, along with Ickx finishing second in the Drivers' championship. Twelve-cylinder boxer Ferrari engines continued to race until the end of 1980, and from 1975 onwards were fitted with the revolutionary transversal gearbox. The list of victories was impressive. Three World Drivers' titles (Lauda in 1975 and 1977, Scheckter in 1979) helped make the flat-12 boxer the Prancing Horse's most successful engine, as well as a unique reference point for the other types of engines used by Grand Prix constructors.

Autodromo di Modena 1970: The Austrian GP version of the Ferrari 312B.

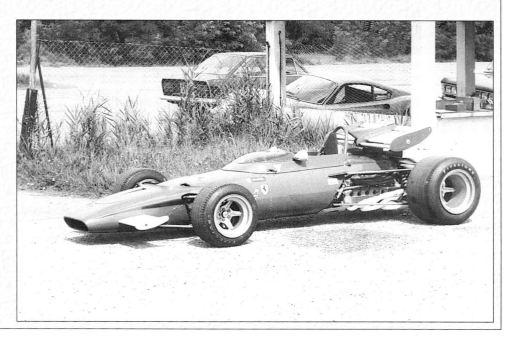

World Championship for Makes: 13 out of 21!

From 1953 to 1973: 21 years of the World Championship for Makes, every one contested by Ferrari, with 13 world titles. These are the details of the title winners over the 20 years:

1953	Ferrari
1954	Ferrari
1955	**Mercedes**
1956	Ferrari
1957	Ferrari
1958	Ferrari
1959	**Aston Martin**
1960	Ferrari
1961	Ferrari
1962	Ferrari
1963	Ferrari
1964	Ferrari
1965	Ferrari
1966	**Ford**
1967	Ferrari
1968	**Ford**
1969	**Porsche**
1970	**Porsche**
1971	**Porsche**
1972	Ferrari
1973	**Matra**

Scenes from the World Sportscar Championship at the end of the 1960s. From above, the Ford GT40 of Hawkins-Hobbs, winners of the 1968 Monza 1000 Kilometers; the Porsche 908 SP of Scarfiotti-Mitter in the same race; the Ferrari of Merzario-Amon at Monza in 1970 .

THE ANDRETTI PHENOMENON

Mario Andretti was the biggest and best surprise for Ferrari early in the 1970s. In South Africa, the opening round of the 1971 World Formula 1 Championship, Mario made his debut with a Ferrari Grand Prix car and won a race packed with excitement. It began with Regazzoni in the other Ferrari powering into a commanding lead, and it concluded with the retirement of Hulme's McLaren, handing victory to Andretti with the 312B1. In 1970, however, Mario had already been the star of an amazing race in the World Championship for Makes. At the Sebring 12 Hours, Andretti and Merzario in the Ferrari 512S dominated the race, but rolled to a halt with mechanical failure just a couple of hours before the checkered flag. There was still the other car of Vaccarella-Giunti, the latter in trouble with the local Florida police after being arrested the day before for speeding. At this point, Franco Gozzi, Enzo Ferrari's famous press officer, but at the ti-

me also sports cars team manager, had a great idea. He put Andretti in Vaccarella's car—and this move made an incredible impact. Thanks to a storming finish, Andretti won the race virtually in a final sprint from the Porsche 908 driven by Peter Revson and film star Steve McQueen.

Mario Andretti at the wheel of the Ferrari 312B2 in 1972 and, below, with the mechanic Gisberto Leopardi in an endurance race with the Ferrari sportscar team.

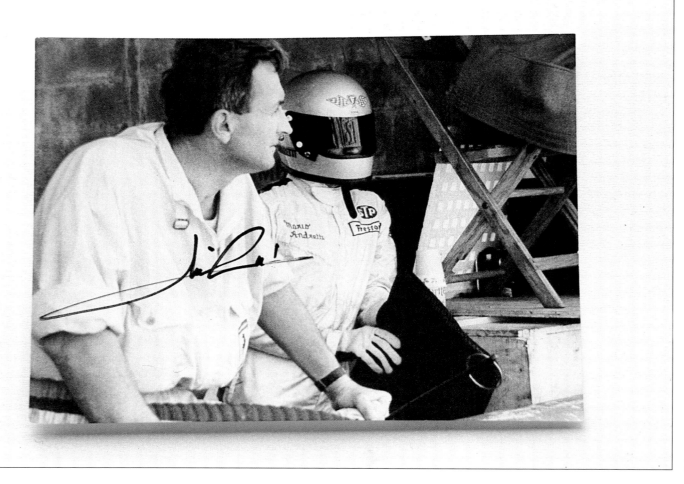

THE PERIOD OF MONTEZEMOLO

Well into 1973, there were signs that an era was coming to an end. The main language of Formula 1 was now English. Lotus wasted a great opportunity: Colin Chapman's single-seater, the 72, held all the right cards, but confusion in running two top drivers, Emerson Fittipaldi and Ronnie Peterson, ended up by the points being ridiculously divided. In the end, victory went to Jackie Stewart. It was his third world title, and his second with a Tyrrell. At the end of the season, Stewart had competed in 99 Grands Prix and won 27 of them. The last few victories were the result of superior class, guaranteed not necessarily by extraordinary performance, but by a level of concentration and an ability to get the best out of the car in driving every single stage of the race, which none of his rivals could match. Someone once said that Stewart killed off the poetry of driving a racing car. When the lights turned to green, his Tyrrell powered straight into the lead. If there were no mechanical problems, it was impossible to catch him. It seemed that for Jackie Stewart everything came easily. In fact the opposite was probably true.

The start of 1976:
Niki Lauda and Clay Regazzoni
present the 312T2 at Fiorano.

In his interesting biography, Faster, Stewart wrote that if a driver tried with all his force to set a fast time, he would never do it: something, either in him or in the car, would go wrong. He could only really go fast when things were done in the most natural way possible, when speed was absorbed and when a lap of the track became long and musical like a film in slow-motion. But in the long run, this pleasure gave way to something else. To fame and glory, and to the money paid generously by the sponsors, who were gradually becoming the major players in Grands Prix. Sponsors names were appearing everywhere, and sometimes replacing the names of the cars. Except for Ferrari. When Jackie Stewart decided to stop racing, he left Formula 1 without a true heir. This unfortunately was not going to be Francois Cévert, his teammate at Tyrrell who had had a fantastic season, picking up six second places, three of which could easily have been victories if Stewart had retired from the races. Cévert lost his life at the Watkins Glen circuit in America, decapitated by a guardrail in Saturday qualifying for the final GP of the year. With Stewart gone and no one ready to take his place, something new was about to happen in Formula 1. It had to happen. That something new was called Ferrari. At Maranello, the historic center of motor racing, which was gradually transferring its central base to Great Britain, a 75- year-old man was conti-

nuing to live and hope with the energy of a 30-year-old. The year for Ferrari was a terrible one. No victories, no pole positions, no fastest laps. The driver pairing was Italo-Belgian,. Alongside the 312B3 for Jacky Ickx, there was also one for Arturo Merzario, who arrived in Formula 1 after good results over the years in sports cars. But the situation was desperate. Two fourth places—in Brazil and South Africa—for Merzario, who in South America finished ahead of Ickx. The victories, however, went the way of cars whose names ended in consonants: Lotus, Lotus, Tyrrell; Lotus, Tyrrell, Tyrrell; McLaren, Lotus again; McLaren, Tyrrell, Tyrrell, Lotus. . . .

It was futile to continue. Ignoring accusations of antisporting behavior, Enzo Ferrari decided not to enter his cars in the Dutch and German Grands Prix. The rumors maintained that the decision was also taken in order to offer a golden opportunity to Ickx to break his contract, something which in fact immediately happened. At the Nurburgring, Ickx appeared, and was immediately competitive, in a McLaren. At the next round in Austria, there was only one red car for Merzario. At Monza the two drivers were back together again, but in the last two Grands Prix, Canada and United States, there was only one car driven by the Italian, and it was at the back of the grid.

It had been a long time since Ferrari had been in such a difficult situation, and there was not even a ray of hope. Despite the good performance of the 12cylinder Boxer engine, the 312B3 could do absolutely nothing against the British competition, which continued to notch up victory after victory, launching itself into frenetic race-by-race development. It was rumored that Ferrari was close to collapse, that the Engineer could not carry on any more, and that Fiat no longer had any desire to continue spending hundreds of millions of lire in this way, without any returns, either technically or in terms of image. It was not true . . . or at least it was true only in part. The Prancing Horse was in fact going round in circles, despite a major effort. On the technical side of things, Mauro Forghieri was the point of refe-

NIKI LAUDA

"At first Niki Lauda reminded me of a young Enzo Ferrari: silent, reserved, maybe a little shy, but blessed with exceptional self-confidence."
These words came from Ferrari himself. At the end of 1973, Lauda arrived at Maranello like a breath of fresh air. He was not yet 25 years of age: rather young to inherit the "mission" of taking Ferrari back to the top. He did have an ally however: Clay Regazzoni, his 1973 teammate at BRM. Clay was summoned by Ferrari: he proposed Lauda as second driver, defining him as ".. inexperienced, but fast and very, very bright."
Maybe Ferrari believed these words. Or instead, and this is easier to accept, three-quarters of a century of a great, insuppressible instinct led him to believe that beneath Lauda and his apparent coolness, his "boy-next-door from a good family" appearance, lay unimaginable skills.
One thing is certain. With the BRM, Lauda stood out in 1973 thanks to a couple of incredible performances. The first was qualifying for the German GP at the Nurburgring, where he was just two seconds off the pole of

The 312B3 with Regazzoni in 1974. The Politoys-sponsored ISO F1 with which the British constructor Frank Williams made his Grand Prix debut the previous year. Henri Pescarolo in the cockpit of the car together with Williams, sitting on the wheel.

brilliant lawyer, who had no experience in Formula 1, but who was clearly backed by the Agnelli family and therefore by Fiat—appeared on the horizon, Ferrari realized that he had to get his man. Not because he was forced to, but because in this rampant, open-minded and above all fresh figure, there was maybe the revolutionary force which would take everyone by surprise and would end up by rewriting history.

rence, but doubts surrounding team management meant that he, too, was involved and was therefore unable to devote much attention to his two specialist fields: tactics and relations with the drivers. Confined to his lair in Maranello, tied increasingly by an umbilical cord to the Grands Prix, which were his only real outlet of activity, and which he followed when he could on television or at the end of the phone, Enzo Ferrari was desperate for success. This was his burning desire. When a certain Luca de Montezemolo—a young and

In the other photos, the CSAI license of Niki Lauda and the driver's license of . . . Elvis Presley.

the incomparable Stewart, but also eight seconds faster than his teammate Regazzoni. Or Canada, where in the pouring rain, Niki had the satisfaction of leading the race for twenty laps, after overtaking Peterson in the Lotus by sheer force, before retiring with transmission failure amidst the cheers of spectators. Clay's suggestion might have been true; but it would be nice to think that on that September 23, while watching television images from the Canadian circuit at Mosport, Ferrari realized that something special lay behind the beaver-like teeth of the young Austrian driver.

Back to the racing. In 1974, the Ferrari line-up was Regazzoni and Lauda. The strictly nonalphabetical order is motivated by the fact that the highest hopes were on Regazzoni. Instead, thanks to the feeling which emerged between the Austrian and Luca di Montezemolo, who was almost the same age, it was Niki who shone. Small, thin and not very talkative, the Austrian driver, heir of an industrial dynasty which had done everything in its power to prevent him from becoming a racing driver, had an iron will, but he did not show it. Gone were the days when to race he had to pledge to a bank his life insurance policy, underwritten in his name by his paternal grandfather, who adored him but who saw him exclusively in the role of future magnate. The contract offered by Ferrari was not a lucrative one— the Engineer's tradition was still intact— but it was good enough for Lauda to be satisfied. This allowed him to concentrate exclusively on the team, the testing work, and the car, which he got to know curve after curve and in which he improved day after day. Lauda had no half measures. Alongside the Austrian, Clay Regazzoni also yearned for success and glory, but the Swiss driver was a lover of the pleasures of life. Niki wasn't. For him, there was only racing and Ferrari. He took up residence at Modena, at the Canal Grande Hotel in the center just a few minutes walk away from Enzo Ferrari's own house. Luca di Montezemolo took care of him at the track. Outside of Fiorano, where the driver spent

endless days testing and asking to test even more, he was looked after by Sante Ghedini, who in the future would leave Ferrari to follow Lauda to Brabham and who would become his right-hand man.

Although it didn't seem that way, Lauda was a man in a hurry. With the much-improved but still far from perfect Ferrari 312B3, he set pole position in his third race. in South Africa.

Lauda at Fiorano, with the Prancing Horse's PR man, Franco Gozzi, and mechanic Borsari; next to the Ferrari BB of Luca di Montezemolo, and posing for photographers on the 1976 312T2.

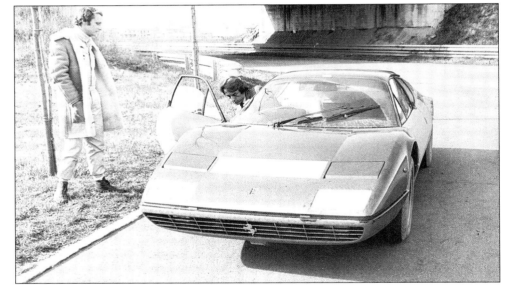

In the next race. in Spain, Ferrari returned to the winner's rostrum—victory Number 50 in the World Championship—with an extraordinary 1-2. It was not a lucky victory either, because Lauda was ahead of Regazzoni. At the end of the season, Lauda had set 9 pole positions out of 15, a massive total. He scored two wins: Spain and Holland (another Ferrari 1-2). At the halfway point, Niki was second in the points table, one point behind Emerson Fittipaldi, who would become champion at the end of the year; he had a two-point lead over Regazzoni, seven over the boisterous, but very fast, Jody Scheckter, who had moved to Tyrrell to replace Stewart. But in the second half of the championship, the Austrian made a few mistakes and there were also some mechanical failures to contend with. He scored few points, eight in seven races, and only finished third overall. On the other hand, Regazzoni won at the Nurburgring and was in with a chance at the title until the final round in the United States, where he retired and handed a second championship victory to Fittipaldi.

Behind his ever-present dark sunglasses, Enzo Ferrari was smiling. Ferrari's return to the big time was complete. All that was needed now was to continue along that path. He had some kind words for Regazzoni: " He has proved himself to be an accomplished driver, and his standard is now very high."

With Niki Lauda, he was more abrupt but did not hide a certain affection: "Niki often obtains fastest laps," he declared, "and knows how to set his own pace."

Shortly, the harmony within the team gave way to tension and jealousy. Toward the end of 1974, no one could deny that Lauda was the darling of the team and that Regazzoni was overshadowed. At the final GP, at Watkins Glen, Niki was out of the title race, Clay wasn't. Yet two Ferrari 312B3s were reserved for Niki, one of which almost brand new; "Rega" only had one, and that was the previous year's model. Public opinion was also divided. Lauda, with his extraordinary ability to be quick almost immediately and apparently without effort, was a fascinating driver but did not stir the

The Team Everest Ferrari 312T at Silverstone in 1976. Below, the press conference for the world title won by Lauda in 1975. From left to right, Luca di Montezemolo, Piero Fusaro, Enzo Ferrari and Franco Gozzi .

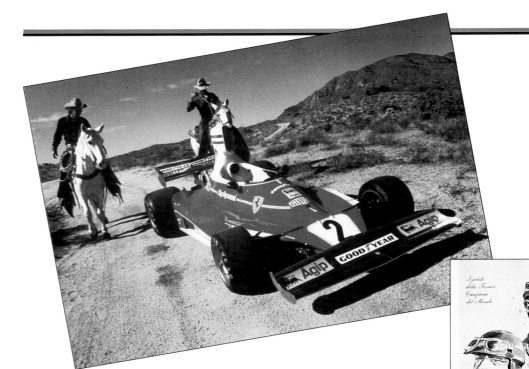

An "exotic" setting in Arizona for the 312T. The T2, below, figured in the official poster for the 1976 Italian GP. Center: The first six F1 World champions with Ferrari cars: Ascari, Fangio, Hawthorn, Hill, Surtees and Lauda.

emotions. Clay aroused a wave of affection because of his personality and his exciting performances on the track. But the important factors, the consideration of Ferrari and Montezemolo, were clearly in favor of the Austrian. This was the situation at the start of 1975. In motor racing circles, Niki was recognized as a brilliant tester, but was not considered to be Number One driver. Above all, his colleagues and rivals envied his Ferrari, particularly his unbeatable 312T.

They asked him what his secret was. The response was icy: "I always wonder what I have to do to finish first." Someone maligned that at least another five drivers were as good as he was, that he was unable to arouse enthusiasm, and so on.

"Patience!" he replied. "On the track, I work to win, not to put on a show." Asked for his opinion about Lauda, Ronnie Peterson lost his patience: "He should remember the Formula 2 days, when he could never overtake me . . . ."

Lauda shrugged his shoulders . . . and won in 1975. Again and again. When he tested the Ferrari 312T, with its 12-cylinder Boxer engine and transversal gearbox. which improved weight distribution at the rear, he did not have a shadow of doubt: "You drive it like a bicycle," he exclaimed to the delight of Forghieri, who had designed it. "We will win a lot with this car."

It was an easy prediction to make. Niki picked up win after win: Monte Carlo, where Ferrari had not won for 20 years, Belgium, and Sweden. Then onto Holland, where he was second behind the Hesketh of James Hunt, a rival who would cross his path again in a dramatic fashion one year later. Another victory in France. The world title was almost won, and it became a mathematical certainty at Monza, where Regazzoni won the race. A Ferrari driver became world champion for the first time in 11 years, since the time of John Surtees. Lauda ended the season on a high note, winning the Watkins Glen round and confirming the first world title for a 12-cylinder engine.

THE FIRE THAT CHANGED HISTORY

At the end of 1975 Niki Lauda was not only World Champion for Ferrari: he was its ambassador, its triumphant face and its credit card for the motor racing world. In a certain sense he was also a star. Success began to bother him, and the search for privacy became more important than the benefits of fame. Maybe it was in those months after the conquest of the 1975 title that something in his rapport with the Prancing Horse began to go wrong.

The results on the track however were no different. Lauda began the championship with a series of wins, first in Brazil, then in South Africa. Regazzoni won the third GP of the season at Long Beach. Niki was second, and turned against the new Sporting Director of the Prancing Horse, Daniele Audetto, accusing him of wanting victory for Clay at all costs and for who knows what reason. Then he got back into the cockpit of the 312T2 and started to win again: Spain (but only after the disqualification of the McLaren of Hunt, who was then reinstated as winner by the sporting tribunal months after),

Belgium, Monte Carlo. Then came Great Britain, again won by Hunt, who was disqualified for sporting irregularities. After 9 of the 16 races on the calendar, the Austrian had what seemed like an unassailable lead: Niki, 61 points; Scheckter, 30; Hunt and Depailler, 26 each. Neither Hunt nor McLaren, not even the revolutionary and immediately competitive six-wheel Tyrrell (four at the front) of Scheckter and Depailler could touch him.

And then came German Grand Prix, which would dramatically mark the turning point of the season and also an era.

Back in July, however, the rapport between Lauda and Ferrari was no longer the same as the previous year. The driver continued to concentrate on the cars and the races, but his mind was occupied with other things, such as lucrative advertising contracts and the house he was building on the hills of Hof near Salzburg. During building work, Niki overturned a tractor and cracked a rib. Nevertheless he took part in the Spanish Grand Prix, which marked the debut of the 312T2, but it was clear that his skill behind the wheel had suffered, and ill feeling began to spread throughout the team. Something also changed in the private life of the driver, whose only real family seemed to be Ferrari. During a party at the house of the actor Curt Jurgens, Niki got to know the beautiful Chilean model Marlene Knaus. It was love at first sight, an impetuous

and uncontrollable relationship, which led him to suddenly break off with Mariella von Reininghaus, the woman who had been at his side, in silence and in the background, since he first arrived in the sport.

From Maranello, Enzo Ferrari was watching, controlling and taking notes. But he refrained from any official comments.

"Niki has discovered the joys of life," he joked. - "but I am sure he will still be the great driver he has always been."

He was wrong. Lauda had something to reproach Ferrari with, first of all, the lower pay he was getting, at least with respect to the British teams. Rumors began to spread about offers from other teams; prompting increasingly embarrassed rejections by the driver. Furthermore, the climate within the team was deteriorating. Despite his massive lead, Niki started to criticize the team and its sporting director. From the Brazilian GP onward, the Brabhams were powered by the 12-cylinder Alfa Romeo Boxer, which soon Niki accredited with greater performance than the similar Ferrari engine. The technical scene also presented the powerful 12-cylinder Matra, suggesting that Prancing Horse supremacy in the engine field would not last much longer.

Volumes have been written about that fateful day, August 1, 1976, at the Nurburgring; Lauda's Ferrari

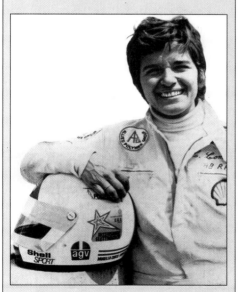
The American photographer (but with an Italian heart) Peter Coltrin, with his wife Gabriella and their much-loved dog.

Ferrari Through the Lens

The best photographs of Ferrari road or racing cars of the 1960s and 1970s bear the name of Peter C. Coltrin. They covered the era when the scarlet red cars dominated worldwide, but before that, they captured some unforgettable days of testing, dialog and interesting meetings at Modena, Maranello and nearby.

Today, more than 15 years after his death, the memories of Peter Coltrin and his intense love for Ferrari live on in the unique photographic archives he left behind.

way over the limit of grip on the wet surface on Lap 3 and the crash against the Bergwerk rock. The 312T2 bounced back onto the track in a crumpled state. The rest of the group arrived: Brett Lunger's Surtees and Harald Ertl's Hesketh hit the Ferrari, which cannoned around like a billiard ball and caught fire. Inside the cockpit, Niki lost consciousness. Without the assistance of several drivers, especially Arturo Merzario, who pulled him out, he would have died amidst the flames. The rest is history. The first images, shot by a spectator, show Niki on a stretcher. He was looking at his hands, but he didn't know his face had been destroyed by the flames. He asked his helpers, "What's my face like?"

What a difference to the Lauda of 1 1/2 months later, when he was blinded by the desire to return to the track and defend his title.

"I prefer to have my right foot than a pretty face," he declared.

Niki was taken to hospital. The consequences, which seemed slight at first, soon turned out to be much more serious. The smoke Lauda had inhaled during the fire caused major respiratory complications. Late in the evening, he was given the last rites, and it was considered unlikely he would live through the night.

The world learnt about Lauda's fate the morning after in the newspapers, especially in Italy, where the GP was not shown on television, either live or delayed. Slowly the alarming news on the health of Niki began to fade away, but no one could say when or if he would return to the track. Meanwhile, after his victory at the Nurburgring, Hunt had begun an incredible fight back, edging him closer and closer to the no longer uncatchable Lauda. The British driver, Niki's friend, was in superb form, and his McLaren M23 was becoming increasingly competitive. As if that wasn't enough, nervousness also began to play its part within Ferrari. The International Federation restored the points and victory in Spain to Hunt; Ferrari, instead of attempting to defend Lauda's lead in the championship, decided as a protest not to take part in the Austrian GP on August 15. The team returned to the track two weeks later in Holland with a sole T2 for Regazzoni, who finished second behind Hunt. The British driver celebrated his 29th birthday in the best possible way, by closing the gap on Lauda to just 14 points.

Niki returned to the track on Friday, September 10, during first practice for the Italian GP. Forty days had passed since the inferno at Bergwerk. He tried to reassure everyone, but he was in a terrible state. The constant vibrations caused his helmet to rub against the healing burns, making them bleed. The rest forms part of the history of Formula 1 and racing. Lauda finished a miraculous fourth at Monza. Hunt retired, but went on to win in Canada and the United States, closing the gap to just three points. Then onto the pouring rain of Fuji for the final

Grand Prix; Lauda abandoned the race, fourth place went to Hunt's McLaren and the championship went to the British driver by just one point.

The divorce between Lauda and Ferrari, officially recorded as taking place in October 1977, actually began in the pits of the Japanese circuit. Niki only completed two laps in the pouring rain. He was almost driving blind because of the bleeding from his wounds. Then he decided to retire. When he abandoned the circuit in a Rolls-Royce, controversy was already brewing in Italy, even though dawn had just broken.

At first, Ferrari defended him.

"I also decided not to race in the Lyon GP in 1924 because I didn't feel like it.

I wasn't feeling well, I was exhausted. I can understand Lauda. He did the right thing."

Strong words, destined to change after a few hours of criticism. Once again, the motor racing world was divided over Lauda. There were those who supported "the courage to be afraid," while others spoke about "the fear of having courage."

Lauda tried not to let it bother him, but it was difficult. For 1977, Ferrari flanked Lauda with Carlos Reutmann, after Regazzoni

A six-wheeled revolution: the Tyrrell P34 of Jody Scheckter at Monza in 1976 and the scale model of the experimental 1977 Ferrari with twin rear wheels.

had been fired without notice, comment or explanation. Reutemann had already been put on stand-by at the end of summer in 1976, in case Lauda couldn't make it back on the track, and he drove a third 312T2 in the Italian GP. In fact, contacts were also made with Ronnie Peterson, who was summoned to Maranello in secret by team manager Daniele Audetto and sent back home again as soon as he landed at Milan airport, because Ferrari was not interested. For Niki Lauda the start of 1977 was an uphill battle. It seemed that the team was betting everything on Reutemann. Fiat had to intervene to give Lauda some help. The Austrian didn't waste any time. Three victories in South Africa, Germany and Holland. Not many but enough to see off the challenge of Mario Andretti's Lotus, the brand-new Wolf of Jody Scheckter

and the McLaren of Hunt, who was victim of "world champion" syndrome with a season of mixed fortunes. These three victories would be enough to guarantee Lauda his second world title. But he was not to finish the season. In open dispute with Ferrari—and attracted by the multimillionaire offer from Brabham, which waved a two-year contract for 1978-79 in front of his nose—Niki did not take part in the final two Grands Prix of the season in Canada and Japan. That was the end of Lauda's wonderful story at Ferrari. A story which marked an era in motor racing and sport in general. Enzo Ferrari, critical toward Lauda and openly hostile when he replied to Niki's harsh anti-Maranello book Protokoll, finally concluded the story two years later with affectionate words.

Monza 1977:
Reutemann at the Italian GP.
The race was won by Andretti in a
Lotus. Lauda, second at the flag, took
his second world title with Ferrari.
He left at the end of the season,
giving rise to controversy not only
in the specialist magazines.

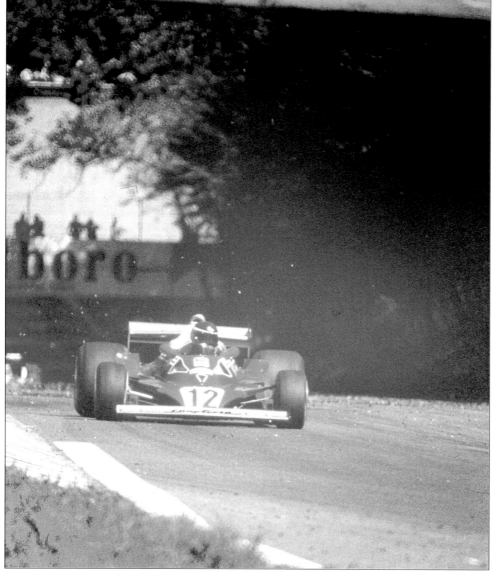

"Lauda sent me a telegram to congratulate me on the title won by Scheckter," he said at the end of 1979. "I replied with this message: 'If you had not decided to leave at the end of 1977, today you would have equaled Fangio's record.'"
Ferrari's appraisal was too kind. Even if he had won the title with Ferrari in 1978 and 1979, Niki would have taken his total to four, whereas Fangio won five titles. Perhaps Ferrari wanted to give an even more contorted and hidden meaning to the period of ill-feeling between the team and the driver.
"Our interpretation is that if at the end of 1976, Niki had kept his faith with Ferrari when he wanted to defend the Austrian's leadership by using Reutemann in the third car for the rest of the championship, he would also have won that title which eventually went to Hunt."
Too complicated and "Macchiavellian"? Maybe so. But the Engineer would certainly have been capable of such an interpretation.

VILLENEUVE FEVER

The world discovered Villeneuve fever in 1979. It first came to Italy, the center of Ferrari. Gilles Villeneuve arrived at Maranello with a traveling bag: a telephone call to his house in Canada, which at first he considered a joke, had convinced him to come for a talk with Enzo Ferrari. For Gilles, the call came out of the blue, just like the decision of Lauda to move to Brabham-Alfa Romeo, despite the fact that with the second title almost certain, the team had tried to reach an agreement for the following year.

Many different stories survive from that meeting, which was destined to end in divorce. What is certain, however, is that Niki was totally outspoken. "Ferrari no longer gives me any more motivation."

What was just as certain was that the Engineer was very disappointed. Deep down, despite the various recent misunderstandings, he was close to Lauda. He had created him from nothing . . . and now he was leaving.

The Engineer also tried to tempt Lauda with the financial card:

"How much do you want to stay?," he shouted to him in his Maranello office.

Lauda's reply was in Austrian schillings, and after getting the company accountant to convert the sum into lire, Ferrari spluttered. It was way beyond Ferrari's means and possibilities. Lauda was lost. He let him go, however not before calling him a name which would remain in history: "Jew!.."

The news of the divorce broke on Monday August 29, the day after Lauda's third win of the season, in Holland, which gave him a lead of 21 points over Scheckter and 28 over his teammate Reutemann, with four Grands Prix left to run.

Talks immediately began over Niki's replacement in Ferrari. First with Mario Andretti, who was blocked by a contract with Colin Chapman of Lotus, who in 1978 was building his fortune around the Italo-American. Then Scheckter, who also could not move

because of an agreement with the team of multimillionaire Walter Wolf. Thoughts also turned to Patrick Tambay, but he was in the McLaren orbit. Who knows why no one contacted Ronnie Peterson, one of Ferrari's old favorites, and free.. Maybe something clicked in the mind of the almost 80-year-old from Maranello: Nothing and no-one could take the place of Lauda in the scarlet red cars better than Villeneuve. The world of Formula 1 knew little about Gilles Villeneuve. A 27-year-old Canadian, who for many years pretended to be two years younger for fear of being too old for Grands Prix, Gilles Villeneuve came from motor sled racing. He had some interesting results in Formula Atlantic, a sort of overseas Formula 2. He made a quiet F1 debut in a McLaren on July 16: 10th in qualifying with an old M23, 27/100ths of a second faster than Jochen Mass, who had a new M26 identical to polesitter James Hunt's. He finished eleventh in the race, but was ahead of everyone in the Sunday morning warm-up in race trim.

Villeneuve arrived at Malpensa airport one sunny morning in September. He was met by Ennio Mortara, the Ferrari translator, who took him to Maranello by car. As soon as he got in, Gilles asked how long the journey would take, then fell asleep. When they introduced him to the living legend of motor racing, Villeneuve didn't seem all that impressed. When they asked him if he would like

to drive the Ferrari that belonged to Lauda, he replied that it would probably be a good idea to talk with McLaren, with whom he had a sort of contract. After Ferrari's calm response, they moved on to financial matters.

"How much would you like to earn to be happy?," asked the Legend.

"Enough to give my family a decent life," replied Villeneuve.

His family: his wife, Joanne, who lived in the shadow of her husband's overriding passion for the sport, their son, 6 1/2-year-old Jacques, and daughter Melanie, who was younger. They all moved together from one Grand Prix to another in a motorhome.

A few words and a handshake. On October 7, Gilles made his official debut in a Ferrari during practice for the Canadian GP. He had not had much time to get to know the 312T2, and qualified in 17th position, slightly more than a half-second slower than teammate Reutemann. In the race he finished 12th, four laps behind the winner, Scheckter (Wolf). Two weeks later, it was the Japanese GP at Fuji. The circuit, situated under the sacred mountain of Japan, is a difficult one, with along pit straight that takes the cars up to over 300 kilometers per hour. In qualifying, Gilles was no higher than the third row from the back of the grid. On the sixth lap of the race, he braked hard and ran into the rear of the six-wheeled Tyrrell of Peterson at the end of the straight. It was later rumored that his brakes had faded. What is certain is that the Ferrari took off and then landed in an area that was banned for the public, leaving two people dead and 10 injured. Villeneuve's fame as an "aviator" started here, as the 1978 championship was to confirm.

The year 1978 was a strange one. The Ferrari 312T3 was not the T2, but without a couple of disastrous starts (Monte Carlo and Belgium), Reutemann could have fought for the title with the Lotus of Andretti, who became World Champion. Alongside the Argentinian driver, Villeneuve was maturing. His times were rapidly approaching his teammate's, but at a high cost: off-road excursions, crashes, jumps. The "Aviator" was on everyone's lips. On July 26, after three victories by Reutemann but with the title virtually in the hands of Andretti, Fer-

Two versions of Gilles Villeneuve: In the cockpit of his 1979 Ferrari 312T4, and relaxing alongside an unusually smiling Enzo Ferrari.

rari signed Jody Scheckter for 1979. It seemed that Villeneuve would have to give up his place to the South African. Instead it was Reutemann who left, and had no alternative but to go to Lotus. Gilles won his first race at the final round of the season, the fifth for the Prancing Horse after four with Carlos. But above all, he began to hold a place in Enzo Ferrari's heart.

The 1979 World Championship saw the debut of the ugly but victorious Ferrari 312T4. Scheckter took it to victory in the championship, which was clinched with victory in front of a delirious crowd at Monza. Villeneuve obeyed orders: He was the Number Two driver and gave way to Jody. He did, however, take three wins, the same number as his teammate. But above all, 1979 was the year when Villeneuve Fever became white-hot. Gilles was no longer an "aviator." On the track he won, convincingly. He guaranteed nonstop excitement. The wheel-to-wheel duel with Arnoux's Renault in the final stages of the French GP at Dijon will remain in the memories of those who follow motor

sport. Not for the win, which went to Jabouille's Renault, the first in the new turbo era in Formula 1, but for second place, which went to Villeneuve by just 0. 64 of a second from Arnoux. The fans celebrated the world title of Scheckter, but went wild over Villeneuve's victory in the final round of the championship, putting him in pole position for the title fight the following year. However, 1980 failed to fulfill its promise. Ferrari, which had moved on to the pretty but outdated 312T5, could do nothing against the ground-effect Williams, which gave the title to Alan Jones, or Piquet's Brabham and Reutemann's Lotus, second and third overall. Gilles was out of luck: 6 points and 10th overall. Scheckter, 2 points and 19th overall, was even more disappointing, and at the end of the year Scheckter left his place to Didier Pironi. The same could be said for 1981, even though it did come with some added excitement. The Formula 1 cars were as rigid as go-karts, ground-effect dominated, and with turbos generating more than 600 horsepower. Ferrari switched to turbo power. With the 126C, Villeneuve won two memorable Grands Prix. In Monte Carlo, he overtook the Williams of an incredulous Jones, with a final dash to the line. In Spain, at Jarama, Gilles had problems in curves because the car was undriveable, but thanks to the power of the six-cylinder turbo, he managed to keep ahead on the straights with sheer horsepower.

"Gilles, you are wild!" was the full-page headline in the Italian weekly magazine Autosprint after the victory at Monte Carlo. But it was all an illusion: Williams and Brabham dominated F1. In the end the title went to the young Brazilian, Nelson Piquet, who was fresher and more lucid at the end of the absurd carpark Grand Prix around the Caesars' Palace Hotel in Los Vegas, where Reutemann said goodbye to yet another title. At the end of 1981, Gilles Villeneuve was tired. He had worked so hard and tested the Ferrari turbo for tens of thousands of kilometers in an attempt to make it competitive and reliable. He had excited crowds all over the world, as in the

1980 Canadian GP, where he scored a legendary third place without a front wing (after a collision) in the rain. He was 31 years old, however, and saw the possibility of becoming World Champion slip further and further away. He listened to offers from other teams, but Enzo Ferrari loved him and knew how to make him understand. He would remain with the Prancing Horse for 1982.

That year was to be the end for Villeneuve. On Saturday, May 8, at Zolder, Gilles Villeneuve lost his life in a stupid accident during qualifying for the Belgian GP. At Imola, 13 days before, he had lost control in a bid for victory, which was "snatched" from him by his teammate Pironi, after orders came from the pits to hold positions with Villeneuve in the lead, seeing as the two Ferraris were uncatchable. In the Terlamen Forest, shortly before 2 o'clock on that terrible afternoon in Belgium, the world's favorite driver said goodbye to Formula 1 forever. For medical records, the time of death was given as the evening at Leuwen hospital. Enzo Ferrari and

Ferrari were filled with grief. The 126C2 Turbo was without a doubt the fastest and most competitive car of the season, and Didier Pironi could not fail to take the title. The Frenchman went on to win in Holland; on the eve of the German GP, the 12th of the 16 rounds on the calendar, he had a 9-point lead over Watson (McLaren) and 14 over Prost (Renault). But on August 7, the final day of qualifying at Hockenheim, Pironi crashed into Prost at 300 kilometers per hour in the pouring rain, and broke both his legs. His career was over. August 7 was Saturday, the same day of the week a Gilles' accident.

At the end of the year, Ferrari won the Constructor's title, thanks to the victory of Patrick Tamblay, who won that fateful race in Germany. However, it is the memory of Gilles that puts the seal on perhaps the most heart-rending season in the history of Ferrari.

Monza 1978: flames and smoke at the start of the Italian GP, in which Swedish driver Ronnie Peterson lost his life.

Villeneuve fever also led to several "fakes." The memorabilia of ex-Ferrari mechanic Gisberto Leopardi also includes this picture dedicated to Gilles and to his famous incident during testing at Imola in 1979.

But look closely, and the photo has obviously been touched up.

Below, Lauda's 312T at the Paul Ricard circuit in France in 1975. In the background, Graham Hill and his driver Tony Brise, who shortly after were to perish in an air crash.

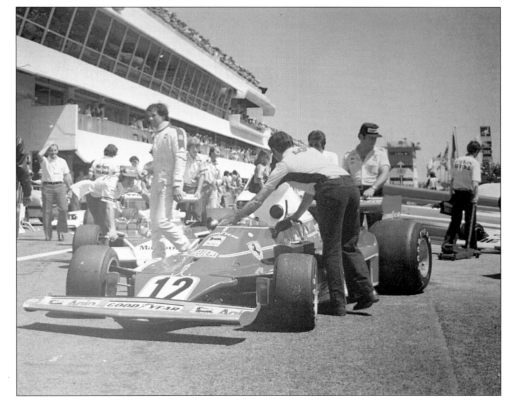

in the world

1978 - In Italy, the Red Brigades kidnapped the Christian Democratic Party Secretary Aldo Moro in March and murdered him on May 9, after holding him hostage for several weeks.

1978 - On October 16, after the brief papacy of John Paul I (August-September), Polish Archbishop Karol Wojtyla became Pope under the name of John Paul II.

1979 - Margaret Thatcher of the Conservative Party became British Prime Minister.

in motor sport

1978 - At Monza, Swedish driver Ronnie Peterson was involved in an incident at the start of the race and was trapped in his burning car. He died in the hospital later that night.

1979 - At Kyalami, Gilles Villeneuve won the South African GP with the new Ferrari 312 T4, designed by Mauro Forghieri.

1979 - Two great drivers of the seventies, Niki Lauda and James Hunt, both retired from motor racing.

Call Montezemolo 3131

Maybe not everyone knows how Luca di Montezemolo, an amateur rally driver with bright hopes but little specific experience of motor racing or even F1, came to be in charge of the Ferrari F1 racing team. Montezemolo was a young lawyer, closely connected to the family of Gianni Agnelli—who at that time, it should be said, was a partner of Ferrari, as he was the owner of Fiat.

In 1972, Luca di Montezemolo was a guest on the famous radio program at the time "Call Rome 3131." The subject of the radio conversation soon moved onto Ferrari and its current bad patch. At this point, Montezemolo replied by defending Ferrari and its work and was so convincing on the air that the Modena constructor got in touch with the young lawyer.

"What are your future plans?," Ferrari asked Montezemolo.

"I'm about to leave for the United States to do a master's degree."

"If you like, when you come back,"—concluded Ferrari, "I would be happy to offer you a position within our sporting activities."

This almost fairy tale story was how Ferrari offered a contract to Montezemolo, who at the end of 1973 took over the F1 team. It won a total of nine Grands Prix over the next two years, the last of which was crowned by Lauda's world title.

Monza 1979: With a 1-2 for Scheckter and Villeneuve at the Italian GP, Ferrari and the South African driver wrapped up the world title. This was also a triumph for the 312T4, the ugly but very competitive Ferrari single-seater car that won six races during the season.

THE LAST WORLD TITLE

The 1979 World Championship began with Ligier and Jacques Laffite winning in Argentina and Brazil. It continued with a remarkable performance by Williams, which began to win with Clay Regazzoni and then dominated the second half of the season with Alan Jones. But 1979 will go down in the annals of motor sport as the year of the world title of Ferrari and Jody Scheckter, who was signed at the end of 1978 to replace the "troubled and troublesome" (another label thought up by Enzo Ferrari) Carlos Reutemann. The days of a fast and over-the-limit Scheckter were long gone. James Hunt used to call him "Fletcher," the name of the sea-gull in Richard Bach's famous book, Jonathan Livingston Seagull, who had ambitions beyond his possibilities. The 1979 version of Jody Scheckter was very different to the young South

African driver who made his debut in 1972 with incredibly fast times and some hair-raising overtaking. The Ferrari version of Scheckter was a fast, consistent, regular driver who had one aim: win the world title with the Ferrari 312T4. The T4 was so ugly that at the official presentation on January 19 it was renamed, rather unkindly, "the Slipper" or "Hippo-nose." Enzo Ferrari, however, wasn't in the least worried about the comments: "Let's hope." he said "that the ugly T4 becomes pretty on the track." And that is exactly what did happen. With the T4, Scheckter and Villeneuve won three victories apiece. The title went to Jody, who scored more placings. No one could have imagined it at the time, but that World Championship victory was the last one for Ferrari until the present day.

THE LAUDA ERA

T for Three, T for Title

From the 312T to the 312T5: From 1975 to 1980, the history of Ferrari cars has only been written with the letter "T." It stands for transversal, the type of gearbox fitted on all the production models, which guaranteed a better balance in the distribution of weight behind the cockpit, and better handling despite the considerable bulk of the 12-cylinder boxer engine. The six years of the "T" Ferraris brought: three world titles: in 1975 (Lauda with the 312T), in 1977 (Lauda with the T2) and in 1979 (Scheckter with the T4). The cars won a total of 27 victories, with 19 pole positions and 25 fastest laps. It was an exceptional performance, and deserves admiration when bearing in mind that all these results were achieved between 1975 and 1979. In 1980 in fact, Scheckter and Villeneuve failed to win a race, set a pole or even one fastest lap.

A "poker" of Ferrari "T" cars. Clockwise from left, the 312T (12) of Lauda's 1975 title; the T2 of Niki's second title, in 1977; the T3 with Reutemann in 1978; the T5 here with Villeneuve in the unlucky 1980 season.

ALBORETO

After the death of Gilles Villeneuve, Enzo Ferrari found that he was 84 years of age. Not in the sense that before he had been unaware of his age, but now the tiredness and pressure were starting to make themselves felt. He was the most famous car constructor in the world, in motor racing and road production. His name and his symbol, the Prancing Horse, were one thing only and told the same story: the dream that turned into a legend, glory, enterprise, innovation, success. But with the death of Gilles Villeneuve, he had to say goodbye to what had remained his personal dream. An unexpressed dream, which he never told to anyone and which he probably only confessed to a few close friends: create a new Nuvolari. There was no doubt that Villeneuve was a creature of Ferrari in the true

meaning of the term. Who amongst Ferrari drivers could, in the past, have been the cause of so many incidents, invent so many incredible spins, destroy so many cars and play so many tricks? No one. Gilles, on the other hand, could do this and a lot more. Without risking anything.

"I was very fond of him," said Ferrari on the death of Gilles Villeneuve. That expression said it all, from the dream of Gilles as a "total driver," to the affection of a father toward his son, without taking into consideration his pros or cons.

It is difficult to imagine whether and how much the great rapport between Gilles and the Engineer derived from the behavior of the driver at the wheel of Formula 1 cars. Certainly fearlessness, indifference to risk and reckless courage were dominant characteristics in Gilles Villeneuve. Enzo Ferrari liked this in a

driver, as he had with Tazio Nuvolari, Guy Moll and very few other champions behind the wheel.

On the death of Villeneuve, Ferrari was a dual industrial and sporting reality. On the one hand, striving for success in the most professional way, using more modern and refined technology and administrative methods; on the other, the almost family-like cohesion linking the protagonists. A tightly-knit staff, on a human and professional level, has always been a special feature of the Prancing Horse. Enzo Ferrari was now more than just old. The problems of asthma, which at the end of the 1970s became serious, requiring innovative surgery by a Turin specialist with the use of human placenta, were a thing of the past. But the high doses of cortisone, which at the time were necessary to combat the asthma, had their effects on Ferrari's kidney functions, and they got worse year after year, weakening the Constructor, subjecting him to daily analysis and making him follow a strict diet. In this situation, the family ties between Ferrari and his closest collaborators were as deep and solid as ever.

Here are just a few examples. Franco Gozzi, who entered Ferrari in the 1950s after being recommended by Ferrari's barber, was for more than a quarter of a century the Prancing Horse spokesman. Born and bred in the Ferrari school (i.e. only say the things which Ferrari wants everyone to know, and deny the rest), Gozzi was an integral part of the "family." Ferrari trusted him blindly, to the point of making him "master of ceremonies" at public occasions and in press conferences, but also in everyday contacts with Italian and foreign journalists. From 1968 to 1970 Gozzi was also team manager, and this expe-

rience helped him to get to know every minor detail of how a racing team worked. This characteristic also helped him to become a vital, irreplaceable piece of the Ferrari jigsaw, and the situation would not change until 1988, the year of the Engineer's death. Mauro Forghieri was the technical "soul" of the Prancing Horse. He arrived at Maranello immediately after graduating in 1959 and a few years later took over the difficult role of Prancing Horse technical director, putting his name to many of the Sport and Formula 1 cars that from then until the 1980s scored some of Ferrari's greatest victories. Foghieri's influence on the "T" series of single-seaters was considerable, and he designed and constructed the successful 12-cylinder boxer, as well as the 312T, which gave Lauda his first title and the T4 of Scheckter's triumph in 1979. At the start of the 1980s, Forghieri was

in the world

1984 - Following an agreement over Hong Kong in September, Britain pledged to hand over the territory to China by the end of 1997.

1984 - Rajiv Gandhi succeeded his mother as Prime Minister of India. The following year in the USSR, Mikhail Gorbachev, the founder of the program of reforms (Perestroika) and compatibility (Glasnost) became Secretary of the Soviet Communist party.

1986 - On April 26, the Chernobyl nuclear power plant in the USSR malfunctioned and caused the world's worst reactor disaster to date. The toxic clouds reached Western Europe.

in motor sport

1986 - The Benetton group arrived in F1 with the purchase of the Toleman team. It was the start of an adventure which would take Benetton to the world title.

1987 - Ayrton Senna scored Lotus' final victory in F1 at Detroit.

1987 - Satoru Nakajima became the first Japanese F1 driver, sparking a wave of interest in F1 in Japan.

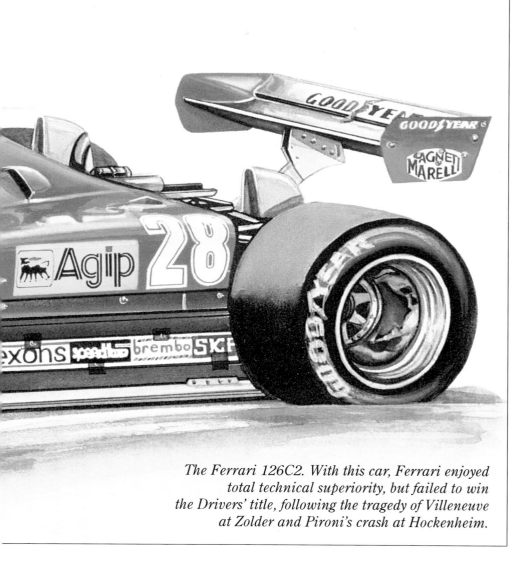

The Ferrari 126C2. With this car, Ferrari enjoyed total technical superiority, but failed to win the Drivers' title, following the tragedy of Villeneuve at Zolder and Pironi's crash at Hockenheim.

BITTER AMARO

involved in the lengthy development work which would take the 6-cylinder turbo to victory in 1982 and 1983, a car which then suffered in the technological battle against foreign manufacturers such as Porsche, Renault and Honda.

Marco Piccinini was manager of the Formula 1 team from 1978 onward. No one held or would hold this post longer than him, and he continued to run the Grand Prix team and drivers until the death of Ferrari in 1988. He would also represent the Prancing Horse in the International Motorsport Federation with an authority which no one, except the Engineer himself, had ever had. Piccinini, like Gozzi and Forghieri, was tied to the Prancing Horse and Ferrari above all by total loyalty, almost a blood tie, forming a bond that no external threat or pressure could change. The last name on this list, but not the least important, was Piero Lardi. At the start of the 1980s, the son of Ferrari was one of the cornerstones of the company and the team. He grew up in the shadows, away from all the official

The presentation of the 126C2 at Maranello. From left to right, Dario Calzavara, Marco Piccinini, Piero Ferrari, Harvey Postlethwaite and Franco Gozzi can be recognized. With the 126C3, in the drawing, Rene Arnoux just missed out on the 1983 title.

dealings but always where it mattered in the company and he had always had a passion for racing, for cars and drivers. He played a key role in the signing of Jody Scheckter in 1978. The driver had also attracted the attention of the Engineer, but it was not easy to persuade him to pay the $ 1 million (more than 1 1/2 billion lire at the time, around 7 billion today) necessary to make him refuse the offers from the British competition. Now Piero was ready to inherit the work of his father, who in 1978 lost his wife Laura with muscular dystrophy, the same disease which had taken away his son Dino many years before. This was the Prancing Horse family that lost Gilles Villeneuve, the adopted son, in such traumatic circumstances. It was clear that it was Enzo Ferrari, the patriarch, who suffered the most. As well as mourning the death of the Canadian driver, Ferrari was passing through a moment which was to say the least, unfortunate. Gilles' place was taken over by the Parisian, Patrick Tambay, a driver whom Ferrari had always liked. Tambay was now available, despite it being late in the season. When Pironi, seriously injured in qualifying for the German GP, was removed from the title race, the superiority of Ferrari's technical "package" was evident. The early days of the Ferrari turbo, powerful yet almost undriveable because it had such a harsh and brutal

power distribution, were a memory of the past. While that turbo could only be controlled by Villeneuve, who took two extraordinary victories in 1981 at Monte Carlo and Jarama, good results could be obtained by almost anyone with the 1982 edition of the 126C2 V-6 turbo. This was demonstrated by Tambay, who won in Germany a few hours after Pironi's crash. Tambay's late arrival on the scene meant he had no chance of going for the title, which went to the Williams-Ford driver Keke Rosberg. It was also confirmed by Mario Andretti, who was called upon by Ferrari to drive in the final two Grands Prix, and who set an extraordinary pole position on his debut at Monza for the Italian GP. He eventually finished third behind Tambay, who lost out to the winner Arnoux in a Renault. Ferrari was left with success—or rather domination—in the World Constructors' Championship, but it was bitter consolation.

128

When the 1982 season was drawing to a close, the Ferrari "family" had to chose the driver to race alongside Tambay the following year. The choice fell upon René Arnoux, the young and fast French driver of the Renault team. Ferrari immediately took a liking to Arnoux, due to the determination he had shown in a year when he fought against, and twice beat, his teammate Alain Prost, a driver tipped to be tomorrow's champion.

But Ferrari also liked another driver. He was Italian, and this was surprising because after the last episode with a home-grown driver, Merzario in 1973, it seemed that the Prancing Horse did not want to repeat this experience, which would clearly have negative repercussions on the press and public opinion, in the event of bad results. The Italian in question was Michele Alboreto; he was 26 and since 1981 had been driving for the Tyrrell team, for whom he had won

his first Grand Prix in the final round of the 1982 championship in the bizarre carpark race at Caesar's Palace in Las Vegas. It was a great moment for Italian drivers in Formula 1. During the 1982 season, before Michele's victory, Riccardo Patrese (at Monte Carlo with Brabham) and Elio De Angelis (at Zeltweg with Lotus after a historic 0.125 of a second photofinish with Rosberg's Williams) had also scored wins. However, this was not the reason why Alboreto earned Ferrari's favor. Between the young Milan driver and the Grand Old Man of Maranello, there was, in fact, the start of a personal friendship, at first kind and affectionate and then increasingly intense. At the end of 1982, Ken Tyrrell, who had a keen eye for drivers, put the brakes on the mutual courtship:

"Michele is a good driver," he declared, "but he still needs more experience.

Another season with us and he'll be

ready to race with Ferrari."

The story, it seemed, had already been written.

In 1983, Ferrari raced with Tambay and Arnoux. It was a great season, totally concentrated on the race for the title. Only McLaren, amongst the top teams, was still tied to the old normally aspirated Cosworth engine, but it still managed to win at Long Beach with Watson. For the rest, the red cars fought an incredible battle with the turbocharged Renaults of Prost and Cheever and the Brabham-BMWs of Piquest and Patrese. The Prancing Horse won four races: one with Tambay at Imola and three with Arnoux in Canada, Germany and Holland. But it wasn't enough. Ferrari again won the World Constructors' Championship, but the Drivers' title—clearly the most important—went for the second time to Piquet and his Brabham. The disappointment at the South African circuit of Kyalami was plain for all to see. The Ferrari cars returned to Maranello without the title they had chased in vain since 1979, and no one could imagine how long this "fasting" was going to go on for. At the ritual end-of-year press conference, the Engineer was totally outspoken: "On Saturday evening they telephoned me from South Africa to tell me that Tambay, on pole position, had requested a bonus to guarantee his support for Arnoux in the final assault on the title," he told the massive numbers of journalists present at Maranello. "'Promise him the moon if you want,' I replied to Piccinini, 'because with our Goodyear tires, we've got no chance of winning anyway.' I was right."

He continued with the presentation of Alboreto for the next season: "One year ago, I said to Alboreto that when his contract had expired, there would be a Ferrari available for him. This moment has arrived, and I am happy to have him with us starting from the 1984 World Championship." Just a few words, therefore, to confirm that the "family" was again complete. René Arnoux, a fast driver whom Ferrari liked, was not the right man, however, to become part of the family. This was confirmed after

129

the first GP of the 1985 season in Brazil, when he was abruptly sacked in a no-nonsense way by the team for reasons never made official, but which certainly had nothing to do with his performance behind the wheel. This was followed punctually by the arrival of Michele Alboreto, who even before taking to the track for his first race with a Ferrari (Brazil 1984, second fastest time on the grid alongside the Lotus-Renault of De Angelis) had been perfectly integrated into the Maranello environment. He wasn't on first name terms with Enzo Ferrari, unlike Villeneuve, but Michele was without a doubt the "son" Ferrari had found again.

Michele Alboreto and the 126C4, in the drawing, with which he won in Belgium in 1984. With the 156/85 (below), the Italian driver scored two wins in Canada and Germany and was in with a shot at the world title, which eventually went to Prost.

DEFEAT AT THE HANDS OF GERMANY AND JAPAN

Alboreto began well in Ferrari. As well as the front row in his first GP in Brazil, the first season with the scarlet red cars stood out for his victory in Belgium. At the end of the season, the record was, however, disappointing: second place in the Constructors Championship, fourth and sixth in the Drivers' with Alboreto and Arnoux. But the year belonged to McLaren with the Tag Porsche turbo engine, which won 12 of the 16 Grands Prix, sharing the victories between its two drivers who, from a certain point in the season onward launched themselves into a sensational head-to-head battle. The two drivers were Alain Prost, who had joined McLaren from Renault, after the French manufacturer abandoned F1 because of lack of results

and never-ending investments without any success, and Niki Lauda. The Austrian was back on the track in 1982, tempted by offers from both McLaren, under the new management of Ron Dennis— a former mechanic of the team—and Arab tycoon Mansour Ojjieh. It was Lauda himself, at the end of a hard-fought season, who took the 1984 title and his third championship by just half-a-point from teammate Prost. After much promise, the Ferrari 126C4 was pensioned off in the wake of a sudden technical and technological disadvantage against the rival cars and engines. The man who came off worse was Mauro Forghieri, who was switched to other responsibilities—to use a sympathetic yet very significant expression. It meant he was removed from his position during 1984. He eventually left Maranello in 1987 for Lamborghini, when the Bologna manufacturer entered F1 as engine-supplier. The technical squad of the Prancing Horse

BITTER TURBO

remained in the hands of the British engineer Harvey Postlethwaite, who came to Maranello in 1981 and who was the first of a long and still unfinished wave of foreign engineers. Track management was in the hands of team manager Marco Piccinini, as well as the engineer Tomaini, and it was already clear by autumn that for the following season the destiny of the Prancing Horse would be entrusted to a new car.

The Ferrari 156/85 was created for the following year. On the face of things, it was a simple evolution of the 126C4. However, it had numerous major changes, starting with the engine, the design of which was

1988 Italian GP at Monza:
A group photograph confirming the
links between Ferrari and Fiat.
From left to right: Piero Ferrari,
Gianni Agnelli, Vittorio Ghidella,
at the time President of Fiat Auto,
and the future President of Ferrari,
Luca di Montezemolo,
can all be recognized.

the same (120-degree six-cylinder V with turbocompressor) but which bore important modifications to the cylinder heads, the timing and the exhausts. Hopes were high for this car. Alboreto set pole position in its first race at Brazil's Jacarapegua circuit and finished second behind Prost's McLaren. It was the same story in Portugal, this time behind a certain Ayrton Senna, who notched up the first victory of his glorious career with a Lotus-Renault. Another second place at Monte Carlo and victory in Canada took Michele to the top of the World Championship, a position he maintained with another win in Germany. Now he was level on 50 points with Prost, after 10 of the 16 races in the calendar.

At Maranello, they were getting ready to celebrate. But it was at this point, after the Austrian Grand Prix halfway through August, that the scarlet cars' progress ground to a halt. The V-6 turbo engine, pushed over the limit in the search for greater power, began to show signs of

yielding. The 156/85 had a series of problems, the McLaren could no longer be caught, and a first long-awaited title went to Prost.

Ferrari was now on a downhill slide. Alboreto and his teammate, Stefan Johansson, the only Swede to drive a Ferrari Formula 1 car, were the drivers in the 1986 World Championship, which turned out to be very disappointing: no victories, no pole positions and no fastest laps; fifth and eighth place overall in the Drivers' Championship with Johansson and Alboreto in that order, a long way behind Prost, who won his second title; fourth in the Constructors' table, behind Williams, McLaren and Lotus. It was at this point that Enzo Ferrari, at the age of 90, realized that the time had come to change once again. At Williams there was a top-class driver whom he liked a lot: Nigel Mansell. At the end of July, he invited him to Maranello. The British driver landed at Bologna airport with a private flight from the Isle of Man, where he lived. He was welcomed and taken to Maranello, where he signed a pre-contract for the 1987 season. He returned home that same evening, a Ferrari driver. Afterward, however, Mansell changed his mind, thanks to a "veto" by Frank Williams, who had helped him mature within the team and had no desire to see him move to Ferrari. Williams had admired Ferrari right from his early days as constructor, and in 1986 managed to equal the number of F1 Constructors' titles (eight) won by the Engineer from Maranello. Mansell was required to pay a penalty for his refusal to go ahead with an already-signed contract: $100,000 at the time (more than $160,000 at the current rate, the equivalent of 260 million lire), which was donated in charity to the Association for the Study of Muscular Dystrophy.

But the Mansell deal was not the only weapon in Ferrari's arsenal. With perfect timing, Ferrari managed to convince the British engineer John Barnard to leave McLaren, for whom he had designed and constructed every World Championship car from 1984 to 1986. The story of Barnard and Ferrari was to be a brilliant one, although full of ups and downs. He left the team in 1989, but came back again in 1992, only to leave Ferrari again in spring 1997 after twice creating a research and development center for the Prancing Horse in Great Britain. On the driver front, it was Enzo Ferrari who chose the Austrian Gerhard Berger in 1987 as teammate to Alboreto after Johansson had left.

Berger, 27, came to Maranello at the end of 1986. The following year, in perfect technical and personal consonance with John Barnard, he took two wins for Ferrari in the final two Grands Prix in Japan and Australia, after spinning away another certain victory in Portugal. However, 1987 was the year when Williams and the Honda turbo dominated.

Against competition from Honda, and before that Porsche and BMW, the once unbeatable Ferrari engines had lost the battle of performance, reliability, fuel consumption and electronic management.

Ferrari's disadvantage would also be evident in the years to come, when because of new international regulations, turbos gave way to normally aspirated engines. This period was characterized first by the continuing domination of Honda and then the entry of new manufacturers, such as Renault and Peugeot. The final season of turbo power in 1988 was marked by both a historic victory at Monza and a lot of disappointment for Ferrari.

Above and below, the Ferrari F1/86 and the F1/87. In the two years they raced, the cars scored totally different results. In 1986, no wins, no pole positions and no fastest laps; the following year, two wins for Berger (Japan and Australia), three poles and three fastest laps.

BITTER TURBO

MANSELL, BUT ONLY "AFTERWARD"

Enzo Ferrari died on Sunday, August 14, 1988. It was a Sunday without Formula 1 and a day that was even quieter than usual because it was the day before the August 15 Bank Holiday, when the whole of Italy was virtually at a standstill. As for the racing, Ferrari left without seeing all his work and the money spent rewarded by the scarlet cars' return to the top, where they had not been since 1982. Until his kidney problems accelerated,

and despite his 90 years, Ferrari had continued to follow Formula 1 race after race, day after day. He lived to see the definitive consecration of Honda as engine builder, its preference for McLaren instead of Williams, despite the titles conquered by the latter in 1987— both Constructors' and Drivers' titles, with Nelson Piquet winning his third World Championship after a season-long duel with his teammate and Number One rival, Mansell, who was injured in the final GP of the year in Japan. But the F1/87 and the F1/87-88 were competitive only on occasions.

On the industrial production side, thanks to the popularity of the marque and its commercial success, Ferrari was a world leader. From 1982, the year of its institution, Ferrari's office was within the new Sporting Management Division building, and this enabled him to follow every aspect and every detail of the industrial activity of the Prancing Horse. The Engineer retired almost full-time, Saturday and often Sunday included, in this new building, which was totally independent of all racing car activity. Here he was able to celebrate the creation of the Ferrari F40: a virtual F1 car with bodywork destined to break a string of production records. The car, which cost almost 400 million lire in 1987-88 ($250,000), equivalent to 600 million lire in 1997 ($375,000) created an unprecedented demand throughout the world.

On June 4, 1988, in the vast area inside the Fiorano circuit, the Ferrari company was visited by Pope John Paul II, an event captured by photographers and broadcast worldwide. The Pontiff made a lap of the track in a Mondial 8, with the "blessing" of all those present. Unfortunately that day, Ferrari himself was only able to greet the Pope by phone, given the gravity of his condition.

Just 71 days later, in fact, Enzo Ferrari departed from this life. On his specific request, news of his death was given the following day. As the daily newspapers in Italy do not come out on the day after August Bank Holiday, the news was only published on Wednesday, August 17. This was yet another "lie" in an entire life spent hiding news from journalists, to whom Ferrari was linked

Translation at page 168

by equal measures of love and hate, respect and dislike, solidarity and, at times, competition.

The world appeared to come to a brief standstill on being told of the news of the death of Enzo Ferrari. The man, a living legend who had constantly modernized the world of the car and of competition, who had changed the balance of world automobile power with his influence, was no longer with us.

Afterward everything resumed as before—work, progress, invention—as if out of respect for the dictates of this man from Modena, whose life had covered almost a century, the first 100 years in the history of the car and motor racing.

On September 11 at Monza, exactly four weeks after the death of the Engineer, Gerhard Berger won the Italian Grand Prix. The victory was purely down to luck: Ayrton Senna, the almost certain winner, was pushed

off the track in his McLaren by Jo Schlesser in a Williams, with just a few corners to go before the checkered flag. That triumph would go down in history as a "lap of honor" for the Grand Old Man who died on the field of battle.

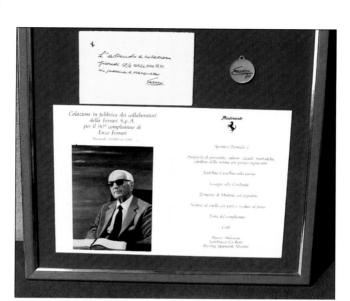

Furthermore, the news that Nigel Mansell, in place of the outgoing Alboreto, was to drive the 1989 Ferrari alongside Gerhard Berger, assumed a special significance. It was the very same Mansell whom Ferrari had wanted in his cars two years before.

The final days of Enzo Ferrari. The company lunch for his 90th birthday (on February 18, 1988) and, on the other page, the notice of death posted up by the local Communist Party and a moving message written by his last Italian driver, Alboreto.

The Visit of the Pope

On Saturday June 4, 1988, something akin to a miracle happened at Fiorano. It had already been visited over the years by a series of presidents and kings, actors and politicians, sportsmen and show business personalities, but this time the doors of Ferrari headquarters were opened for a special guest: Pope John Paul II. The visit, organized by way of Team Manager Marco Piccinini's excellent relations with the Vatican, had a purely pastoral purpose, with the blessing of the factory and a Holy Mass at the Fiorano circuit. But even before the day began, the implications of the event for the mass media had far exceeded every expectation.

When the Pope arrived at Ferrari, the only person missing was Enzo Ferrari himself. His increasingly grave health condition had confined the Constructor to his Modena house: only a telephone call connected the two Grand Old Men, the

Pope taking Ferrari's call inside the headquarters at the Ferrari circuit.

A few hours later, a sudden idea presented the world with a totally unprecedented image. When the Pope was just about to get into his bulletproof Land Rover for the blessing during a lap of the track, someone objected, in all good faith, that at Fiorano a similar moment "must" take place in a Ferrari car. And John Paul, far from being embarrassed, immediately got into a Mondial 8 driven

by Piero Ferrari. He remained standing up, holding on to the upper part of the windscreen for an entire lap, blessing an enthusiastic crowd of Ferrari workers and employees, guests, journalists and photographers from all over the world, thrilled by what was happening right before their very eyes.

Pictures of the Pontiff in the Ferrari Mondial 8 went all around the world and were published worldwide in newspapers and magazines.

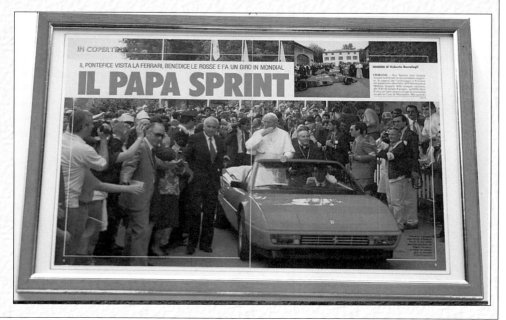

THE ARRIVAL OF PROST

Mansell's rapport with Ferrari couldn't have got off to a better start—with a win. It happened on March 26, 1989, at the Jacarepagua circuit south of Rio de Janeiro. It was a "first" for many reasons: for Mansell at the wheel of a Ferrari; for the semiautomatic gearbox constructed by Barnard; and for Cesare Fiorio at the helm of the Maranello team. Although it was true that Nigel should have driven for Ferrari back in 1987 as the Engineer had wanted, it was also true that without the death of the Modena constructor Fiorio would probably never have been put in charge of the team.

Cesare Fiorio was from Turin and had been a brilliant team manager for Fiat and Lancia in rallies and endurance racing. He was without a doubt the most highly qualified and successful team manager in the history of Italian motor sport. For some time, the appointment of Fiorio as team manager of Ferrari had been one of the mysteries of the sport, especially considering the frequent turnover of managerial staff inside the Scuderia. Maybe it was a lack of genuine feeling between Fiorio and the Engineer, or maybe because at Maranello there was no intention of handing over control to a man - despite his clear professional and sporting capacity—who was the incarnation of Fiat power. Once Ferrari had

Alain Prost: In close-up on the podium of the Spanish GP he won at Jerez in 1990, and with Mansell, then in the company of Cesare Fiorio and current president of FIA, Jean-Marie Balestre. The French driver lost all chance of winning the 1990 title at the penultimate round.

left this world, the Competitions Director of Lancia and Alfa Romeo was put directly in charge of the Prancing Horse's sporting activities. The month of March had just begun, and in a few days time the team was due to leave for Brazil and the first GP of the 1989 season. With Fiorio and the car, officially called "640" but unofficially baptized "the duck" due to its

strange nose, Mansell won in Brazil and Hungary. Berger also gave a hand to its success, winning in Portugal in September, when he was officially McLaren-bound for the next season. Halfway through July, in fact, on the Friday before the British Grand Prix, Alain Prost announced that he would be leaving McLaren. There had been too many rows with his teammate Ayrton Senna, 1988 World Champion and the favorite of the British team, despite an open battle for the 1989 championship.

"I'm leaving McLaren," said Prost, "even if I win the championship at the end of the year. I don't know if or for whom I will be driving in 1990." That was all, a cold and concise declaration. Rumors went around that his place, alongside Senna, would be taken by Berger, who was now second-string driver behind Mansell at Ferrari, and who had a close personal friendship with Ron Dennis, the McLaren owner. Even without thinking of the future of his driver, Cesare Fiorio was the first to welcome Prost's decision, and he approached him in the Silverstone paddock. "Are you interested in the possibility of an agreement?," he asked him point-blank. "Yes," was the reply, "but give me a few more races."

In the Japanese Grand Prix on October 22, Senna was disqualified in the race and Prost obtained the world title with mathematical certainty. The three-time winner was already officially with Ferrari for the next two seasons. In 1990, with Prost behind the wheel of a scarlet red car with the number 1 on its nose for the first time since Jody Scheckter's title, Ferrari came very close to winning the World Championship. It came about with the F1 90 car, better known as the 641 from its design project number. Without John Barnard in the team, following the engineer's transfer to Benetton the previous autumn after refusing to move to Maranello, the 641 was an evolution of the successful but unreliable car of the previous year. The problems were all gradually corrected by the vast experience of Prost, who won five Grands Prix in the year—including France, the 100th victory for Ferrari in Formula 1. - Pro-

st was still in with a chance at the final round, the Japanese GP at Suzuka. In Japan, however, Senna with the Mc-Laren-Honda did not hesitate to knock Prost's Ferrari off the track at the first turn after the start. By taking revenge (as he would officially admit one year later) for the collision which gave a third title to Prost at Suzuka '89, Senna was crowned World Champion for the second time.

The dream did not come true and all eyes were on 1991. At this point, however, the rapport between Prost and Fiorio was strained to breaking point. During the summer, the team manager had come to a sort of agreement with Ayrton Senna for the Brazilian to drive a Ferrari from 1991 onward. The news alarmed Prost, who was not prepared to have Senna in his team once again and who turned to the support of Fiat for appropriate guarantees. Alain was also defended by the President of Ferrari, Piero Fusaro, who, by assuming this stance, embarked on a collision course with Fiorio. The outcome of this intricate web of friendships and rivalries is still fresh in the memory. Jean Alesi arrived in place of Senna in 1991, Fiorio was fired in May the same year, Prost left one race before the end of his contract, and later Fusaro abandoned the presidency of Ferrari. In between, however, there was the 1991 World Championship which once again saw Ferrari in deep trouble. And that was only the beginning . . .

Seventy Years of Team Managers

Team manager of the Prancing Horse is undoubtedly one of the most difficult jobs in motor sport. As well as representing the scarlet red cars at circuits and road races throughout the world, the Ferrari team manager (or sporting director, to use Italian terminology), also had to be aware that the day after the race he was required to carry out an even more difficult task: brief Enzo Ferrari in person at Maranello. Ferrari had never been soft with his representatives at the races, as demonstrated by the long list of names who held the job from 1930, shortly after the constitution of Scuderia Ferrari, to the present day. From 1989 onward, immediately after the death of Ferrari, the figure of team manager was modified into responsible for Sporting Management (Italian terminology again), clearly maintaining the previous role. Frenchman Jean Todt is the latest Ferrari sporting director to hold the job. Former rally codriver (he was 1981 World Rally Championship runner-up with Guy Fréquelin), from 1983 to halfway through 1993, Todt was responsible for Peugeot's sporting activities, winning in world rallies and endurance racing. He was called to Ferrari by President Montezemolo in spring 1993, and took charge of the Ferrari F1 team on July 1, immediately after winning the Le Mans 24 Hours race with the Group C Peugeot 905.

Year	Name	Year	Name
1930-1931	Saracco Ferrari	1971-1972	Peter Schetty
1932-1933	Mario Lolli	1973	Sandro Colombo
1934	Federico Giberti	1974-1975	Luca di Montezemolo
1935-1940	Nello Ugolini	1976	Guido Rosani e Daniele Audetto
1947-1951	Federico Giberti		
1952-1955	Nello Ugolini	1977	Roberto Nosetto
1956	Eraldo Sculati	1978-1988	Marco Piccinini
1957	Mino Amorotti	1989-May 1991	Cesare Fiorio
1958-1961	Romolo Tavoni	May-end 1991	Claudio Lombardi
1962-1966	Eugenio Dragoni	1992-June 1993	Sante Ghedini
1967	Franco Lini	June 1993	Jean Todt
1968-1970	Franco Gozzi		

Thirty Years of Presidency at Maranello

The first Prancing Horse president other than Ferrari himself was appointed in 1978. Already in 1970, as soon as the purchase of the majority of Ferrari shares by Fiat was made official, the founder of Ferrari decided to leave the presidency of the company, opening the door to a series of new presidents, who clearly had to come from Fiat.
Here is the list year by year:

Period	President
Until 1977	Enzo Ferrari
1978 - 1980	Nicola Tufarelli
1980 - 1984	Giovanni Sguazzini
1984 - 1988	Vittorio Ghidella
1988 - 1991	Piero Fusaro
Since November 1991	Luca di Montezemolo

Luca di Montezemolo returned to Maranello as President of Ferrari 16 years after the triumphs of Niki Lauda, when he was team manager. It was November 1991, and the date coincided with the start of the commercial and sporting recovery of Ferrari.

The Technological Centre

Almost everything that can be said has been said about John Barnard, his merits and his defects as designer. What is certain, however, is that his arrival at Maranello as technical director at the end of 1986 will forever remain unique in the history of Ferrari. As soon as he began work at Ferrari, the British engineer clashed with the ways of doing things of the Italian factory. The ban on the mechanics having their customary bottle of wine at lunchtime in 1987 virtually said it all, and it caused such a violent uproar that a quick about-turn was necessary to allow the staff to resume their habits, which in any case had never had any ill effects on how they worked. Barnard will also be remembered for the good things he did. The semiautomatic gearbox, introduced on the 1989 Ferrari 640, paved the way for its use by all the major Formula 1 teams. The aerodynamic solutions, which gave form to the 1989-90 and the 1993-97 Ferraris, were also valuable, even though not to the same degree as those with McLaren in the first

half of the 1980s. The same can be said for the plate suspension mounts, which no longer used mechanical joints, an innovation by Barnard in 1993, to be copied by other designers.

Another success was the creation of a Ferrari R&D center in Shalford, England, in what was called the Formula 1 "Silicon Valley," due to the high technological concentration of teams and technical suppliers in the area. Without a doubt, the Technological Center gave positive results, but its distance from the Ferrari factory and the production departments had a negative impact. This included the lack of harmonization of the various phases of design and construction, making the work of Barnard and his British team go way over the time scale.

This had a negative effect on the construction of the cars, which were never ready on time and which, as in 1996, prevented an adequate test program from being carried out.

Almost the Last Ferrari World Champion

The Ferrari that came close to taking the 1990 world title with Prost was called F1 90. Better known as 641, from its project number, the car, which was initially designed by John Barnard and then taken over by Enrique Scalabroni and Steve Nichols, won a total of six Grands Prix in the 1990 World Championship: five with Prost and one with Mansell, and it only said good-bye to the title at the penultimate round of the series.

Powered by a normally-aspirated 65-degree 12-cylinder Vee engine with 5 valves per cylinder (maximum power was around 710 horsepower at almost 14,000 rpm), the Ferrari F1 90 had a longitudinal, electronically controlled 7-speed gearbox.

This semiautomatic box worked by means of a balance-lever located behind the steering wheel, and was an evolution of the first system of this kind ever seen in Grands Prix, which was mounted on the previous year's Ferrari 640.

The Ferrari F1-90 (641) on the track with Mansell in the 1990 World Championship. With this car, Prost almost took victory in the championship.

THE MAN OF THE FUTURE

ALESI

Prost liked him, Fiorio was interested in him, and the same could be said for the rest of the Formula 1 world, impressed by his ability to drive fast almost immediately and in any conditions, whether or not he was familiar with the circuit. The man in question was Jean Alesi, who made his Grand Prix debut halfway through 1989 and who immediately became the New Man in F1. Ferrari was also secretly impressed by the Frenchman, and it was clear that sometime in the future he would become part of the Prancing Horse team, completing the plans that had started

the wheel could still be a benefit for the red cars. Furthermore, there was the question of the "offense" perpetrated the year before at the Portuguese GP, when Nigel (involuntarily?) damaged Prost's Ferrari at the start, thus preventing him from winning a crucial race in his championship battle against Senna.

With Mansell gone, fresh air was required within the team. The choice of Alesi was perfect—a youngster full of hopes, happy to come to Maranello, which a few months ago was seen as an impossible dream. Above all, he was liked by Prost, who couldn't wait to have by his side a noncompetitive teammate, who wa-

young future Ferrari driver. Alesi's tendency to talk too much was already in evidence. He talked in good faith, but often complicated situations. In a moment of difficulty, with Ferrari involved in negotiating far away from the spotlights, Jean burst out with, "I'd rather retire than drive for Williams," something that illustrates the impetuosity of the man. The agreement was only reached after considerable delay, and Alesi eventually arrived in Maranello.

This was the start of a marriage that was to last five seasons. A marriage of love, without a shadow of doubt, but also one full of arguments and moments of great tension. The only

Prost signs an autograph for a French policeman. In 1991 Alain wanted the rising star Jean Alesi as his team-mate. He was to remain with Ferrari until the end of 1995. His team-mate from 1993 to 1995 was Gerhard Berger (below, other page).

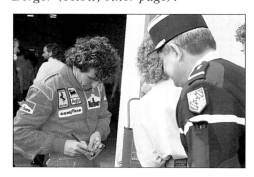

with the successes of 1989 and 1990 and were destined to form an all-French pairing for a new cycle of victories. All this happened in the summer of 1990, a season of growing enthusiasm and incredible results with Prost, who only said goodbye to the title at the penultimate round of the championship. All the team's energies were absorbed in 1990, but Ferrari was looking ahead. They had to replace Mansell, who pulled out after being suffocated by the presence of Prost on the team. With Nigel, the laws of Ferrari - but also F1 in general—were implacable. On a team increasingly dominated by the natural charisma of Prost and his "political" capacities, the British driver was slowly but surely overshadowed. It didn't matter that his ability behind

sn't anxious to beat him. Basically, Alesi was a driver who was not a threat to Prost. And so it was. Cesare Fiorio's offer convinced the young French driver of Italian origin (his father was from Alcamo in Sicily). It was a pity that Alesi's enthusiasm in the face of this sudden surge in popularity led him to exaggerate things. Jean still had an option with the Tyrrell team, with whom he had made his F1 debut at the 1989 French GP and with whom he had competed in his first full season in 1990. He signed an agreement with Ferrari; a few weeks later, however, it was discovered that he had already signed one with Williams as well. There followed a long period of uncertainty, which ended by unsettling (and we are only at the beginning of the story) the

negative factor in Alesi's period at Ferrari was to be the almost total lack of race victories—just one, Canada in 1995. Too few to prevent a divorce which was not entirely devoid of controversy. This part of the story, however, belongs to the future, let's go back to the start of the relationship. Alesi arrived at Ferrari and the driver and the team already had high expectations for the 1991 World Championship. Unfortunately for both of them, the situation was no longer the same as the year before. Hopes for a crisis of the McLaren-Hondas in the face of a Ferrari onslaught soon vanished with the victory of Senna in the first four rounds of the championship. The situation in Ferrari was close to boiling point and exploded with the sacking of Fiorio as team manager.

Jean Alesi

Born in France on 11th June 11, 1964 from a family of Italian origin, Jean Alesi made his Formula 1 debut for Tyrrell at the French GP in 1989, the season in which he contested a total of eight Grands Prix and at the same time won the International F3000 Championship. He also took part in the 1990 F1 season with Tyrrell, obtaining two splendid second places at the United States GP (Phoenix) and at Monte Carlo, results which opened the door at Ferrari. He raced five full seasons with the red cars, scoring numerous remarkable results including dozens of podium positions. His last season at Maranello, in 1995, saw Alesi's only victory with Ferrari, at the Notre Dame circuit in Montreal. The long period of Jean without a victory was over and all signs were that from this moment onward things would be different. But his Ferrari career brought no more wins. The closest he came was at Monza, when he was robbed of certain victory by mechanical failure. Three races later, the rapport between Alesi and Ferrari was over. The Frenchman ended up in the Benetton team, where he took the place of newly signed Ferrari driver Schumacher and where he is also driving this year.

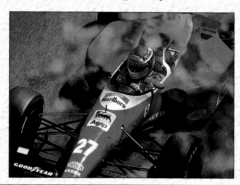

The results clearly went some way to explaining the decision, but they weren't the whole reason. Divorce between Ferrari and Fiorio, which came on May 15 like a bolt from the sky, was the final episode in a rapport of growing disagreement between the team manager and Prost, who had already been shocked the previous summer by negotiations to bring Senna to Ferrari in 1991. News reports from that summer, in 1990, which have never been confirmed by the people involved, spoke of a meeting between Fiorio and Senna off the "Costa Smeralda" coast in Sardinia, on the yacht of the team manager, who was taking his summer holidays there. On that occasion, Ayrton is reported to have even signed a draft agreement. But the plans were destined to fail. Ferrari President Piero Fusaro brought it to an end, assuring Prost that no one would force him to be teammates with the Brazilian champion, his much-disliked teammate in McLaren in the 1988-1989 period. On top of this, Fusaro also guaranteed Alain a key role on a political and decision-making level.

The departure of Fiorio left Alesi without any real reference points. While before he had clearly been the team's Number Two driver, but with the support of the people who had wanted him in the team, now he was the Number Two to a Prost who was increasingly nervous, discouraged, and on a collision course with the team. The team, in fact, was to get rid of Prost one race before the end of the championship. At this point, Alesi's role in Ferrari clearly assumed different connotations. From young Number Two, he became the reference point for the team, which for 1992 flanked him with Ivan Capelli, and then from 1993 to 1995 with Gerhard Berger. Alongside the Austrian driver, who returned to Maranello, where he

Prost testing in 1991.
The driver and the team were
to go separate ways at the end of the
season, one race before the end
of the championship, amidst
blazing controversy.

had worked from 1987 to 1989, Alesi confirmed and maintained his position as a driver who was much-loved, especially by Italian fans. This was despite the fact that Berger was more reliable in technical feedback, testing ability and car development. Although the team officially recognized the role of Number One for Berger, Jean continued to love the red cars and drive them sometimes over the limit, often setting extraordinary times, to the delight of spectators. His disappointment, however, grew at the same rate as his stretch without a win, as well as his diminishing chances of taking a world title. When he found out halfway through the 1995 World Championship that he was to make way for Schumacher, Alesi had to resign himself to the decision. It was impossible to win with his much-loved Ferrari, especially now that the team had very little faith in the French driver. The memory lingers on of five years of high excitement, but also real tension. Five successive seasons with the Prancing Horse—few other drivers had managed to last so long.

MONTEZEMOLO - PART TWO

Luca di Montezemolo came back to Ferrari once again in an official capacity on November 20, 1991. Sixteen years had passed since he had left, since he had relinquished his job of team manager, which had culminated with the conquest of the 1975 world title by Niki Lauda.

The Montezemolo years had seen a rebirth of Ferrari. Two seasons, were especially significant: In 1974, the car returned to its winning ways. But 1975 will go down in history for a number of different reasons. It was the year of the 312T, characterized by a revolutionary transversal gearbox, and the year of a certain Andreas Nikolaus Lauda, Niki to his friends, who was reared into a great champion by Luca. This success demonstrates how Luca di Montezemolo, at the time a man full of great temperament and the capacity to motivate those around him, managed to forge a winning Ferrari, by

Luca di Montezemolo shares a joke with Michael Schumacher and Jean Todt. This is the Ferrari of the present, and the future.

forgetting all the dark days at Maranello and welding together a strong and unbeatable team of capable men and sheer determination.

These memories probably had a major influence on Fiat's decision to find a successor to President Fusaro. For Luca, the telephone call was an offer which just could not be refused: The invitation to take over the position that once belonged to Enzo Ferrari was mixed with recollections of a time he had always said had been one of the best of his life. Luca di Montezemolo arrived at Maranello and immediately indicated that his plans within Ferrari were on a long-term basis. First he had to resolve the difficult situation linked to the worldwide automobile market: the sale of Ferrari road cars in a period of general economic depression. Once restructuring in this field had got going, the new president could deal with the racing team.

A few weeks into 1992, Luca di Montezemolo decided to intervene. The situation within the team saw all powers concentrated in the hands of Claudio Lombardi. Lombardi, an engineer from Fiat, was an engine genius and the technical brains behind extraordinary rally cars such as the Lancia Delta S4 Group B and the subsequent Delta Group A, which won six successive world rally titles. Lombardi had been summoned to Ferrari by Fusaro in May 1991 to fill the power gap left by the traumatic firing of Cesare Fiorio; the very same Fiorio he had replaced at the start of 1989 as head of Lancia and

Alfa Romeo's competition activities, when Fiorio moved to Maranello. Lombardi's management era was a difficult one. Under his leadership, two ex-Ferrari engineers, Harvey Postlethwaite and Claude Migeot, were recalled to Maranello. Together the two designed the F1/92, an innovative single-seater that was characterized by a double flat bottom offering considerable aerodynamic advantage, at least in theory. In practice, the 1992 Ferrari was never competitive and was overwhelmed not only by Mansell's Williams, but also by the McLaren.

At this point, once he realized the situation was disastrous, Luca di Montezemolo decided to step in with authority, especially at a planning level. He gradually limited Lombardi to a technical role, and then started talks with John Barnard. In the three years since his divorce from Ferrari in the autumn of 1989, the British designer had not had a happy time. First he was with Benetton F1, then with the team responsible for the Toyota project run by Tom Walkinshaw, who was at the time not yet involved in Grands Prix. Barnard had not changed. He still wanted to stay and work in England, so a new "technological center" was set up for him near Shalford, Surrey, in an area called the "F1 Silicon Valley."

The motivations of the newly appointed president of the Prancing Horse were clear. Enzo Ferrari had passed away almost four years before. In this period, the scarlet red cars had occasionally been very competitive, but this was punctuated by confused management and disastrous internal warfare.

Fusaro, Fiorio, Mansell, Prost, Lombardi, Alesi, Capelli . . . a lot of projects, planning and ambitions and a lot of disappointments. As the days passed, Luca di Montezemolo began to sit more and more firmly on the throne at Maranello.

He began to feel the shadow of the Ferrari legend and he was asked to intervene even more directly and more resolutely within the company. He felt that the team above all needed a real heir to Enzo Ferrari—and he was the man for the job. And so it was.

Luca di Montezemolo took control of the team's sporting activities. Once John Barnard had been taken on, Montezemolo realized that the technical and manpower situation at Maranello did not hold out great hopes for the future. In 1992, the red cars were struggling and not only were no victories obtained that year, but Ferrari was nowhere near being competitive.

The dark days continued in 1993, with Berger and Alesi carrying out endless testing and disappointing results on the track. Meanwhile, the technical structure of the team was changing. In the engine division, full powers were given to Martinelli, who had come up from within the company. Ferrari also resorted to the experience of the Japanese engineer Goto, formerly with Honda and McLaren. The decision to re-employ Gerhard Berger, who had been with Ferrari from 1987 to 1989, and since then had been the teammate of Senna with McLaren, was also part of this new logic. Berger's experience with the Brazilian, and the British team, was seen as being of great value.

But the piece that completed the new Ferrari jigsaw was called Jean Todt. The French ex-rally codriver (he came close to winning the 1981 world title with Guy Fréquelin) was the team manager of the Peugeot team, which dominated in rallying and the World Sports Car Championship. Todt came to Maranello on July 1, 1993, and this was the first stone in the construction of the Ferrari of the future.

THE LAST ITALIAN

Let's take a step back to 1991, the year of Prost's sensational divorce with Ferrari, and the start of an announced new course by Ferrari management, at the time closer than it had ever been to Fiat, its men and its methods. Claudio Lombardi was in command of the team when the Prost "time-bomb" stopped ticking. The French champion was in increasing disagreement with the team, with its decisions and its methods. Ferrari came to the Japanese GP, the penultimate round of the championship. The race finished with Prost in difficulty, and after the checkered flag he said to a journalist:

"My Ferrari was like a truck to drive." Nothing special, nothing traumatic, at least for a great communicator such as Prost, who had always been able to accompany his driving skills with speaking ability. But this time Prost's declaration left its mark, and it was the straw that broke the camel's back. It was immediately decided to end his contract. At the final GP of the year, in Australia, Prost's Ferrari was given to team tester Gianni Morbidelli. That was a bitter end to a marriage that was born under the best of omens and which was a whisker away from reaching the pinnacle, the world title, which had been eluded since Scheckter in 1979 and which Alain had come so close to winning in 1990. The turning-point, however, was much more significant.

Lombardi's Ferrari was oozing with Fiat influence; the influence which Prost had wanted at first, then defended and supported (at the time of the Fiorio-Senna negotiations in summer 1990) and finally abandoned, after realizing how much the driver and his opinions had become awkward.

The problem was now to find a new Ferrari driver to join the already-confirmed Alesi, who after a difficult 1991 in the political shadow of Alain Prost, now wanted to be the Number One driver. The choice of his future teammate was, however, pretty limited. The idea of signing Senna, who was not convinced of Ferrari's potential for 1992, was dropped; the possible choices of Mansell and Patrese were considered and rejected, so Lombardi decided to go for Ivan Capelli, for at least two reasons. First, an Italian driver would be positive for the new image of the team, which was capable of standing on its own two feet once again without external intervention. Second, Capelli was fast. Memories if the 1990 French GP, won by Prost, the third victory of the season for the Frenchman and the 100th for Ferrari in Formula 1, were still fresh. At Paul Ricard, Prost had a terrific battle with the Leyton House of Ivan Capelli, who was leading for much of the race and was eventually beaten by the Frenchman by nine seconds.

At the end of 1991, the idea of having Capelli in the team seemed an extremely good one. A fast and extremely reliable driver, a good tester, a calm and positive character; in short he had everything required for Ferrari to complete the team along with the fast but unsettled Alesi. It all seemed perfect. Ferrari couldn't wait to welcome another Italian driver to the team, the first since the split with Alboreto in 1988. What a pity that this idyllic situation was not destined to last very long. Ivan arrived at Maranello and everything seemed marvelous. He tried hard to live up to the sweetness of the Ferrari dream. His statements were full of happiness, gratitude for Ferrari and those who had wanted him in the team, as well as for Alesi, with whom he promised he would work well. But as soon as he tried out the F92A, the famous double flatbottom Ferrari, the driver's dreams came crashing to the ground. "The car is fantastic>" pouted Alesi to the national and international press. "With this Ferrari, no result will be impossible." "The car is undriveable," responded Capelli. "It's got major problems resulting from design errors."

The split was immediate. Not only between the two drivers, with Alesi accusing Capelli of a politically negative attitude with the team, but also between Capelli and the team, the large majority of whom preferred to believe in the illusory declarations of Jean, and not the criticism of the new driver. The results of the season, when the red cars were sinking into technical and performance trouble despite the numerous modifications made race after race, seem to demonstrate indirectly that Capelli was right. But the split with the team was now irreversible. No one would admit it, but the causes of the problems of the Ferrari

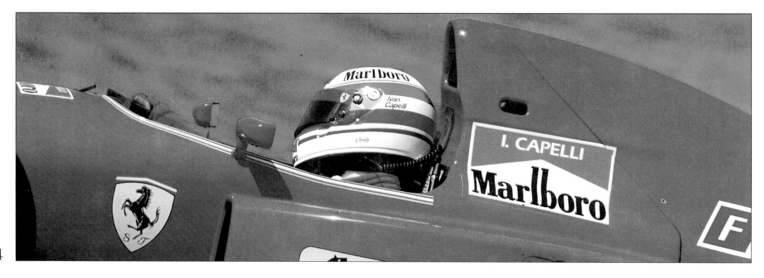

were partly down to Ivan and his scarce competitivity, his lack of desire to risk everything with a car far from perfect. The car was certainly a lot better than the unmitigated engineering disaster the driver described it to be. Not even the views of Niki Lauda, the newly appointed Ferrari adviser, who clearly absolved the drivers of any responsibility for the car's weaknesses, helped to smooth things over. Capelli now had the entire team against him. At least, he had Alesi against him, which was practically the same thing.

Ivan Capelli's experience at Maranello concluded in the worst possible way—one race before the end of the World Championship, exactly the same as what happened to Prost one year before. The man who was "fired" by Ferrari was by now dejected and demotivated. He was not given help by anyone within the team, let alone

by Alesi, who did not appreciate the lack of obedience by Capelli. Alesi felt that Capelli, as "Number Two" driver, should have been subject to his (Alesi's) opinions. Capelli's exit from Ferrari was difficult to digest, and it concluded a totally disappointing season for the Italian; not necessarily from a results point of view, but because a gulf had been created between him and the team and its managers, and because he was pushed to one side out of the way. Capelli found another drive for 1993 with Jordan, who welcomed him with open arms, but who dumped him even more brutally after just one GP for reasons which seriously undermined the professional credibility of the driver.

Ivan Capelli's adventure in Formula 1 terminated here. It was impossible to heal the wounds, especially moral ones, left by his time with Ferrari.

The last Italians at Maranello. Other page, Capelli, Ferrari driver in 1992. Above, Nicola Larini, long-time Ferrari test driver, who has driven for the team in four Grands Prix.

The Cook

A new figure came into being within Ferrari 1979: the team cook. The man given the job was Luigi Montanini, a young 25-year-old who was full of initiative, and wasted as a mechanic. Moreover, he had a certain experience in the kitchen, having worked in a famous pastry shop close to Ferrari headquarters. The idea came from Piero Ferrari. Why not organize our own restaurant service, instead of continuing to call on the caterers? The choice clearly fell upon Montanini, already nicknamed "Pasticcino" (Mr. Pastry).

Ferrari's trackside cook made his debut in Formula 1 in 1979, when the scarlet cars were driven by Jody Scheckter and Gilles Villeneuve. The initial idea was to prepare a few rolls, but Montanini soon converted that idea into multistar cuisine. Since then, Pasticcino has fed a generation of Ferrari drivers, falling back on his experience and imagination to satisfy everyone's tastes.

"I remember one thing above all of Gilles," said Montanini. "He liked chocolate. He used to consume vast quantities of chocolate and milk.

But he also liked special dishes, such as mushrooms with cream, and generally speaking, anything with cream, sauces and butter. Scheckter was the complete opposite. He was obsessed with carrots. He used to eat them in slices or in salads, but often just munch them whole, even during technical briefings."

From 1979 to 1993, when he switched to the Benetton team on request from Flavio Briatore, Pasticcino practically "invented" F1 cuisine, and was followed by all the other teams. At his tables have sat drivers of the caliber of Alboreto and Berger, Mansell and Prost.

"Michele used to eat like all Italians: very little breakfast, light lunch, dinner at the track with plain or tomato-flavored pasta, a slice of meat. Berger was different. Yogurt for breakfast, a couple of slices of bread with some cheese or butter and jam. At lunch he would often have chicken and rice."

And the menu continued . . . with Mansell and Prost.

"Nigel wanted carrots for breakfast. He ate them grated with Parmesan cheese. In the morning, Prost wanted milk and yogurt with muesli and fruit salad. Both of them, for lunch

and dinner, easily adapted to Italian food: pasta, meat or fresh fish."

Luigi Montanini also has memories of when he used to prepare lunch at the Fiorano track for Enzo Ferrari, who often followed the testing at the track in the early 1980s.

"Ferrari's lunch was light, but complete," he remembered. - "Usually I prepared him a risotto with Parmesan cheese, which he liked, then a grilled sirloin seasoned with a good balsamic vinegar and a green salad."

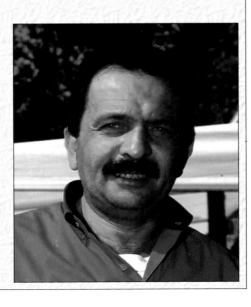

ALMOST SENNA

The long story of the never-to-be marriage between Ferrari and Senna covered almost the final five years of the life of the Brazilian champion, who died in May 1994. If one considers the respect and admiration expressed by Enzo Ferrari for the great champion and the fact that the story of Ferrari and Senna would almost certainly have continued to the present day, it can safely be said that the rapport between these two cornerstones of the history of motor sport lasted more than a decade.

At the start of the 1990s, it was clear that sooner or later Ferrari and Senna were destined to meet. There were many reasons for this, but they all boiled down to one in particular. In a world, sporting or otherwise, in which legends are all too rare, Ferrari had always managed to resist and preserve its aura of being something that went far beyond mere results. When Senna's superiority over all the other drivers became clear halfway through the 1980s, his joining Maranello became one of those social events, like a VIP marriage, that went far beyond love and attraction. It had to take place, for the good of the sport. Moreover, in the case of Ayrton and the Prancing Horse, mutual love and attraction were an undeniable value, maybe mitigated by the convenience of the moment, the debatable competitive qualities of the red cars and the presence of Prost in Ferrari, but in any case undeniable.

We have already spoken of how Fiorio in 1990 had convinced Ayrton to go to Maranello the next season. Perhaps only a top-secret test with the scarlet cars convinced the driver of the technical validity of the project, as suggested by a number of sources. And perhaps—as suggested by other rumors at the time—after not putting Senna alongside his

"enemy" Prost, but at the side of Mansell, leaving Alain free to move at the end of the 1990 championship. The agreement was never concluded, as already mentioned, above all due to the opposition of Prost, who was supported by the then-president of Ferrari, Fusaro. When Luca di Montezemolo found himself having to deal with the question of Senna in 1992, his position was perfect: No one, either in Ferrari or Fiat, could interfere in the plan.

In 1992 the situation within Ferrari was rather serious. From an engineering point of view, the gap with the main competitors (Williams, McLaren and the rapidly improving Benetton) was plain for all to see. The car was not competitive enough, and there was no engineering program that promised a better short-term future. From a technology point of view, Ferrari was undoubtedly way behind the competition, and this became dramatic in the en-

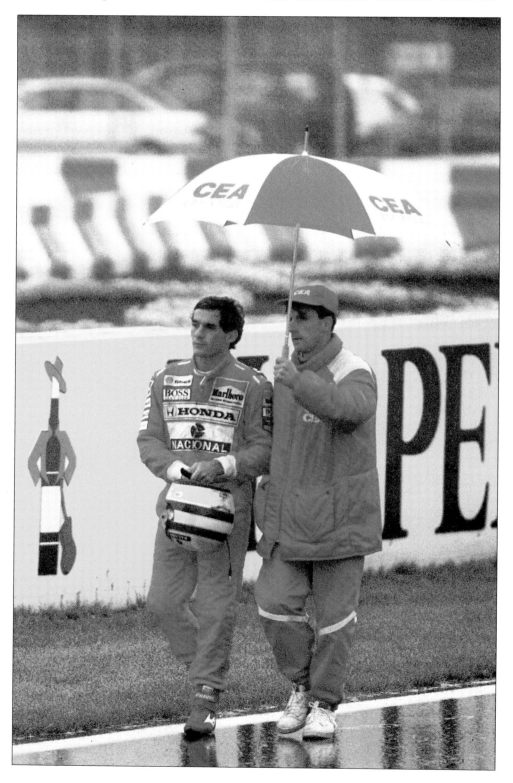

Ayrton Senna and Ferrari:
A long-lasting affair, which only
the premature death of the driver
on May 1, 1994, prevented
from turning into a
full-scale relationship.

gine field, where not even the traditional supremacy of the Prancing Horse could catch up with Honda and Renault. Furthermore, Alesi and Capelli were not the right drivers to guarantee that extra advantage that only top drivers can.

This was why the choice of Ayrton Senna was almost a compulsory one. In this area, Ferrari had learnt from recent experience. In 1989-1990, its driver was Nigel Mansell, who had a powerful competitive urge and a ca-

pacity to always give 101 percent, often way over the risk threshold. In 1990-1991, its driver was Alain Prost, who was highly skilled in becoming the focal point of the team, creating a perfect car through extraordinary technical finesse. Two top drivers, two aces, two very different human beings. How could the two be united? How could all of this be found in one single driver? Obviously, the answer was Senna. The Brazilian driver was a combination of Mansell

in the world

1994 - On 6th May, Queen Elisabeth II and French President Francois Mitterand inaugurated the 50 km long Channel Tunnel. Construction work had started in 1987 and regular service began in August 1994.

1994 - The World Cup was held for the first time in the United States. Brazil won its fourth title, defeating Italy on penalties in the final.

in motor sport

1994 - The tragedy of Imola. Roland Ratzenberger (in qualifying) and Ayrton Senna (in the race) were both killed. The Brazilian champion went off the track on lap five and died in the hospital four hours later.

THE MAN OF THE FUTURE

and Prost. Furthermore, he knew how to catalyze the team around himself, how to urge it on, how to talk straight with engineers, gaining their utmost respect.

In addition he would have brought with him all the undeniable experience accumulated in the years spent with McLaren and Honda. Finally Senna was not just any champion, he was The Champion.

Everyone who loved Ferrari, loved Senna: both inside and outside the team. The team and the driver would in both cases be a perfect match.

The courtship started at once. Niki Lauda, Luca di Montezemolo's special envoy at the circuits, approached the three-time World Champion and told him basically that Ferrari was waiting for him. Ayrton listened, evaluated the situation, asked for and obtained detailed information. He then replied in a way that could have been "Yes, but not yet." This meant: "I would like to come, I will come; but first Ferrari must improve and guarantee, as a minimum

condition, a competitive team and car. At that point, it's all up to me."

That was the summer of 1992. The Prancing Horse found itself in a corner and was in desperate need of finding a vastly experienced driver, so it opted for Gerhard Berger. The deal was finalized at the end of August and announced on the eve of the Belgian GP at Spa—with the blessing of Senna, who remained with McLaren, yet did not lose contact with the president of Ferrari.

In fact, in September the contacts became even more frequent. Ayrton indicated that he was confident in Ferrari's progress the following year, and said he was interested for 1994. Maranello said they were ready for him. The feeling in Ferrari and in the outside world was that the team and the driver were as close as ever to making a deal.

The 1993 World Championship got under way. Alain Prost, Senna's sworn "enemy," and his Renault-powered Williams dominated the season. Halfway through the year,

the French driver announced that he was leaving Formula 1 at the end of the season. For Ayrton, suffocated by the technical superiority of the Williams, which thwarted any possibility of fighting for the championship on level terms, the temptation was irresistible. Frank Williams' swift offer was greeted with an immediate "Yes." The perfect technological partnership between the British car and the powerful French Renault engine not only paved the way toward a fourth world title for Senna, equaling Prost, but also toward a le-

Summer 1995:
Jean Alesi learns that from
the next season onward, his place
in Ferrari will be taken
by Michael Schumacher.
The German driver came
to Maranello after winning two
successive F1 titles with Benetton.

gendary fifth title, which only Fangio had ever achieved.

Senna's arrival at Ferrari, however, was only postponed. Commenting on the decision to leave McLaren for Williams, the champion from Sao Paolo did not hesitate to mention that Ferrari would be part of his future plans. Probably it would be the final chapter in a brilliant career,

which now looked like being unique. It was a real tragedy therefore that fate turned its back on these plans and dreams. On May 1, 1994, the life of Ayrton Senna was cruelly ended at the Imola circuit . . . without a fourth title, which would almost certainly have been his that year . . . and without a fifth title, which he might have won with Ferrari.

Not Only Formula 1

Halfway through the 1990s, Ferrari discovered two new categories of motor sport in which it could aim for victory. In 1994, the 333SP made its debut in the North-American IMSA Sports Car Championship, even though it was run by Ferrari clients, not the factory. With the colors of Team Scandia Motorsport, below,

the sports car would dominate the 1995 IMSA season, winning the Drivers' title with Spain's Fermin Velez. Below: Heated competition in a Challenge Ferrari race. At first reserved for the 348 and then the 355, the one-make championship has achieved extraordinary success among competitors and popularity among spectators, and races are organized in many countries of the world.

SCHUMACHER

His name is Michael Schumacher. He is young, he has clear ideas, and he bases his great driving ability on a strong personality that leaves little space for compromise. Ferrari had already been in touch in 1994, the year of his first title with the Ford-powered Benetton, which came about after the death of Senna. At this point, defining the German driver as the heir to Ayrton is a logical step. It is not an exact definition, even though the motorsport "blood" links between him and the Brazilian champion were already clear when Senna was still alive. Like Ayrton, Schumacher is a naturally fast driver. His performances, often irrespective of the logic imposed by technique and imagination, appear to be so simple, without frills, without the spectacular ability of other drivers. Like Ayrton, Schumacher makes physical training a vital part of his life. When he gets out of the car, at the end of a victorious Grand Prix, he appears to be well rested, often without a drop of sweat, as if the race had just started. Like Ayrton, Schumacher immediately proved himself to be the focal point of the team. He spends hours and hours in the pits at the end of practice, following the work on his car in never-ending dialog with the engineers. He spurs the team on to give its all, motivating it, while not producing any ill-feeling. Halfway through 1995, a deal was finally reached for the next two seasons. What Luca di Montezemolo and his entourage—especially team ma-

nager Jean Todt—maybe did not expect, was that Schumacher would almost immediately become an object of worship for Ferrari fans, those hundreds of thousands throughout the world who have a common passion for Ferrari, but not necessarily for its drivers.

The miracle came about, almost immediately. Schumacher succeeded in winning with the F310 in Spain, the seventh Grand Prix of the 1996 championship, in a race which was flooded by a downpour. This highlighted the abilities of the driver and leveled the technical performance of the car. Schumacher's incredible performance in the first few laps, when he overtook one car after another and grabbed the lead from a

"rain-master" such as Alesi, was one of those that immediately earn a place in the history of motor racing. The confidence with which he defended his lead in the last few laps, despite an engine which was showing worrying signs of not lasting the distance, proved that Schumacher was a great champion. Up there on the Barcelona podium, soaked in rain and champagne, Schumacher earned a place in the hall of fame of drivers dear to Ferrari fans. In fact, he had already booked that place months before, right from his first tests with the red cars, right from his first declarations of cautious but firm confi-

Other page, a young Schumacher, with Mansell and Patrese on his first podium, in the 1992 Mexican GP, where he finished third. Since 1996, Michael has been a Ferrari driver. His team-mate is Eddie Irvine, here with Stirling Moss. Below, the big difference between a Ferrari pit garage in 1924 (Italian GP) and now. In this page: the World Championship aspirations of Schumacher and the Prancing Horse lie with the F310B.

dence that the results would come. Two more wins came in the 1996 World Championship: in Belgium and at Monza. The wins came about due to the misfortunes of others, but in any case they more than lived up to the expectations of the "Ferraristi," and clearly also to the those of the driver, who slowly but surely was being caught up by the legend that was being woven around him. "Schummy" ended up by being seduced by Ferrari. He finally yielded by accepting a renewal of the contract that would make him a Ferrari driver until the end of 1999, signing one year before the first contract ran out at the end of 1997. As far as Ferrari was concerned, an extension of the contract was the best thing they could have possibly hoped for. There were no doubts about the technical and driving abilities of the German champion; it was the commitment of the man and his involvement in the Ferrari project which had raised a few doubts. At the end of 1996, Ferrari and Schumacher were forged together. The words of Jean Alesi a

few years before, when the moment for the renewal of his contract came up, spring to mind. At the time, Jean was torn between a declaration of love and accusations of scarce technical continuity within the team.

"The truth is,' confessed Alesi, "that I am in love with Ferrari. I criticize and rebuke Ferrari because they will not guarantee me a contract as Number One driver or because they do not pay me as much as I would like. But in reality, when I get into a Ferrari I can feel the weight of motor racing history behind me. I would pay from my own pocket to drive for Ferrari."

For Schumacher, things are different. Given the fee guaranteed by his record contract, declarations of this kind would appear to be out of place. But almost certainly, Schumacher himself, when he gets behind the wheel of his single-seater red Ferrari, also feels a presence; the presence of a man, Enzo Ferrari, who almost 100 years ago, first came into the world on the outskirts of Modena, with a mission: To create out of nothing the legend that is Ferrari.

The Future FERRARI

This is the F310B in all its secrets.
Right from the first round of the 1997 season, the Ferrari F310B has shown excellent reliability and good performance. It was the progress shown throughout the season that was the F310B's extra weapon. There was a constant improvement that allowed Schumacher to take five victories and gave him a chance of winning the Driver's title right down to the final Grand Prix on the calendar. Twenty-three laps from the end of the GP at Jerez, Schumacher was leading the race and was virtually sure of the 1997 title . . . but the dream was soon to fade. When his rival Jacques Villeneuve in the Williams made his attack, the two cars touched . . .For the Ferrari driver, it meant retirement, while the young Canadian managed to keep going. He finished the race in the points and was World Champion, twenty years and a few days after the debut in Ferrari of his father, the unforgettable Gilles.

ONE STEP AWAY FROM THE DREAM

RAIN OF THE CENTURY

May 11, 1997 to February 20 (or 18, referring to the original enigma), 1998: celebrations for the entire history of the Prancing Horse were spread over these nine months. these are fundamental dates. Last year the fifth round of the 197 Formula 1 World Championship was held at Monte Carlo on the second Sunday in May, but memories went back to May 11 fifty years before. It was the same date and the same day of the week—a Sunday. That Sunday in 1947 was a day to remember because the first Ferrari—prepared, entered, and raced by a Ferrari team—made its debut at the Piacenza circuit. It was driven by Franco Cortese, who led the race until a few laps before the checkered flag. Fuel Problems ended the Ferrari 125's race. There were no problems a fortnight later however, at Rome's Caracalla circuit. Here the superiority of the 125 gave Cortese and Ferrari their first victory in a series that was destined to rewrite the history of motorsport.

On the February 18 or 20, and the second month of 1998 marked the centenary of the birth of Enzo Ferrari. This is the reason why theses nine months contain the entire legend of the Prancing Horse, the weight of its history and its irresistible triumph not only in motorsport but also in social history and costume. Nine months of celebrations, of memories of the revolutionary human figure of Enzo Ferrari, of considerations and viewpoints on the splendid reality called Ferrari. On May 11,

LA "FERRARI 125" DI CORTESE

this period started off in the best possible way with Ferrari and Schumacher winning the Monaco GP under a downpour to take the lead of the World Championship. The street circuit in the Principality, dangerous when it rains, appeared to have sealed a "pact" with the number five Ferrari. After Williams, which had dominated three of the first four rounds of the championship, made a wrong tire choice at the start, Michael set a cracking pace. The determination with which he pulled out a massive lead was incredible. As if by magic, the F310B lost all resemblance with the average car seen at the start of the championship, and began to put on a brilliant display at every curve. Two hours before, Jacques Villeneuve, the winner in Brazil and Argentina but who was retired twice in Australia and Imola had appeared to be the dominate force in the 1997 championship. his Williams, which won at Imola in the hands of teammate Frentzen (who set his first-ever pole at the Monte Carlo), was on the way toward a triumphant victory: the Driver's and Manufacturer's titles for Williams. Monte Carlo had something to say about that . . .

The two hours of the Grand Prix were never-ending. Despite the impression of total confidence that appeared from his driving, Schumacher was complaining to his pits by radio. He had started on intermediate tires that were performing less and less as the rain increased. After the pit-stop, he put on a set of rain tires and his control of the race became total. Lap after lap, the tension in the Ferrari pits was becoming increasingly unbearable. Victory was closer and closer. The tension increased corner after corner: Michael himself mana-

Michael Schumacher on podium and (bottom left) the editorial published in 1947 with the photo of the first Ferrari car.

ged to make things worse by making an error at the first curve after the pits, with just a few laps to go before the checkered flag. A late-braking maneuver at St. Devote, the Ferrari went straight on into the run-off area, but stopped before the barriers. No fear: Schummy did it deliberately to avoid sliding off the wet track and losing all his lead.

*Gilles Villeneuve
and his Ferrari 126 CK
in the last lap of his victorious
GP at Monaco - May 1981.*

After this moment of terror for Ferrari had passed, Schumacher made it to the checkered flag—and victory. It was the German's fourth win as a Ferrari driver, the first of the 1997 season that was now shaping up nicely.

Ferrari had last won the "Monaco roulette" race in 1981 with an extraordinary exploit by Gilles Villeneuve. At the time, his race ability was counterbalanced by the powerful but heavy and clumsy turbo Ferrari, which was difficult to drive on the Monaco street circuit. If we remember that the Monte Carlo sky had been bright blue less than an hour before the race, this rain was defined as the "rain of the century." From a Ferrari point of view, it was probably the "rain of a half-century," because 50 years of history could not have been celebrated in a better way.

MAGIC . . .
WITHOUT
A MAGICIAN

At the presentation of the Ferrari F310B, Maranello's forecasts were cautiously optimistic.

"We will be satisfied if we win more races than last year, " admitted the President of the Prancing Horse, Luca di Montezemolo. "One year ago we scored three wins. This year, we'll be happy with at least four. If at that point we can start talking about the title, then OK. For the moment, however, none is thinking about that."

True. At the start of the 1997 season, no one at Maranello dared to think about the possibility of winning the title. The F310B arrived on time after a lot pressure on John Barnard, who had designed the car in England. Maybe Barnard, the ex-magician of design, really thinks about the competitive potential of his

cars before designing them, but he thinks twice about underlining it, especially when the car begins to show a few problems on the track.

The F310B in fact was struggling. Michael Schumacher immediately declared it was difficult to drive, understeered virtually everywhere, and not even the 10-cylinder engine seemed to be powerful. When the championship got underway, the situation was clear. After lengthy preseason tests (an improvement over past years!), the F310B was found to be robust, reliable, and it never broke down. As for its speed . . .

The Williams team was on another planet. They dominated in the opening round in Argentina (Villeneuve) and then Frentzen took his first-ever GP win at Imola. For Maranello, hopes for a win were slim, to say the least. Unlike Villeneuve, who either won or retired with a breakdown, Schumacher only abandoned a race in Argentina, and that wasn't due to mechanical failure. At the

ONE STEP AWAY FROM THE DREAM

Bernie Ecclestone, Eddie Irvine, Michael Schumacher, Jean Todt, Luca di Montezemolo, Ross Brawn.

start of the fifth round of the championship therefore at Monte Carlo, the German was not far behind the Canadian who was leading the table for Williams. What counted however was that at Ferrari, they wee starting to see signs of progress.

This was not thanks to John Barnard, who at the end of his contract, finished his period in Ferrari by acquiring Design Centre in England and moving to Tom Walkinshaw's Arrows team. The credit must go to the new technical pairing in Ferrari, designer Rory Byrne and technical director Ross Brawn. A few months before, they had both been lured away form Benetton, where they had contributed to the car's numerous victories in 1994 and 1995.

The two foreigners had a difficult job. They had to improve the F310B in the race, overcoming the difficulties of a calendar in which the races followed think and fast and planning a series of small improvements. They also had to think about the following year's car, when Formula 1 would have totally new and different regulations form those of the current season. The results began to appear, however. At Imola the F310B

was much faster. It was still a little slow in qualifying, but in the race it ran a lot closer to the two Williams cars. At Monte Carlo, the rain falsified matters somewhat: If the race had been dry, then Schumacher would never have dominated. A difficult GP in Spain was next. At the Montmelo circuit north of Barcelona, the Ferrari rarely goes well . . . while the Williams cars wee flying. The race was dominated by Villeneuve, while Schumacher lost the lead of the points table and had to settle for a finish in the points. The total reliability of the F310B had been confirmed, and that was going to bring a smile to the face of easy-going Ross Brawn, whose lengthy list of technical improvements was beginning to show its first results.

The rest of the story can be told by looking at the championship standings after each race. Schumacher won in Canada and France. In Montreal, he was helped by a crazy incident by Villeneuve, who went off the road on lap two and by the retirement with a broken clutch of the McLaren of Coulthard, who had the victory in his pocket. At Magny-Cours, the domination of the Ferrari was total. Schumacher dominated in practicing , qualifying, and the race. He was far superior in the dry and in the wet an moved ahead in the championship. The list of improvements to

the F310B had not finished yet. At the next race in Great Britain, a number of aerodynamics and suspension improvements appeared. The result was that Schumacher was heading for his third successive victory, when a wheel bearing forced him into retirement. this was Ferrari's first retirement of the year because of mechanical problems, and it was made worse by the almost contemporary driveshaft breakage on Irvine's car, which could have gone on to win. Even harder to digest was that the win again went to Villeneuve, who took the checkered flag after the engine of leader Hakkinen's McLaren gave up wit just a few laps to go.

The damage was acceptable, however. In Germany the Ferraris had all sorts of problems, but neither was it Villeneuve's day. The F310B appeared to be at the end of its development, but at this point it was the only car that could face up to the Williams. In Hungary, Schumacher appeared with a new lightened Ferrari, the latest development from the Byrne-Brawn duo. the operation produced it first result: Michael's set pole position. In the race however, he had to abandon hopes of using the new car, when it was damaged during the Sunday morning warmup. The race finished badly for Ferrari. The scarlet cars suffered from massive tire wear on the abrasive tarmac and the extraordinary mid-August heat in Budapest. Williams and Villeneuve wee not enjoying a good day either, but a few kilometers from the end, race dominator Damon Hill had gearbox problems and the young Canadian driver luckily scored his fifth win of the year.

The season continued. The World Championship battle is increasingly becoming a private affair between Villeneuve and Schumacher. Michael hit the target in Belgium, the twelfth round of the season. Again, the rain came to his aid. It was due to the downpour that hit the heights of Spa-Francorchamps a few minutes before the start of the Grand Prix. As in Monte Carlo, Schummy and Ferrari were the most astute or the most reckless with their choice of tire setup for what was going to be an unpredictable race. On the track, Michael again showed all of his class: he overtook Alesi's Benetton and Villeneuve's Williams in the wet and increased his lead on every lap.

Incredible as it may seem, Ferrari's 1997 crisis began here. The F310B was not even a far-off relative of the car seen at the start of the year. After improving rapidly race by race with the development modifications, in the post-Belgium period its performance leveled out considerably. It all went wrong at Monza, where luckily the win went to Coulthard and McLaren, while Villeneuve also had to settle for a few points. Expectations were high for the race at the new and rather faceless Spielberg track in Austria, where Formula 1 cars had competed until 1987, but victory went to Villeneuve. What was worse is that "lady luck" appeared to desert the scarlet red cars. Schumacher, who had problems in qualifying, could have finished at least third, had he not made a fantastic overtaking maneuver under yellow flags, which earned him a 10-second stop-and-go in the pits. Afterwards, he furiously recovered to finish in the points. At the Nürburgring, seven days later, things deteriorated even more. Villeneuve won again and leapt into the lead of the championship after Schumacher was taken out at the first corner by his brother Ralf, who had rocketed away from the start.

M. Schumacher (1°)
and J. Villeneuve (6°)
under the rain during the
GP of Belgium - August 1998.

Damon Hill formerly
World Championship 1996
at Hungaroring. An unlucky race.

MORE THAN PRANCING ... HORSE

Ferrari's 1997 season will go down in history as the year of the missed title, the year that almost ended a long period of failure that began with Jody Scheckter's conquest of the 1979 title. Away from all the glories and tensions of the Grand Prix season, Maranello's year will also go down in history for its industrial and market success. In 1997, the Prancing Horse set a new sales and production record for its GT cars, with considerable increases recorded in every area of the world, often going against local commercial tendencies. The merit for this must go to a production line that today can count on models of enormous technological and sporting fascination that closely respects the demands of an increasingly sophisticated and challenging market. An example of this was the F355 which obtained success in every continent. Credit must also go to the results of a company marketing and strategic restructuring policy, which Luca di Montezemolo began to put into place in 1991, the year he was appointed president of Ferrari. Since then, the modernization of Maranello has continued at the same pace: in sport as well as production. Today the Ferrari of the next century is based on a reinforced legend, but above all on a diversified structure that helps it to become one of the best examples of "Made in Italy" throughout the world.

Luca di Montezemolo,
President of Ferrari since 1991
and two pictures of the
new Ferrari F355.

There were two rounds left: Japan and again Spain, for the European Grand Prix. The Manufacturer's title was in the hands of Williams; the Driver's title was slipping away but within Ferrari there were still those who believed it could be won. Thanks to more technical developments, the Ferraris had a fantastic day in Suzuka. Even Eddie Irvine could have won, but he respected the interests of the team and let Schumacher, though the German's victory this time was worth double because of the disqualification of Villeneuve. During the qualifying, the Canadian was alleged to have overtaken under yellow flags and he completed the race under appeal. in the end he knew he was even going to lose the two points he earned for fifth place.

The points situation couldn't have been closer as they arrived at Jerez for the final race of the season. Schumacher led Villeneuve by one point. The driver who finished in front would be the World Champion. With millions of TV spectators watching, Schumacher led the race until two thirds distance. The track was narrow and twisty, without any real overtaking points. After the second and final pitstop, Villeneuve's Williams recovered and latched onto Schumacher's tail. Michael committed the error of not believing Jacques would attack. When he found the Canadian alongside on the inside line, his wheels almost blocked in a reincarnation of his father Gilles, it was too late. The rest is history and controversy: Schumacher's maneuver, the contact between the two, the Ferrari in the gravel, and the Williams making it to the finish. Villeneuve handed the victory over to Hakkinen in the McLaren, but third place earned him the title.

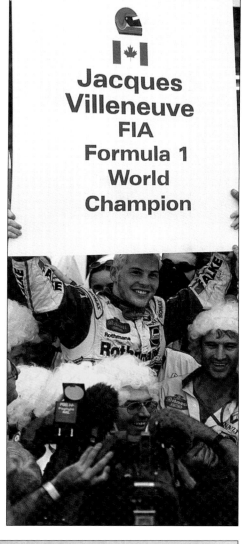

Ralf Schumacher caused the taken out of his brother Michael at the Luxembourg GP, and J. Villeneuve in triumph as World Champion '97.

ONE STEP AWAY FROM THE DREAM

FERRARI 100

Only those few people who knew him personally are able to imagine how Enzo Ferrari would approach the final two years of the twentieth century. His son, Piero; Franco Gozzi, who was alongside him for decades as press officer; and adviser, sporting director, and friend Luca di Montezemolo, discovered by him and thrown into the fray a quarter of a century ago. Maybe only these people can imagine how Ferrari would enter his second century.

One must not forget his first steps I the Modena fog at the turn of the century, his raw adolescent passion that was still unaware of the life ahead. Ferrari today would probably look back and ahead with pride. Admiring the splendid road cars produced by the Prancing Horse today, he would probably smile at the memory of those first hand-worked auto panels, hammered out by his friend

Scaglietti. Following the Williams cars of the British constructor, who has overtaken him by 9 to 8 in the number of Manufacturer's Championship victories, he would play down his anger and recognize the worth of this British rival. In this way, this would increase his anxiety and determination to win the next race and the next world title.

"The best victory?" he once said, "is the one that is still to come."

This remarkable declaration is atypical; example of the slightly overwrought communications that for decades have characterized Ferrari. But it is also true, exceptionally true, because Ferrari did no only race to win—he won to race: to continue to measure himself against others, but above all against himself, with his capacities and those of his collaborators: men who he chose and appointed as living appendages of himself, his immense sensitivity and his innovative way (in sport as well as in production) of thinking and designing.

A photomontage with Enzo Ferrari and Michael Schumacher seated in Ferrari F310B, the car of the dream in the '97 World Championship. A scene that Enzo Ferrari would have appreciated so much.

Although ten years have gone by since his death, it is not difficult to imagine a hundred-year-old Ferrari, ready to launch himself into the third millennium. For the man himself, not even a long-awaited title twenty years after Scheckter's would be the ultimate compensation. What everyone at Maranello and throughout the world is waiting for as the "duty" of Michael Schumacher, for him would be anything but the final word.

HISTORYCAL DATA

1948

Modello: **125 F1**
Drivers: **Bira - Farina - Sommer**
President: **E. Ferrari**
Technical Director: **G. Colombo**
Sporting Director: **F. Giberti**

Driver	Nat.	GP	Circuit	1°	2°	3°
R. Sommer	FRA	ITA	Del Valentino (Torino)			•

1949

Modello: **125 F1**
Drivers: **Ascari - Villoresi** (Folland - Mays - Richardson - Whitehead)
President: **E. Ferrari**
Technical Director: **G. Colombo**
Sporting Director: **F. Giberti**

Driver	Nat.	GP	Circuit	1°	2°	3°
L. Villoresi	ITA	BEL	Spa		•	
A. Ascari	ITA	BEL	Spa			•
A. Ascari	ITA	SUI	Bremgarten	•		
L. Villoresi	ITA	SUI	Bremgarten		•	
P. Whitehead	GBR	FRA	Reims			•
L. Villoresi	ITA	NED	Zandvoort	•		
A. Ascari	ITA	ITA	Monza	•		
P. Whitehead	GBR	TCH	Brno	•		

1950

Modelli: **125 F1 - 166 F2 - 275 F1 - 375 F1**
Drivers: **Ascari - Serafini - Sommer - Villoresi** (Whitehead)
President: **E. Ferrari**
Technical Director: **G. Colombo - A. Lampredi**
Sporting Director: **F. Giberti**
F1 World Drivers' Champion: **G. Farina** (Ita)

Driver	Nat.	GP	Circuit	1°	2°	3°
A. Ascari	ITA	MON	Montecarlo		•	
P. Whitehead	GBR	FRA	Reims			•
D. Serafini- A. Ascari	ITA	ITA	Monza		•	

1951

Modelli: **125 F1 - 212 F1 - 375 F1**
Drivers: **Ascari - Gonzalez - Taruffi - Villoresi** (Fischer - Whitehead)
President: **E. Ferrari**
Technical Director: **A. Lampredi**
Sporting Director: **F. Giberti**
F1 World Drivers' Champion: **J.M. Fangio** (Arg)

Driver	Nat.	GP	Circuit	1°	2°	3°
P. Taruffi	ITA	SUI	Bremgarten		•	
A. Ascari	ITA	BEL	Spa		•	
L. Villoresi	ITA	BEL	Spa			•
A. Ascari-F. Gonzalez	ITA ARG	FRA	Reims		•	
L. Villoresi	ITA	FRA	Reims			•
F. Gonzalez	ARG	U.K.	Silverstone	•		
L. Villoresi	ITA	U.K.	Silverstone			•
A. Ascari	ITA	GER	Nürburgring	•		
F. Gonzalez	ARG	GER	Nürburgring		•	
A. Ascari	ITA	ITA	Monza	•		
F. Gonzalez	ARG	ITA	Monza			•
F. Gonzalez	ARG	ESP	Pedralbes		•	

1952

Modelli: **500 F2 - 166 F2**
Drivers: **Ascari - Farina - Taruffi - Villoresi** (Carini - De Tornaco -Fischer - Hirt - Laurent - Rosier - Salvadori - Schoeller - Simon)
President: **E. Ferrari**
Technical Director: **A. Lampredi**
Sporting Director: **N. Ugolini**
F1 World Drivers' Champion: **A. Ascari** (Ita)

Driver	Nat.	GP	Circuit	1°	2°	3°
P. Taruffi	ITA	SUI	Bremgarten	•		
R. Fischer	SUI	SUI	Bremgarten		•	
A. Ascari	ITA	BEL	Spa	•		
G. Farina	ITA	BEL	Spa		•	
A. Ascari	ITA	FRA	Rouen	•		
G. Farina	ITA	FRA	Rouen		•	
P. Taruffi	ITA	FRA	Rouen			•
A. Ascari	ITA	U.K.	Silverstone	•		
P. Taruffi	ITA	U.K.	Silverstone			•
A. Ascari	ITA	GER	Nürburgring	•		
G. Farina	ITA	GER	Nürburgring		•	
R. Fischer	SUI	GER	Nürburgring			•
A. Ascari	ITA	NED	Zandvoort	•		
G. Farina	ITA	NED	Zandvoort		•	
L. Villoresi	ITA	NED	Zandvoort			•
A. Ascari	ITA	ITA	Monza	•		
L. Villoresi	ITA	ITA	Monza		•	

1953

Modelli: **550 F2 - 553 F2 - 166 F2**
Drivers: **Ascari - Carini - Farina - Hawthorn - Maglioli - Villoresi** (Adolff - De Terra - Hirt - Rosier -Swaters)
President: **E. Ferrari**
Technical Director: **A. Lampredi**
Sporting Director: **N. Ugolini**
F1 World Drivers' Champion: **A. Ascari** (Ita)

Driver	Nat.	GP	Circuit	1°	2°	3°
A. Ascari	ITA	ARG	Buenos Aires	•		
L. Villoresi	ITA	ARG	Buenos Aires		•	
A. Ascari	ITA	NED	Zandvoort	•		
G. Farina	ITA	NED	Zandvoort		•	
A. Ascari	ITA	BEL	Spa	•		
L. Villoresi	ITA	BEL	Spa		•	
M. Hawthorn	GBR	FRA	Reims	•		
A. Ascari	ITA	U.K.	Silverstone	•		

Driver	Nat.	GP	Circuit	1°	2°	3°
G. Farina	ITA	U.K.	Silverstone			•
G. Farina	ITA	GER	Nürburgring	•		
M. Hawthorn	GBR	GER	Nürburgring			•
A. Ascari	ITA	SUI	Bremgarten	•		
G. Farina	ITA	SUI	Bremgarten		•	
M. Hawthorn	GBR	SUI	Bremgarten			•
G. Farina	ITA	ITA	Monza		•	
L. Villoresi	ITA	ITA	Monza			•

1954

Modelli: **553 F1 - 625 F1**
Drivers: **Ascari - Farina - Gonzalez - Hawthorn - Maglioli - Manzon - Taruffi - Trintignant** (Parnell - Rosier - Swaters)
President: **E. Ferrari**
Technical Director: **A. Lampredi**
Sporting Director: **N. Ugolini**
F1 World Drivers' Champion: **J.M. Fangio** (Arg)

Driver	Nat.	GP	Circuit	1°	2°	3°
G. Farina	ITA	ARG	Buenos Aires		•	
F. Gonzalez	ARG	ARG	Buenos Aires			•
M. Trintignant	FRA	BEL	Spa		•	
R. Manzon	FRA	FRA	Reims			•
F. Gonzalez	ARG	U.K.	Silverstone	•		
M. Hawthorn	GBR	U.K.	Silverstone		•	
F. Gonzalez-	ARG					
M. Hawthorn	GBR	GER	Nürburgring		•	
M. Trintignant	FRA	GER	Nürburgring			•
F. Gonzalez	ARG	SUI	Bremgarten		•	
M. Hawthorn	GBR	ITA	Monza		•	
F.Gonzalez-	ARG					
U.Maglioli	ITA	ITA	Monza			•
M. Hawthorn	GBR	ESP	Pedralbes	•		

1955

Modelli: **555 F1 - 625 F1**
Drivers: **Castellotti - Farina - Frere - Gonzalez - Hawthorn - Maglioli - Schell - Taruffi - Trintignant** (Claes)
President: **E. Ferrari**
Technical Director: **A. Lampredi**
Sporting Director: **N. Ugolini**
F1 World Drivers' Champion: **J.M. Fangio** (Arg)

Driver	Nat.	GP	Circuit	1°	2°	3°
Gonzalez-Farina-	ARG/ITA					
Trintignant	FRA	ARG	Buenos Aires		•	
Farina-Maglioli	ITA/ITA					
Trintignant	FRA	ARG	Buenos Aires			•
M. Trintignant	FRA	MON	Montecarlo	•		
G. Farina	ITA	BEL	Spa			•
E. Castellotti	ITA	ITA	Monza			•

1956

Modello: **D50**
Drivers: **Castellotti - Collins - De Portago - Fangio - Frere Gendebien - Musso - Pilette**

President: **E. Ferrari**
Technical Director: **A. Fraschetti**
Sporting Director: **E. Sculati**
F1 World Drivers' Champion: **J.M. Fangio** (Arg)

Driver	Nat.	GP	Circuit	1°	2°	3°
L. Musso-	ITA					
J.M. Fangio	ARG	ARG	Buenos Aires	•		
P. Collins-	GBR					
J.M. Fangio	ARG	MON	Montecarlo		•	
P. Collins	GBR	BEL	Spa	•		
P. Frere	BEL	BEL	Spa		•	
P. Collins	GBR	FRA	Reims	•		
E. Castellotti	ITA	FRA	Reims		•	
J.M. Fangio	ARG	U.K.	Silverstone	•		
A.De Portago-	SPA					
P.Collins	GBR	U.K.	Silversone		•	
J.M. Fangio	ARG	GER	Nürburgring	•		
P.Collins-	GBR					
J.M.Fangio	ARG	ITA	Monza		•	

1957

Modelli: **D50 - 801 F1**
Drivers: **Castellotti - Collins - De Portago - Hawthorn - Musso - Perdisa - Trintignant - Von Trips**
President: **E. Ferrari**
Technical Director: **A. Fraschetti**
Sporting Director: **R. Tavoni**
F1 World Drivers' Champion: **J.M. Fangio** (Arg)

Driver	Nat.	GP	Circuit	1°	2°	3°
L. Musso	ITA	FRA	Rouen		•	
P. Collins	GBR	FRA	Rouen			•
L. Musso	ITA	U.K.	Aintree		•	
M. Hawthorn	GBR	U.K.	Aintree			•
M. Hawthorn	GBR	GER	Nürburgring		•	
P. Collins	GBR	GER	Nürburgring			•
W. Von Trips	GER	ITA	Monza			•

1958

Modello: **246 F1**
Drivers: **Collins - Gendebien - Hawthorn - P. Hill - Musso - Von Trips**
President: **E. Ferrari**
Technical Director: **C. Chiti**
Sporting Director: **R. Tavoni**
F1 World Drivers' Champion: **M. Hawthorn** (GBR)
F1 Manufacturers' Cup: **Vanwall**

Driver	Nat.	GP	Circuit	1°	2°	3°
L. Musso	ITA	ARG	Buenos Aires		•	
M. Hawthorn	GBR	ARG	Buenos Aires			•
L. Musso	ITA	MON	Montecarlo		•	
P. Collins	GBR	MON	Montecarlo			•
M. Hawthorn	GBR	BEL	Spa		•	
M. Hawthorn	GBR	FRA	Reims	•		
W. Von Trips	GER	FRA	Reims			•
P. Collins	GBR	U.K.	Silverstone	•		
M. Hawthorn	GBR	U.K.	Silverstone		•	
M. Hawthorn	GBR	POR	Oporto		•	
M. Hawthorn	GBR	ITA	Monza		•	
P. Hill	USA	ITA	Monza			•
M. Hawthorn	GBR	MAR	Casablanca		•	
P. Hill	USA	MAR	Casablanca			•

Driver	Nat.	GP	Circuit	1°	2°	3°
R. Ginther	USA	U.K.	Aintree			•
W. Von Trips	GER	GER	Nürburgring		•	
P. Hill	USA	GER	Nürburgring		•	
P. Hill	USA	ITA	Monza	•		

1959

Modello: **256 F1**
Drivers: **Allison - Behra - Brooks - Gendebien - Gurney - P. Hill - Von Trips**
President: **E. Ferrari**
Technical Director: **C. Chiti**
Sporting Director: **O. Tavoni**
F1 World Drivers' Champion: **J. Brabham** (AUS)
F1 Manufacturers' Cup: **Cooper**

Driver	Nat.	GP	Circuit	1°	2°	3°
T. Brooks	GBR	MON	Montecarlo		•	
T. Brooks	GBR	FRA	Reims	•		
P. Hill	USA	FRA	Reims		•	
T. Brooks	GBR	GER	Avus	•		
D. Gurney	USA	GER	Avus		•	
P. Hill	USA	GER	Avus			•
D. Gurney	USA	POR	Monsanto			•
P. Hill	USA	ITA	Monza		•	
T. Brooks	GBR	USA	Sebring			•

1960

Modelli: **256 F1 - 256 P F1**
Drivers: **Allison - Ginther - Gonzalez - P. Hill - Mairesse - Von Trips**
President: **E. Ferrari**
Technical Director: **C. Chiti**
Sporting Director: **O. Tavoni**
F1 World Drivers' Champion: **J. Brabham** (AUS)
F1 Manufacturers' Cup: **Cooper**

Driver	Nat.	GP	Circuit	1°	2°	3°
C. Allison	GBR	ARG	Buenos Aires		•	
P. Hill	USA	MON	Montecarlo			•
P. Hill	USA	ITA	Monza	•		
R. Ginther	USA	ITA	Monza		•	
W. Mairesse	BEL	ITA	Monza			•

1961

Modello: **156 F1**
Drivers: **Baghetti - Gendebien - Ginther - P. Hill - Mairesse - R. Rodriguez - Von Trips**
President: **E. Ferrari**
Technical Director: **C. Chiti**
Sporting Director: **O. Tavoni**
F1 World Drivers' Champion: **P. Hill** (USA)
F1 manufacturers' Cup: **Ferrari**

Driver	Nat.	GP	Circuit	1°	2°	3°
R. Ginther	USA	MON	Montecarlo		•	
P. Hill	USA	MON	Montecarlo			•
W. Von Trips	GER	NED	Zandvoort	•		
P. Hill	USA	NED	Zandvoort		•	
P. Hill	USA	BEL	Spa	•		
W. Von Trips	GER	BEL	Spa		•	
R. Ginther	USA	BEL	Spa			•
G. Baghetti	ITA	FRA	Reims	•		
W. Von Trips	GER	U.K.	Aintree	•		
P. Hill	USA	U.K.	Aintree			•

1962

Modello: **156 F1**
Drivers: **Baghetti - Bandini - P. Hill - Mairesse - R. Rodriguez**
President: **E. Ferrari**
Technical Director: **M. Forghieri**
Sporting Director: **E. Dragoni**
F1 World Drivers' Champion: **G. Hill** (GBR)
F1 Manufacturers' Cup: **BRM**

Driver	Nat.	GP	Circuit	1°	2°	3°
P. Hill	USA	NED	Zandvoort			•
P. Hill	USA	MON	Montecarlo		•	
L. Bandini	ITA	MON	Montecarlo			•
P. Hill	USA	BEL	Spa			•

1963

Modello: **156 F1-63**
Drivers: **Bandini - Mairesse - Scarfiotti - Surtees**
President: **E. Ferrari**
Technical Director: **M. Forghieri**
Sporting Director: **E. Dragoni**
F1 World Drivers' Champion: **J. Clark** (GBR)
F1 Manufacturers' Cup: **Lotus**

Driver	Nat.	GP	Circuit	1°	2°	3°
J. Surtees	GBR	NED	Zandvoort			•
J. Surtees	GBR	U.K.	Silverstone		•	
J. Surtees	GBR	GER	Nürburgring	•		

1964

Modelli: **156 F1-63 - 158 F1 - 512 F1**
Drivers: **Bandini - P. Rodriguez - Scarfiotti - Surtees**
President: **E. Ferrari**
Technical Director: **M. Forghieri**
Sporting Director: **E. Dragoni**
F1 World Drivers' Champion: **J. Surtees** (GBR)
F1 Manufacturers' Cup: **Ferrari**

Driver	Nat.	GP	Circuit	1°	2°	3°
J. Surtees	GBR	NED	Zandvoort		•	
J. Surtees	GBR	U.K.	Brands Hatch			•
J. Surtees	GBR	GER	Nürburgring	•		
L. Bandini	ITA	GER	Nürburgring			•
L. Bandini	ITA	AUT	Zeltweg		•	
J. Surtees	GBR	ITA	Monza	•		
L. Bandini	ITA	ITA	Monza			•
J. Surtees	GBR	USA	Watking Glen		•	
J. Surtees	GBR	MEX	C. del Messico		•	
L. Bandini	ITA	MEX	C. del Messico			•

1965

Modelli: **158 F1 - 512 F1**
Drivers: **Bandini - Bondurant - P. Rodriguez - Scarfiotti - Surtees - Vaccarella**
President: **E. Ferrari**
Technical Director: **M. Forghieri**
Sporting Director: **E. Dragoni**
F1 World Drivers' Champion: **J. Clark** (GBR)
F1 Manufacturers' Cup: **Lotus**

Driver	Nat.	GP	Circuit	1°	2°	3°
J. Surtees	GBR	SAF	East London		•	
L. Bandini	ITA	MON	Montecarlo		•	
J. Surtees	GBR	FRA	Clermont			•
J. Surtees	GBR	U.K.	Silverstone			•

1966

Modelli: **246 F1-66 - 312 F1-66**
Drivers: **Bandini - Parkes - Scarfiotti - Surtees**
President: **E. Ferrari**
Technical Director: **M. Forghieri**
Sporting Director: **E. Dragoni**
F1 World Drivers' Champion: **J. Brabham** (AUS)
F1 Manufacturers' Cup: **Brabham**

Driver	Nat.	GP	Circuit	1°	2°	3°
L. Bandini	ITA	MON	Montecarlo		•	
J. Surtees	GBR	BEL	Spa	•		
L. Bandini	ITA	BEL	Spa			•
M. Parkes	GBR	FRA	Reims		•	
L. Scarfiotti	ITA	ITA	Monza	•		
M. Parkes	GBR	ITA	Monza		•	

1967

Modello: **312 F1-67**
Drivers: **Amon - Bandini - Parkes - Scarfiotti**
President: **E. Ferrari**
Technical Director: **M. Forghieri**
Sporting Director: **F. Lini**
F1 World Drivers' Champion: **D. Hulme** (NZL)
F1 Manufacturers' Cup: **Brabham**

Driver	Nat.	GP	Circuit	1°	2°	3°
C. Amon	NZL	MON	Montecarlo			•
C. Amon	NZL	BEL	Spa			•
C. Amon	NZL	U.K.	Silverstone			•
C. Amon	NZL	GER	Nürburgring			•

1968

Modello: **312 F1-68**
Drivers: **Amon - Bell - De Adamich - Ickx**
President: **E. Ferrari**
Technical Director: **M. Forghieri**
Sporting Director: **F. Gozzi**
F1 World Drivers' Champion: **G. Hill** (GBR)
F1 Manufacturers' Cup: **Lotus**

Driver	Nat.	GP	Circuit	1°	2°	3°
J. Ickx	BEL	BEL	Spa			•
J. Ickx	BEL	FRA	Rouen	•		
C. Amon	NZL	U.K.	Brands Hatch		•	
J. Ickx	BEL	U.K.	Brands Hatch			•
J. Ickx	BEL	ITA	Monza			•

1969

Modello: **312 F1-69**
Drivers: **Amon - P. Rodriguez**
President: **E. Ferrari**
Technical Director: **M. Forghieri**
Sporting Director: **F. Gozzi**
F1 World Drivers' Champion: **J. Stewart** (GBR)
F1 Manufacturers' Cup: **Matra**

Driver	Nat.	GP	Circuit	1°	2°	3°
C. Amon	NZL	NED	Zandvoort			•

1970

Modello: **312 B**
Drivers: **Giunti - Ickx - Regazzoni**
President: **E. Ferrari**
Technical Director: **M. Forghieri**
Sporting Director: **F. Gozzi**
F1 World Drivers' Champion: **J. Rindt** (AUT)
F1 Manufacturers' Cup: **Lotus**

Driver	Nat.	GP	Circuit	1°	2°	3°
J. Ickx	BEL	NED	Zandvoort			•
J. Ickx	BEL	GER	Hockenheim		•	
J. Ickx	BEL	AUT	Osterreichring	•		
C. Regazzoni	SUI	AUT	Osterreichring		•	
C. Regazzoni	SUI	ITA	Monza	•		
J. Ickx	BEL	CAN	St. Jovite	•		
C. Regazzoni	SUI	CAN	St. Jovite		•	
J. Ickx	BEL	MEX	C. del Messico	•		
C. Regazzoni	SUI	MEX	C. del Messico		•	

1971

Modelli: **312 B - 312 B2**
Drivers: **Andretti - Ickx - Regazzoni**
President: **E. Ferrari**
Technical Director: **M. Forghieri - A. Colombo**
Sporting Director: **P. Schetty**
F1 World Drivers' Champion: **J. Stewart** (GBR)
F1 Manufacturers' Cup: **Tyrrell**

Driver	Nat.	GP	Circuit	1°	2°	3°
M. Andretti	USA	SAF	Kyalami	•		
C. Regazzoni	SUI	SAF	Kyalami			•
J. Ickx	BEL	ESP	Montjuich Park		•	
J. Ickx	BEL	MON	Montecarlo			•
J. Ickx	BEL	NED	Zandvoort	•		
C. Regazzoni	SUI	NED	Zandvoort			•
C. Regazzoni	SUI	GER	Nürburgring			•

1972

Modello: **312 B2**
Drivers: **Andretti - Galli - Ickx - Merzario - Regazzoni**
President: **E. Ferrari**
Technical Director: **A. Colombo**
Sporting Director: **P. Schetty**
F1 World Drivers' Champion: **E. Fittipaldi** (BRA)
F1 Manufacturers' Cup: **Lotus**

Driver	Nat.	GP	Circuit	1°	2°	3°
J. Ickx	BEL	ARG	Buenos Aires			•
J. Ickx	BEL	ESP	Jarama		•	
C. Regazzoni	SUI	ESP	Jarama			•
J. Ickx	BEL	MON	Montecarlo		•	
J. Ickx	BEL	GER	Nürburgring	•		
C. Regazzoni	SUI	GER	Nürburgring		•	

1973

Modelli: **312 B2 - 312 B3-73**
Drivers: **Ickx - Merzario**
President: **E. Ferrari**
Technical Director: **A. Colombo - M. Forghieri**
Sporting Director: **G. Rosani - L. di Montezemolo**
F1 World Drivers' Champion: **J. Stewart** (GBR)
F1 Manufacturers' Cup: **Lotus**

1974

Modello: **312 B3-74**
Drivers: **Lauda - Regazzoni**
President: **E. Ferrari**
Technical Director: **M. Forghieri**
Sporting Director: **L. di Montezemolo**
F1 World Drivers' Champion: **E. Fittipaldi** (BRA)
F1 Manufacturers' Cup: **McLaren**

Driver	Nat.	GP	Circuit	1°	2°	3°
N. Lauda	AUT	ARG	Buenos Aires		•	
C. Regazzoni	SUI	ARG	Buenos Aires			•
C. Regazzoni	SUI	BRA	Interlagos		•	
N. Lauda	AUT	ESP	Jarama	•		
C. Regazzoni	SUI	ESP	Jarama		•	
N. Lauda	AUT	BEL	Spa - Francorchamps		•	
N. Lauda	AUT	NED	Zandvoort	•		
C. Regazzoni	SUI	NED	Zandvoort		•	
N. Lauda	AUT	FRA	Digione		•	
C. Regazzoni	SUI	FRA	Digione			•
C. Regazzoni	SUI	GER	Nürburgring	•		
C. Regazzoni	SUI	CAN	Mosport		•	

1975

Modelli: **312 B3-74 - 312 T**
Drivers: **Lauda - Regazzoni**
President: **E. Ferrari**
Technical Director: **M. Forghieri**
Sporting Director: **L. di Montezemolo**

F1 World Drivers' Champion: **N. Lauda** (AUT)
F1 Manufacturers' Cup: **Ferrari**

Driver	Nat.	GP	Circuit	1°	2°	3°
N. Lauda	AUT	MON	Montecarlo	•		
N. Lauda	AUT	BEL	Zolder	•		
N. Lauda	AUT	SWE	Anderstorp	•		
C. Regazzoni	SUI	SWE	Anderstorp			•
N. Lauda	AUT	NED	Zandvoort		•	
C. Regazzoni	SUI	NED	Zandvoort			•
N. Lauda	AUT	FRA	Paul Ricard			•
N. Lauda	AUT	GER	Nürburgring			•
C. Regazzoni	SUI	ITA	Monza	•		
N. Lauda	AUT	ITA	Monza			•
N. Lauda	AUT	USA	Watkins Glen	•		

1976

Modelli: **312 T - 312 T2**
Drivers: **Lauda - Regazzoni - Reutemann**
President: **E. Ferrari**
Technical Director: **M. Forghieri**
Sporting Director: **D. Audetto**
F1 World Drivers' Champion: **J. Hunt** (GBR)
F1 Manufacturers' Cup: **Ferrari**

Driver	Nat.	GP	Circuit	1°	2°	3°
N. Lauda	AUT	BRA	Interlagos	•		
N. Lauda	AUT	SAF	Kyalami	•		
C. Regazzoni	SUI	USA West	Long Beach	•		
N. Lauda	AUT	USA West	Long Beach		•	
N. Lauda	AUT	ESP	Jarama		•	
N. Lauda	AUT	BEL	Zolder	•		
C. Regazzoni	SUI	BEL	Zolder		•	
N. Lauda	AUT	MON	Montecarlo	•		
N. Lauda	AUT	SWE	Anderstorp			•
N. Lauda	AUT	U.K.	Brands Hatch	•		
C. Regazzoni	SUI	NED	Zandvoort		•	
C. Regazzoni	SUI	ITA	Monza		•	
N. Lauda	AUT	USA	Watkins Glen			•

1977

Modello: **312 T2**
Drivers: **Lauda - Reutemann - Villeneuve**
President: **E. Ferrari**
Technical Director: **M. Forghieri**
Sporting Director: **R. Nosetto**
F1 World Drivers' Champion: **N. Lauda** (AUT)
F1 Manufacturers' Cup: **Ferrari**

Driver	Nat.	GP	Circuit	1°	2°	3°
C. Reutemann	ARG	ARG	Buenos Aires			•
G. Reutemann	ARG	BRA	Interlagos	•		
N. Lauda	AUT	BRA	Interlagos			•
N. Lauda	AUT	SAF	Kyalami	•		
N. Lauda	AUT	USA West	Long Beach		•	
C. Reutemann	ARG	ESP	Jarama		•	
N. Lauda	AUT	MON	Montecarlo		•	
C. Reutemann	ARG	MON	Montecarlo			•
N. Lauda	AUT	BEL	Zolder		•	
C. Reutemann	ARG	SWE	Anderstorp			•
N. Lauda	AUT	U.K.	Silverstone		•	
N. Lauda	AUT	GER	Hockenheim	•		

N. Lauda	AUT	AUT	Osterreichring		•	
N. Lauda	AUT	NED	Zandvoort	•		
N. Lauda	AUT	ITA	Monza		•	
C. Reutemann	ARG	JPN	Fuji		•	

1978

Modelli: **312 T2 - 312 T3**
Drivers: **Reutemann - Villeneuve**
President: **E. Ferrari**
Technical Director: **M. Forghieri**
Sporting Director: **M. Piccinini**
F1 World Drivers' Champion: **M. Andretti** (USA)
F1 Manufacturers' Cup: **Lotus**

Driver	Nat.	GP	Circuit	1°	2°	3°
C. Reutemann	ARG	BRA	Rio	•		
C. Reutemann	ARG	USA West	Long Beach	•		
C. Reutemann	ARG	BEL	Zolder			•
C. Reutemann	ARG	U.K.	Brands Hatch	•		
G. Villeneuve	CAN	AUT	Osterreichring			•
C. Reutemann	ARG	ITA	Monza			•
C. Reutemann	ARG	USA	Watkins Glen	•		
G. Villeneuve	CAN	CAN	Montreal	•		
C. Reutemann	ARG	CAN	Montreal			•

1979

Modelli: **312 T3 - 312 T4**
Drivers: **Scheckter - Villeneuve**
President: **E. Ferrari**
Technical Director: **M. Forghieri**
Sporting Director: **M. Piccinini**
F1 World Drivers' Champion: **J. Scheckter** (SA)
F1 Manufacturers' Cup: **Ferrari**

Driver	Nat.	GP	Circuit	1°	2°	3°
G. Villeneuve	CAN	SAF	Kyalami	•		
J. Scheckter	SA	SAF	Kyalami		•	
G. Villeneuve	CAN	USA West	Long Beach	•		
J. Scheckter	SA	USA West	Long Beach		•	
J. Scheckter	SA	BEL	Zolder	•		
J. Scheckter	SA	MON	Montecarlo	•		
G. Villeneuve	CAN	FRA	Digione			•
G. Villeneuve	CAN	AUT	Osterreichring			•
J. Schectker	SA	NED	Zandvoort			•
J. Scheckter	SA	ITA	Monza	•		
G. Villeneuve	CAN	ITA	Monza			•
G. Villeneuve	CAN	CAN	Montreal			•
G. Villeneuve	CAN	USA	Watkins Glen	•		

1980

Modello: **312 T5**
Drivers: **Scheckter - Villeneuve**
President: **E. Ferrari**
Technical Director: **M. Forghieri**
Sporting Director: **M. Piccinini**
F1 World Drivers' Champion: **A. Jones** (AUS)
F1 Manufacturers' Cup: **Williams**

1981

Modello: **126 CK**
Drivers: **Pironi - Villeneuve**
President: **E. Ferrari**
Technical Director: **M. Forghieri**
Sporting Director: **M. Piccinini**
F1 World Drivers' Champion: **N. Piquet** (BRA)
F1 Manufacturers' Cup: **Williams**

Driver	Nat.	GP	Circuit	1°	2°	3°
G. Villeneuve	CAN	MON	Montecarlo	•		
G. Villeneuve	CAN	ESP	Jarama	•		
G. Villeneuve	CAN	CAN	Montreal			•

1982

Modello: **126 C2**
Drivers: **Andretti - Pironi - Tambay - Villeneuve**
President: **E. Ferrari**
Technical Director: **M. Forghieri**
Sporting Director: **M. Piccinini**
F1 World Drivers' Champion: **K. Rosberg** (FIN)
F1 World Manufacturers' Champion: **Ferrari**

Driver	Nat.	GP	Circuit	1°	2°	3°
D. Pironi	FRA	SMR	Imola	•		
G. Villeneuve	CAN	SMR	Imola		•	
D. Pironi	FRA	MON	Montecarlo		•	
D. Pironi	FRA	USA East	Detroit			•
D. Pironi	FRA	NED	Zandvoort	•		
D. Pironi	FRA	U.K.	Brands Hatch		•	
P. Tambay	FRA	U.K.	Brands Hatch			•
D. Pironi	FRA	FRA	Paul Richard			•
P. Tambay	FRA	GER	Hockenheim	•		
P. Tambay	FRA	ITA	Monza		•	
M. Andretti	USA	ITA	Monza			•
P. Tambay	FRA	USA	Las Vegas		•	

1983

Modelli: **126 C2 - 126 C3**
Drivers: **Arnoux - Tambay**
President: **E. Ferrari**
Technical Director: **M. Forghieri**
Sporting Director: **M. Piccinini**
F1 World Drivers' Champion: **N. Piquet** (BRA)
F1 World Manufacturers' Champion: **Ferrari**

Driver	Nat.	GP	Circuit	1°	2°	3°
R. Arnoux	FRA	USA	Long Beach			•
P. Tambay	FRA	SMR	Imola	•		
R. Arnoux	FRA	SMR	Imola			•
P. Tambay	FRA	BEL	Spa		•	
R. Arnoux	FRA	CAN	Montreal	•		
P. Tambay	FRA	CAN	Montreal			•
P. Tambay	FRA	U.K.	Silverstone			•
R. Arnoux	FRA	GER	Hockenheim	•		
R. Arnoux	FRA	AUT	Osterreichring		•	
R. Arnoux	FRA	NED	Zandvoort	•		
P. Tambay	FRA	NED	Zandvoort		•	
R. Arnoux	FRA	ITA	Monza	•		

HISTORYCAL DATA

1984

Modello: **126 C4**
Drivers: **Alboreto - Arnoux**
President: **E. Ferrari**
Technical Director: **M. Forghieri - H. Postlethwaite**
Sporting Director: **M. Piccinini**
F1 World Drivers' Champion: **N. Lauda** (AUT)
F1 World Manufacturers' Champion: **McLaren**

Driver	Nat.	GP	Circuit	1°	2°	3°
M. Alboreto	ITA	BEL	Zolder	•		
R. Arnoux	FRA	BEL	Zolder			•
R. Arnoux	FRA	SMR	Imola		•	
R. Arnoux	FRA	USA	Dallas		•	
M. ALboreto	ITA	AUT	Osterreichring			•
M. Alboreto	ITA	ITA	Monza		•	
M. Alboreto	ITA	Europe	Nürburgring		•	

1985

Modello: **156-85**
Drivers: **Alboreto - Arnoux - Johansson**
President: **E. Ferrari**
Technical Director: **H. Postlethwaite**
Sporting Director: **M. Piccinini**
F1 World Drivers' Champion: **A. Prost** (FRA)
F1 World Manufacturers' Champion: **McLaren**

Driver	Nat.	GP	Circuit	1°	2°	3°
M. Alboreto	ITA	BRA	Rio		•	
M. Alboreto	ITA	POR	Estoril		•	
M. Alboreto	ITA	MON	Montecarlo		•	
M. Alboreto	ITA	CAN	Montreal	•		
S. Johansson	SWE	CAN	Montreal		•	
S. Johansson	SWE	USA	Detroit		•	
M. Alboreto	ITA	USA	Detroit			•
M. Alboreto	ITA	U.K.	Silverstone		•	
M. Alboreto	ITA	GER	Nürburgring	•		
M. Alboreto	ITA	AUT	Osterreichring			•

1986

Modello: **F1-86**
Drivers: **Alboreto - Johansson**
President: **E. Ferrari**
Technical Director: **H. Postlethwaite**
Sporting Director: **M. Piccinini**
F1 World Drivers' Champion: **A. Prost** (FRA)
F1 World Manufacturers' Champion: **Williams**

Driver	Nat.	GP	Circuit	1°	2°	3°
S. Johansson	SWE	BEL	Spa			•
M. Alboreto	ITA	AUT	Osterreichring		•	
S. Johansson	SWE	AUT	Osterreichring			•
S. Johansson	SWE	ITA	Monza			•
S. Johansson	SWE	AUS	Adelaide			•

1987

Modello: **F1-87**
Drivers: **Alboreto - Berger**
President: **E. Ferrari**
Technical Director: **J. Barnard**
Sporting Director: **M. Piccinini**
F1 World Drivers' Champion: **N. Piquet** (BRA)
F1 World Manufacturers' Champion: **Williams**

Driver	Nat.	GP	Circuit	1°	2°	3°
M. Alboreto	ITA	SMR	Imola			•
M. Alboreto	ITA	MON	Montecarlo			•
G. Berger	AUT	POR	Estoril		•	
G. Berger	AUT	JPN	Suzuka	•		
G. Berger	AUT	AUS	Adelaide	•		
M. Alboreto	ITA	AUS	Adelaide		•	

1988

Modello: **F1-87/88C**
Drivers: **Alboreto - Berger**
President: **E. Ferrari**
Technical Director: **H. Postlethwaite - J. Barnard**
Sporting Director: **M. Piccinini**
F1 World Drivers' Champion: **A. Senna** (BRA)
F1 World Manufacturers' Champion: **McLaren**

Driver	Nat.	GP	Circuit	1°	2°	3°
G. Berger	AUT	BRA	Rio		•	
M. Alboreto	ITA	MON	Montecarlo		•	
G. Berger	AUT	MON	Montecarlo			•
G. Berger	AUT	MEX	C. del Messico			•
M. Alboreto	ITA	FRA	Paul Ricard			•
G. Berger	AUT	GER	Hockenheim			•
G. Berger	AUT	ITA	Monza	•		
M. Alboreto	ITA	ITA	Monza		•	

1989

Modello: **F1-89**
Driver: **Berger - Mansell**
President: **P. Fusaro**
Technical Director: **J. Barnard**
Sporting Director: **C. Fiorio**
F1 World Drivers' Champion: **A. Prost** (FRA)
F1 World Manufacturers' Champion: **McLaren**

Driver	Nat.	GP	Circuit	1°	2°	3°
N. Mansell	GBR	BRA	Rio	•		
N. Mansell	GBR	FRA	Paul Ricard		•	
N. Mansell	GBR	U.K.	Silverstone		•	
N. Mansell	GBR	GER	Hockenheim			•
N. Mansell	GBR	HUN	Hungaroring	•		
N. Mansell	GBR	BEL	Spa			•
G. Berger	AUT	ITA	Monza		•	
G. Berger	AUT	POR	Estoril	•		
G. Berger	AUT	ESP	Jèrez		•	

1990

Modello: **F1-90**
Drivers: **Mansell - Prost**
President: **P. Fusaro**

166

Team Manager: **C. Fiorio**
F1 World Drivers' Champion: **A. Senna** (BRA)
F1 World Manufacturers' Champion: **McLaren**

Driver	Nat.	GP	Circuit	1°	2°	3°
A. Prost	FRA	BRA	Interlagos	•		
N. Mansell	GBR	CAN	Montreal			•
A. Prost	FRA	MEX	Città Messico	•		
N. Mansell	GBR	MEX	Città Messico		•	
A. Prost	FRA	FRA	Paul Ricard	•		
A. Prost	FRA	U.K.	Silverstone	•		
A. Prost	FRA	BEL	Spa		•	
A. Prost	FRA	ITA	Monza		•	
N. Mansell	GBR	POR	Estoril	•		
A. Prost	FRA	POR	Estoril			•
A. Prost	FRA	ESP	Jèrez	•		
N. Mansell	GBR	ESP	Jèrez		•	
N. Mansell	GBR	AUT	Adelaide		•	
A. Prost	FRA	AUS	Adelaide			•

1991

Modello: **F1-91**
Drivers: **Alesi - Morbidelli - Prost**
President: **P. Fusaro - L. di Montezemolo**
Team Manager: **C. Fiorio - C. Lombardi**
F1 World Drivers' Champion: **A. Senna** (BRA)
F1 World Manufacturers' Champion: **McLaren**

Driver	Nat.	GP	Circuit	1°	2°	3°
A. Prost	FRA	USA	Phoenix		•	
J. Alesi	FRA	MON	Montecarlo			•
A. Prost	FRA	FRA	Magny Cours		•	
A. Prost	FRA	U.K.	Silverstone			•
J. Alesi	FRA	GER	Hockenheim			•
A. Prost	FRA	ITA	Monza			•
J. Alesi	FRA	POR	Estoril			•
A. Prost	FRA	ESP	Barcellona		•	

1992

Modello: **F92 A**
Drivers: **Alesi - Capelli - Larini**
President: **L. di Montezemolo**
Team Manager: **C. Lombardi**
F1 World Drivers' Champion: **N. Mansell** (GBR)
F1 World Manufacturers' Champion: **Williams**

Driver	Nat.	GP	Circuit	1°	2°	3°
J. Alesi	FRA	ESP	Barcellona			•
J. Alesi	FRA	CAN	Montreal			•

1993

Modello: **F93 A**
Driver: **Alesi - Berger**
President: **L. di Montezemolo**
Team Manager: **H. Postlethwaite - J. Todt**
F1 World Drivers' Champion: **A. Prost** (FRA)
F1 World Manufacturers' Champion: **Williams**

Driver	Nat.	GP	Circuit	1°	2°	3°
J. Alesi	FRA	MON	Montecarlo			•

1994

Modello: **412 T1**
Drivers: **Alesi - Berger - Larini**
President: **L. di Montezemolo**
Team Manager: **J. Todt**
F1 World Drivers' Champion: **M. Schumacher** (GER)
F1 World Manufacturers' Champion: **Williams**

Driver	Nat.	GP	Circuit	1°	2°	3°
J. Alesi	FRA	BRA	Interlagos			•
G. Berger	AUT	Pacific	Aida		•	
N. Larini	ITA	SMR	Imola		•	
G. Berger	AUT	MON	Montecarlo			•
J. Alesi	FRA	CAN	Villeneuve			•
G. Berger	AUT	FRA	Magny-Cours			•
J. Alesi	FRA	U.K.	Silverstone			•
G. Berger	AUT	GER	Hockenheim	•		
G. Berger	AUT	ITA	Monza		•	
J. Alesi	FRA	JPN	Suzuka			•
G. Berger	AUT	AUS	Adelaide		•	

1995

Modello: **412 T2**
Drivers: **Alesi - Berger**
President: **L. di Montezemolo**
Team Manager: **J. Todt**
F1 World Drivers' Champion: **M. Schumacher** (GER)
F1 World Manufacturers' Champion: **Benetton**

Driver	Nat.	GP	Circuit	1°	2°	3°
G. Berger	AUT	BRA	Interlagos		•	
J. Alesi	FRA	BRA	Interlagos			•
J. Alesi	FRA	ARG	O. F.Galvez		•	
J. Alesi	FRA	SMR	Imola		•	
G. Berger	AUT	SMR	Imola			•
G. Berger	AUT	ESP	Catalunya			•
G. Berger	AUT	MON	Montecarlo			•
J. Alesi	FRA	CAN	G. Villeneuve	•		
J. Alesi	FRA	U.K.	Silverstone		•	
G. Berger	AUT	GER	Hockenheim			•
G. Berger	AUT	HUN	Hungaroring			•
J. Alesi	FRA	Europe	Nürburgring		•	

1996

Modello: **F310**
Drivers: **Irvine - Schumacher**
President: **L. di Montezemolo**
Team Manager: **J. Todt**
F1 World Drivers' Champion: **D. Hill** (GBR)
F1 World Manufacturers' Champion: **Williams**

Driver	Nat.	GP	Circuit	1°	2°	3°
E. Irvine	IRL	AUS	Melbourne			•
M. Schumacher	GER	BRA	José C. Pace			•
M. Schumacher	GER	Europe	Nürburgring		•	
M. Schumacher	GER	SMR	E. e D. Ferrari		•	
M. Schumacher	GER	ESP	Catalunya	•		
M. Schumacher	GER	BEL	Spa	•		
M. Schumacher	GER	ITA	Monza	•		
M. Schumacher	GER	POR	Estoril			•
M. Schumacher	GER	JPN	Suzuka		•	

HISTORYCAL DATA

1997

Modello: **F310B**
Drivers: **Irvine - Schumacher**
President: **L. di Montezemolo**
Team Manager: **J. Todt**
F1 World Drivers' Champion: **J. Villeneuve** (CAN)
F1 World Manufacturers' Champion: **Williams**

Driver	Nat.	GP	Circuit	1°	2°	3°
M. Schumacher	GER	Australian	Albert Park		•	
E. Irvine	IRL	Argentine	Oscar A.Galvez		•	
M. Schumacher	GER	S.Marino	E. e D. Ferrari		•	
E. Irvine	IRL	S.Marino	E. e D. Ferrari			•
M. Schumacher	GER	Monaco	Monaco	•		
E. Irvine	IRL	Monaco	Monaco			•
M. Schumacher	GER	Canadian	G. Villeneuve	•		
M. Schumacher	GER	French	Magny-Cours	•		
E. Irvine	IRL	French	Magny-Cours			•
M. Schumacher	GER	German	Hochenhëim		•	
M. Schumacher	GER	Belgian	Spa	•		
M. Schumacher	GER	Japanese	Suzuka	•		
E. Irvine	IRL	Japanese	Suzuka			•

I was asked to write a few words about Enzo Ferrari, but I've got to admit it wasn't an easy job. Having shared moments of great joy as well as moments of deep dejection with such a legendary figure, I had to watch out and not let my emotional involvement make me say banal or obvious things, and I especially didn't want to go overboard. What I also felt was important was not to repeat what so many others have already said about him. In brief, therefore, I can say, first of all, that having had the privilege of collaborating with Enzo Ferrari is something that I'm indeed very proud of.

Furthermore, during the five years I was at Maranello, there was never a day that went by that I wasn't able to see for myself what an uncomplicated man he was, in contrast to what many have said about him. What seemed to be an enigmatic behavior on his part was actually a pose and not the way he really was, because he fully realized that the secret to his success lay in the fact that others considered him to be unapproachable, and he stuck to this principle through thick and thin.

He also had a rare gift when it came to overcoming problems. His interior force and composure, even when things got rough, was an example and inspiration for all of his collaborators.

Racing was his life, his sustenance, the air he breathed. Building and selling prestigious automobiles was only an expedient for obtaining his principle objective: To race, win and continue reaping greater glory.

Although becoming a legend was never Enzo Ferrari's real intention, it was inevitable.

Michele Alboreto